INTRODUCTION TO EDUCATION STUDIES

Steve Bartlett is Reader in Education at Chester College of
Higher Education. Diana Burton is Head of Education Programmes,
Manchester Metropolitan University. Nick Peim lectures
at the University of Birmingham in teacher education and
professional development.

INTRODUCTION TO EDUCATION STUDIES

Steve Bartlett, Diana Burton
and Nick Peim

P·C·P

Paul Chapman
Publishing

Paul Chapman Publishing
A SAGE Publications Company
6 Bonhill Street
London EC2A 4PU

SAGE Publications Inc
2455 Teller Road
Thousand Oaks, California 91320

SAGE Publications India Pvt Ltd
32, M-Block Market
Greater Kailash - I
New Delhi 110 048

A catalogue record for this book is available from the
British Library

ISBN 0 7619 7015 0
ISBN 0 7619 7016 9 (pbk)

Library of Congress catalog record available

Typeset by Dorwyn Ltd, Rowlands Castle, Hants
Printed in Great Britain by Cromwell Press, Trowbridge,
Wilts

Contents

Acknowledgements

The authors and publishers wish to thank the following for permission to use copyright material:

Blackwell for P.K. Smith and H. Cowie (1988) *Understanding Children's Development*.
Harper & Row for H. Bee (1985) *The Developing Child*, 4th Edition.

Every effort has been made to trace the copyright holders but if any has been inadvertently overlooked the publishers will be pleased to make the necessary arrangement at the first opportunity.

Introduction: What Is Education Studies?

Until the mid-1970s the academic study of education was a substantial element in courses preparing students for careers in teaching. Carr has called this the academic era of teacher education, in which a significant part of the curriculum was 'concerned with making larger sense of education and teaching in value-driven and culturally significant enterprises' (1997: 56). The 'field' drew significantly on the disciplines of philosophy, sociology, psychology and history for the purposes of critical reflection and analysis. Rather than becoming a unified subject these disciplines generally remained as discrete units and were taught in this way. For many students they were presented in isolation and did not sufficiently link with the other parts of their professional training courses to make them appear worthwhile. For such students their prime focus was on the subjects they were going to teach, the teaching practice itself and, particularly, aspects of classroom management and control. Due to various political and economic pressures of the 1970s and 1980s the theoretical study of education as part of teacher training courses fell into disrepute. Teacher education was criticized as being too removed from the classroom. It was perceived as largely ignoring the practical nature of teaching while also promoting progressive ideologies of education. Thus the study of education as such was largely abandoned and teacher training became just that, training in how to teach. Wider questioning of the purpose, nature and effects of education upon individuals and larger social groups was not seen as appropriate (Barton et al., 1994). The emphasis was on the practical skills of the teacher at the expense of theoretical underpinning and critical analysis (see Burton, 1998, for an extended discussion of this area).

Since the early 1990s there has been a move in higher education towards modular degrees allowing greater variation in student programmes. This has enabled a return to the study of education as a 'subject'. It is taken as part of a degree along with one or two other subjects to which it is often seen as complementary. Thus students combine education studies with sports science, English, drama, religious studies, geography and the like. These students are very different to those on the teacher training programmes of 30 years ago. They may or may not be considering a future career in teaching, they may be studying education as a major or a minor part of their degree or they may be just taking several education modules to broaden their horizons. However, at this point in their studies, they have chosen education as an academic rather than a professional area of study and they wish to approach it in a critical fashion. They are seeking answers to key questions such as: What is education and what are its purposes? How does learning take place and how far is achievement dependent upon natural ability or social factors such as income, gender and race? The attention of the student is also drawn to educational policy and political issues surrounding education.

With the resurgence of the academic study of education, and an increasing number of students with education studies in their degree title, the significance of the traditional disciplines once again becomes apparent. Rather than being taught as separate disciplines these are now used in an eclectic manner to study key education issues. This is useful in that education is a field of study which draws on the approaches of several other disciplines. However, a multidisciplinary approach can be difficult for the new student who, by definition, is unlikely to be experienced in all of these different areas of study. Consider how the Quality Assurance Agency (QAA) sees it:

> Education studies is concerned with understanding how people develop and learn throughout their lives. It facilitates the study of the nature of knowledge, and a critical engagement with a variety of perspectives, and ways of knowing and understanding, drawn from a range of appropriate disciplines. [Education studies courses] all involve the intellectually rigorous study of educational processes, systems and approaches, and the cultural, societal, political and historical contexts within which they are embedded. (QAA, 2000: 4)

The QAA also lists a set of principles to which all programmes of education studies should relate. Programmes should:

● draw on a wide range of intellectual resources, theoretical perspectives and academic disciplines to illuminate understanding of education and the contexts within which it takes place

- provide students with a broad and balanced knowledge and understanding of the principal features of education in a wide range of contexts
- encourage students to engage with fundamental questions concerning the aims and values of education and its relationship to society
- provide opportunities for students to appreciate the problematic nature of educational theory, policy and practice
- encourage the interrogation of educational processes in a wide variety of contexts
- develop in students the ability to construct and sustain a reasoned argument about educational issues in a clear, lucid and coherent manner
- promote a range of qualities in students including intellectual independence and critical engagement with evidence. (QAA, 2000: 4)

This approach to the study of education can be seen to be far more searching than simply training how to teach specific content and how to 'control' classes.

Aspects of education are studied within various disciplines, specifically philosophy, psychology, sociology and history, as part of their particular interest in the human condition. However, education is also seen as a legitimate area of study in its own right by QAA. This means that education is at the centre of the study and therefore draws on the other disciplines as appropriate. Thus while psychology students will study aspects of education as appropriate, for instance, in relation to cognitive development, education studies students will study some aspects of psychological theory when looking at the process of learning within schools or colleges. It is interesting to consider the status relations between these older and newer subjects, the longer-standing disciplines having a better developed theoretical base to consider as their own.

Many students are surprised by their early encounters with education studies. They have all been through formal systems of education which has taken them many years, either recently or in the more distant past. They may have gone through their formal education without really questioning what was happening to them. By and large they were not encouraged to probe the nature of the process, just the content which was presented to them. In schools pupils study history, mathematics, science and other subjects but not usually the education process itself. They are therefore unsure of what to expect when beginning their studies of education. To some students just embarking on their course education is assumed to be a straightforward process and an uncomplicated area of study. Perhaps it will involve such things as accounts of how to teach, how schools or colleges should be organized, how to revise and get good results. They may not have thought of education as anything more than a clearly defined process and therefore expect their studies to be descriptive. Many express surprise that education is so 'political' with so much argument and no absolute answers. They may not have previously looked at education in a critical manner. There is also surprise that research into, and discussion of, education takes place across such diverse fields of study. Students soon realize that there is more to the study of education than the schooling of 5- to 18-year-olds.

In their other degree studies these students often have experience of the subjects' content and methodologies, having studied them at school. This is not the case with education studies. While the education process is something which all students have experience of it has not actually been a focus of study for them unless they took sociology and psychology at school or college and studied aspects of education within these. For many students with no previous experience of the subject, embarking on an education studies course can be an unsettling time and insecurities can be felt. This is perhaps because they are questioning something which they had previously regarded as one of the fixed entities in their lives. For others, of course, it may be a relief to find alternative accounts and analyses of education which align with their own feelings about the difficult times they spent in educational institutions.

There are many interesting journals and books to which students are directed from the beginning of their courses, but generally these assume a level of understanding and knowledge which the student does not yet have. Thus, while there are many texts suitable for the knowledgeable student, there are very few which may be used by the novice as an introduction into the field. This book aims to introduce students to the study of education and to provide a starting point from which they can progress. It outlines several major areas of education studies and the key issues therein. In the text we refer, wherever possible, to current literature which the student should be able to access. We are also aware that to deal with the overarching questions and issues in such a short space can actually do them a disservice and cause distortion by oversimplification. We want, therefore, to emphasize that the purpose is to introduce the student to the study of education, outline the theoretical arguments and encourage deeper exploration.

1

The Nature of Education

This chapter considers the complex nature of education as an area of study, looking at the meaning of the term 'education' and moving on to a discussion of the purposes of an education system which can be seen from a number of different perspectives. Ideological positions are analysed together with the theories of teaching, learning and assessment which derive from them. Education is seen to be inextricably linked to belief and value systems. The multidisciplinary nature of education studies is illustrated by reference to the disciplines of philosophy, psychology, sociology and history. The chapter concludes by emphasizing the importance of a critical approach to the study of education.

Introduction

Education is an activity we all feel that we know something about, having had practical experience of it. In a systematic study of education, however, two fundamental questions will be posed: 'what do we mean by education?' and 'why is education important?' Finding the answers to these two questions is a complex endeavour. As students of education, the answers we give are likely to vary over time. Thus the meaning of the term 'education' and its purpose is not universally fixed and is not the same for all of us.

The meaning of education

Personal resonances of the term education are shaped by a number of individual experiences. Coming top of the class, passing examinations, going on school trips, being made fun of by pupils or teachers, or being in the bottom set. Various groups of people are usually positioned differently in relation to education and its purposes. Political leaders, parents, pupils at school, university students, teachers, the police and factory managers will espouse different views. These groups might themselves be differentiated, for instance, parents may be classified by income levels, single parents, age group, number of children in the family and so on. More specific questions about education help to elicit a deeper analysis.

1 *Is education a process?* Something which we go through over a period of years? Does this process vary over time? For instance, how is education for 4-year-olds in nursery different from that for 20-year-olds at university?

2 *Is education a product to be consumed?* Can it be quantified? Is the product defined as what someone can do at the end of it, i.e. a demonstration of competence at something, or is the product about examination passes? Where does intellectual development fit in here? Does the product vary? For instance, is the education of an unskilled worker different from that of a nation's leaders? Should it be different?

3 *What does education involve?* Is it about sitting at desks, learning important facts and answering questions? Does it mean being absorbed by interesting tasks or solving challenging problems? Should it make us happy or serious and should we be put under pressure and 'extended' to our limits?

4 *Where does education take place?* Is it mainly in schools, colleges and universities? Can we do it at home using information and communications technology (ICT) and learning packages delivered 'on line'? Does it carry on throughout life beyond school, college or university?

It is interesting to analyse our perceptions of education using such questions. Yet the range of responses, when we compare our views with those of others, can also be disconcerting. The complexity of the area of study becomes very apparent. All the possible interpretations implied by the questions above are emphasized in various ways by different people when looking at the meaning of the term 'education'. We also need to ask if education has to be intended or if it can happen by accident in an unplanned and, sometimes, perhaps unrecognized manner.

Peters (1966) was well aware of the problems in attempting to define 'education'. He suggested that the term had been used in many different ways and, as such, was difficult to capture in any precise definition, though he was able to outline a range of 'normative' and 'cognitive' aspects associated with it (Peters, 1966; 1967). For Peters education was deeper than just learning facts or how to do something. This more superficial approach he associated with training. Education involved a linking of concepts by the learner to gain a wider understanding of the world. In his view, for something to count as education it had to be regarded as worthwhile. In this way it was inseparable from judgements of value. It should also be learnt in a morally acceptable manner, it should not involve coercion or brainwashing. This implies some agreement by the learner to take part (Peters, 1967). This view of education could certainly cause us to question some of our own experiences within compulsory education.

Consider the life history of a convict and the questions one could ask concerning their education. What has their education involved? Could it be that they learned different things than the teachers intended? What skills have they developed? Once in prison what do convicts learn and from whom? Do they go to education classes and listen attentively to the advice of the warders or do they 'pick up tips' from listening to and being with other inmates? Using Peters's view of education, unreformed convicts would see their learning of how to be criminals as useful. They entered into this voluntarily and so it is morally acceptable from their position, unlike their experiences at school where they had perhaps been chastised. It also fits with their wider view of the world and how they can survive in it.

In its broadest sense education is normally thought to be about acquiring and being able to use knowledge, and developing skills and understanding – cognitive capabilities. It can be claimed that, as humans, we are identified by our capacity to learn, communicate and reason. We are involved in these things throughout our lives and in all situations. From the earliest times people have learnt from one another in family and social groups. As society became larger scale and more complex, so systems of education became formalized and expanded. We still learn from those around us but the education system now also plays a large part in all our lives.

Formal education developed first for the elite minority and, over time, became compulsory for all. This is not to say that schools for the elite and those for the masses gave the same education or had the same purposes. Those being groomed to rule and those subject to being ruled have traditionally been educated in different ways and with different expectations. Steadily the time spent in educational institutions increased as children started younger and finished older than their predecessors. This trend of an increasing number of years spent in formal education continues today. The development of post-16 and higher education in recent years is testament to this while, at the same time, nursery and pre-school provision is also rapidly expanding.

Education has become a large industry employing many thousands of people in Britain alone. It is supposedly an important part of ensuring future economic development yet it also imposes a major financial cost. It is presented by politicians as an investment in our future, the 'our' referring to the nation as a whole as well as to the individual. Thus education plays a central role in society and also in all of our lives.

The purposes of education

We may accept, then, that it is appropriate to take a broad view of the meaning of education. Turning our attention to the second question to look at why education is important may help us to understand more fully the meaning of the term. When looking at the purposes of education we are generally referring to the purposes of the education 'system'. It should be apparent from the previous discussion that this is likely to exclude a great deal of interesting material. While a wide detour may be made into education at the 'university of life', space does not permit this here. We will limit our concern to the 'official', or 'formal', processes of education.

The functionalist approach

Over the years many theorists and commentators have listed what they believed to be the purposes of the education system. The functionalist approach stresses how education benefits the whole of society (consider the work of sociologists such as Davis and Moore, 1967; Durkheim, 1947; Parsons, 1964. In Chapters 4 and 5 there is a further discussion of the functionalist perspective.) Education is seen alongside other social institutions as working to create and maintain a stable society. The functionalist analogy compares society to a machine or a living organism. The different social institutions, such as the forces of law and order, the political system and also education, function to maintain the whole society. This is in the same way that the different parts of a machine or a body contribute to the working of the whole. If any of the parts does not function properly then this affects the whole society and may even lead to a breakdown, in the same way as a machine breaks down or a body becomes sick and dies. Though the lists vary, the main functions of education may be seen as:

Development of basic academic skills

In order to participate in a modern society certain skills are seen as very important. Most notably we need to be able to read, write and perform basic arithmetical tasks. These are needed in all areas of modern life. Consider how many times you use reading skills in any one day. You could conclude that life as we know it is virtually impossible to live without them. It is amazing to think that some people do actually survive without highly developed reading skills, but they are at a distinct disadvantage and need to seek help frequently. This is not easy for them because of the social stigma attached to an adult being unable to read proficiently. The ability to use ICT is now also regarded as an essential skill. The importance of, and increasing emphasis on, the development of what are variously called 'transferable', 'key' or 'core skills' is part of the rhetoric surrounding the development of an adaptable, flexible workforce for the 'skills economy'. Thus interpersonal, communication, literacy and numeracy skills have been promoted up the educational agenda particularly within post-16 learning.

Socialization

Functionalists see this as the way in which we become human. It is a process which begins at birth when we start effectively as blank slates. We develop our 'selves' as we learn what we need to know to live and operate with others in social groups. This includes language, right and wrong, expectations of ourselves and others, how to behave in different situations and so on. It is, of course, a subject of debate as to how much our development depends upon social learning or biological processes. This is looked at in more detail in Chapter 4.

Socialization is a process of induction into society's culture, norms and values. This ensures a level of social cohesion necessary for society to continue. It is a process which continues throughout life but which is certainly of central importance in our early years. Thus the family and schooling have a crucial role in the socialization process.

Social control and maintaining social order

For us to live our lives and for established social life to exist we must be assured of a level of order and safety as we go about our daily business. This involves the rule of law but also certain expected ways of behaving. These may be seen as norms of behaviour or manners. Consider how we behave in an orderly manner for much of our lives without really thinking about it. We queue up for things in shops or when waiting for public transport. We say 'please' and 'thank you' in appropriate circumstances. In public places we walk without bumping into or touching other people. We maintain appropriate eye contact and distance when conversing with others depending upon who these others are. These norms are learned and education helps in this process. Control mechanisms may be overt and show outward force as in the case of riot police quelling trouble on the streets. Control may, however, be more covert and subtle when compliance is expected, as in the case of a disparaging look from a teacher when work has not been completed.

Preparing for work

In small-scale and self-sufficient societies children would learn about survival from adults. In these communities adults are multiskilled and can satisfy most of their wants by using their own abilities. There may be only a few specialist roles such as healer or midwife in such groups. As forms of employment diversified and became specialized then increasingly specific training needed to take place. Payment, in the form of wages, generally reflected the level, scarcity and importance of the skill required. General qualities needed for employment such as those expressed in the transferable skills can be developed at all levels of education. Job-specific training is likely to be workplace based but also to involve further and higher education.

The functions of education may be seen to overlap. The preparation for work involves the developing of minds and learning of important skills. Socialization is an important part of preparing for adulthood and elements of internalized social control form part of this. Different functions may be to the fore at times during a pupil's education. Whereas it may be appropriate to stress the development of the mind and individual freedom to experiment at particular stages, it may be important to stress discipline and the need for self-control at others. Each of these functions can be seen to be appropriate but, taken together, there are potential tensions between them. For example, developing minds means encouraging a questioning attitude. The image is of a learner exploring and experimenting. However, the need to maintain social order involves pupils showing obedience to authority and 'correct' behaviour. This could be interpreted as the creation of accepting, rather than questioning, individuals.

Pupils may be encouraged to question within the topics chosen by a teacher. Much primary work, for instance, involves investigations by pupils into the world around them. The children may ask questions to do with friction, life cycles, different materials and so on. They carry out investigations designed to find the answers. However, other areas of school life must not be questioned beyond a superficial level: 'Why must we wear this uniform?' 'Will all of this homework help our progress?' 'Why are we studying "this" as opposed to "that"?' Obedience is an important part of any pupil's schooling. When the characteristics of a 'good' school leaver are listed they include independence and initiative, yet prospective employers also look for a willingness to obey instructions and for a neat (in other words, conforming) appearance.

It seems there is a need for both self-development and self-control. The difficulty is striking a balance. We can see the importance of order, direction, control and discipline, but not to the extent that it prevents questioning and individual development. The balance struck rests upon beliefs about human nature, the working of society and, thus, the purposes of education.

The stress placed upon the different functions of education may be different depending upon the pupil. Some pupils may be pushed academically while others may be prepared for low-level employment. Indeed some functionalists, such as Davis and Moore (1967), saw the sifting of talent and allocating of individuals to appropriate roles in society as an important function of a formal education system. Some pupils may be given freedom to express themselves whereas for others, the emphasis may be on modifying their behaviour. Chapters 4 and 5 examine this potential for treating pupils differently and posit some explanations for it.

The rhetoric of consensus

When considering the functionalist perspective on education we need to ask for whose purposes education exists. By saying that education functions for the whole society it is assumed that what is good for the society is good for us all. The implication is that we all have the same needs and wants and also that there is equality of opportunity to benefit from such a system. In short it takes a consensus view of society and ignores the fact that significant differences and conflicts of interest may exist. Inequality, in terms of income or wealth, is actually seen as something which itself performs a function of encouraging us to better ourselves and, in the process, benefits the society as a whole.

The rhetoric of consensus also ignores the power differentials between separate sections of society and how this can be used to maintain superior positions. Children from certain groups are significantly more successful in education and it has been posited that this is a reflection of their economic and social background (Bourdieu and Passeron, 1977). Research has also shown that the labelling which attaches to children in lower socio-economic groups serves to further disadvantage them (Hargreaves, 1967).

Functionalists assume that the system must be maintained if society is to survive. By reinforcing the status quo these functions actually benefit those who are in the best positions. They maintain stability and thus it is easier for those at the top to ensure that their children follow in their footsteps. Those at the bottom are, by and large, kept there. It is pointed out that it is largely their own fault for not taking the opportunities on offer. Thus inequality is perpetuated and regarded as the 'natural' order of things. Education is seen as an important part of the unifying process needed to help maintain a level of consensus within society.

Conflict theories

Conflict perspectives also viewed education as preparing people for a place in society. However, rather than the consensus envisaged by functionalism, conflict theorists, Marxists for example, see education as reinforcing a class system. Marxism perceives a conflict of values in society, with those of the capitalist ruling class being dominant. The education system, by operating as an agency of the state, serves to reinforce these values. It helps to keep the working class in their place while preparing middle-class pupils to 'legitimately' take over the powerful positions held by their class. Bowles and Gintis (1976) saw a close correspondence between how schools treat pupils and the later experiences they can expect at work. This plays an important part in preparing working-class youth for menial forms of employment. Bourdieu and Passeron (1977) used the concept of cultural capital to explain how the middle classes are able to maintain their position in the process of social reproduction while making this inequality legitimate. By claiming to be a meritocracy the education system helps to keep social order and perpetuate the existing inequalities. This is, for the classic Marxist analyst, the purpose of formal education.

Many conflict theorists would consider it possible for subversive elements to work within the system and some may hold an image of a young idealistic revolutionary teacher but, generally, Marxists see capitalism as too powerful to be threatened by individuals. Idealists working within education to change society will, in the long term, become incorporated into the system themselves. In fact, by helping individual working-class pupils to succeed, these teachers may ultimately be perpetuating the myth of a meritocracy. They are in the end legitimating the very education system which is helping to sustain the existing structural inequalities. In the novel *Kes*, (Hines, 1974) an English Literature reader for many 14- and 15-year-olds in the 1970s and 1980s, the teacher who befriends and guides the poor, badly treated working-class pupil makes no difference to the overall order of things. Thus it might be argued that both functionalism and Marxism conceive of the purposes of education as maintaining the current order of society but from very different standpoints. However, contemporary Marxists (after Gramsci, Althusser and Habermas) may see education as a legitimate field of conflict to be contested in detail at every point. The functionalist and Marxist perspectives are outlined in more detail in Chapter 6.

Ideologies in education

Systems of broad beliefs and values about the nature of the world are termed 'ideologies'. They are relevant to all areas of life and are often related. Thus understandings about human nature may be linked to beliefs about law, order, political life, the economic system, the purposes of education and so on. We have explored the purposes of education from a largely functionalist perspective. There are, however, other ideologies which analyse both the purposes and nature of education slightly differently. Carr and Hartnett (1996) suggest that the education system has a purpose of social reproduction, in terms of cultural, economic and political life, as well as a purpose to do with social transformation. There is a tension between the need for stability and the desire for change. It is apparent that education is based on beliefs about the things that need to be socially reproduced and those that need transforming. They suggest that as education is to do with the creation of the 'good society' there is a strong link between political philosophy and educational theory.

There are many differing positions on the human condition. These lead to alternative visions of what is desirable and what is humanly possible in the organization of society. These views have tended to be presented as polarized alternatives which offer differing perspectives as to the purposes of a formal education system and its concomitant structure.

Plato and Hobbes

Plato argued that humans are naturally predisposed to perform certain tasks. In the Greek state he identified three levels of society – workers, soldiers and leaders. Society will be 'in balance' when people are performing the tasks for which they have a natural disposition. Thus the purpose of the education system is to prepare different pupils in the most appropriate way for their future roles. This means different teaching methods and content as appropriate. Plato saw traditional, high-status knowledge being appropriate for some people only and practical instruction appropriate for others. Everyone 'in their place' doing what they do best leads to a stable society. It is interesting to compare this view of society and the education system appropriate with the tripartite system set up in post-war England (see Chapter 3).

In Plato's analysis to go against this natural order is to threaten the whole existence of society. Encouraging those not suited to rise above their station will cause social unrest, instability, disobedience and civil strife. Ultimately this must be put down by force or it will lead to revolution, anarchy and a total breakdown of the social fabric. In this way everyone in society will suffer. Thus, for Plato, order was important for the maintainance of society (see Carr and Hartnett, 1996, for a very lucid account of the views of Plato).

The 'utilitarians' held a similar view of the need for enforced social order. In the seventeenth century Hobbes suggested that we all have natural desires which we wish to satisfy. Humans in this respect are no different from other animals. Survival is of the fittest and life can be seen as potentially 'nasty, brutish and short'. We are, ultimately, all on our own trying to satisfy our needs and live in a totally hostile world. For the utilitarians life is a dog-eat-dog existence. Humans do thrive in larger social groups where trade and cooperation can take place. However, the constant pressure to revert back to our natural state needs to be guarded against. Thus for social life to be made possible there need to be rules, laws and sanctions which are rigorously enforced. So, for example, to take a life or to commit a crime against property leads to severe punishment.

Hobbes explained that parameters of behaviour need to be clear and enforcement strict. Anything less, any sign of weakness, will threaten the superficially stable and secure lives of us all. The line between a well-ordered society and a state of brutal chaos is slim. Respect and fear of the law is what enables a society to exist (see Parsons, 1970, for an account of Hobbes and the problem of social order). For Plato and Hobbes the importance of education in maintaining order, and thus the existence of society, is clear. People need strict guidelines to operate within and discipline needs to be instilled in mind and body. Order is of central importance if society, and the individuals within it, is to have a chance to prosper.

Rousseau

An alternative view of human nature is put forward by the 'romantics'. In the eighteenth century Rousseau took the view that, far from maintaining society, power in the hands of the few will lead them to reinforce their position which itself results in tyranny. He saw this increasing oppression as leading to violent uprisings from the oppressed in their struggle for freedom. In his view what was needed was to educate all citizens fully. This involved encouraging the development of questioning minds and giving everyone the widest of educational experiences. As our intellects develop we can all contribute to the evolution of society by continuous discussion and reason. Rousseau saw the development of a 'social contract' whereby to maintain their own freedom people respected the rights of others. This would only happen when all felt involved in the society and it would be the height of democratic development. The common good is presented as the 'general will' of the people (see Carr and Hartnett, 1996).

Thus self-discovery and individual development form the basis of education, for Rousseau, leading to a more liberated society. Without this freedom there would always be oppression based on physical force. These freedoms were the very things that Plato saw as dangerous to the fabric of society. On the one hand there is the view that education should be about individual development and fulfilment. All citizens will then be able to play an active part in social life resulting in tolerance of the views of others. This will lead to a 'better' and more just society. On the other, there is the belief that this freedom will lead to instability due to the innate selfishness of human nature. What is needed is social order and a structure which will enable us to lead our lives without fear and within which we can earn our living. A prime purpose of education is to develop individual discipline with a respect for authority and tradition which will ensure this. These opposing views can both be detected when examining political developments in recent education policy (see Chapters 3 and 8).

We can see how our own experiences in schools, colleges and universities mirror one or other of these sets of beliefs. When thinking of our secondary schooling we may recall the ways order was enforced: lining up outside classrooms, detentions, threat of exclusion. Rules were enforced even down to the way work had to be laid out in exercise books. While being critical of the exercise of control over our freedom, we are also aware of what it's like to be pupils in a classroom where order has broken down and the teacher has lost authority. This situation is often regarded by pupils as being fun at first but quickly turns to boredom and frustration at the lack of any constructive activity and direction. A desire grows for a return to an orderly learning environment as pupils themselves begin to complain to wider authorities. The majority of school children, without openly admitting it, welcome the structure and direction a teacher is able to give. Often, however, learning involves both individual choice and external direction and control. Most adults can recall important learning experiences which affected their personal development, such as a moving poem or story read with feeling by another pupil or a teacher, a word of encouragement from a form tutor, finishing a piece of craftwork and taking it home. Such experiences are generated as a result of this complex interaction between self-determination and teacher control.

A typology of ideologies in education

The views of Plato and Rousseau apply to the whole of society and social life. Now let us consider education specifically. Meighan and Siraj-Blatchford define ideologies of education as: 'The set of ideas and beliefs held by a group of people about the formal arrangements for education, specifically schooling, and often, by extension or implication, also about informal aspects of education, e.g. learning at home' (1998: 185). There have been various attempts to classify ideologies in education and Meighan and Siraj-Blatchford outline the dichotomous approach which uses polarized types such as teacher-centred v. child-centred, authoritarian v. democratic and so on. The juxtaposition of only two ideologies may prove rather simplistic especially when examining long lists of polarized opposites which may or may not be related to other 'pairs' on the list. Meighan and Siraj-Blatchford suggest that other more complex typologies attempt to go beyond this.

Lawton (1992) pointed out that ideologies are used at different levels of generality. There is the broad level which is about the nature and purposes of education within a wider society, such as those of Plato and Rousseau considered above. There is the interest group level, which is concerned with how the system should be organized, for instance, whether education provision should be a totally free market where schools offer and charge for a service and the customer pays according to what is on offer, or a totally comprehensive state system for all with no choice. Then there is the teaching or pedagogic level which is concerned with the organization and delivery of the curriculum at classroom level. This involves what should be taught and how it should be taught.

Lawton (1992) suggests that these different levels are very much linked and overlapping. For instance, views on the nature and purposes of education are influential when it comes to considering the organization of schools, colleges and universities. They will also be significant in deciding what is the most appropriate content and methods of teaching to be applied. How individual teachers view content and teaching methods will, in turn, be linked to how they see the purposes of what they are involved in. For this reason Meighan and Siraj-Blatchford (1998) prefer to use the concept of a network of ideologies to show how they operate between, as well as at, these different levels.

Throughout this book there are issues concerning the nature of education, how the system should be organized, what should be taught and how. The relationship and overlap between the three levels of ideology identified by Lawton will be continually stressed. One level cannot be considered without reference to the other two levels.

Ideologies of education may be categorized in various ways in many permutations. Scrimshaw (1983) suggested organizing educational ideologies in terms of their stress upon the individual, knowledge or society as a useful means of categorizing such a wide range of ideas. Morrison and Ridley (1989) also use these three headings to neatly summarize clusters of educational ideologies in the following way.

Ideologies which emphasize the individual

Under this heading they place ideologies labelled variously as progressivism, child/student centredness and romanticism. The emphasis is on

individual development with the needs and interests of the learner being central. The learning process is seen as vital, with discovery and experimentation being at its heart. Learning is held to be rewarding in itself and pupils/students maintain high motivation because of this. The emphasis is on development at different rates with students following their own learning programmes according to their interests. Learning is individualized and lifelong, and the concept of failure is not appropriate as it only applies to set courses and fixed parameters of progress. Formative purposes of assessment are favoured over summative ones. Thus student portfolios are regarded as more valid in showing progress than mass examinations at the end of the year.

The child-centred approach had made some headway in the 1960s, with the Plowden Report (CACE, 1967) doing much to endorse these ideas, particularly in primary schools. The development of this approach was a reaction partly to the notion which influenced much post-Second World War education policy that intelligence and aptitude were largely innate. There was a growing belief in the significance of environmental influences on the development of the individual (see Chapter 4 for theories of development and Chapter 8 for changes in education policy).

Various questions and issues are raised concerning the practicalities of this 'romantic' approach which puts pupils, with their interests, needs and wishes, to the fore. In an age of mass education the development and management of individual programmes becomes difficult if not impossible. There is the issue of the pupil who does not particularly want to progress. For instance, the child in the reception class may be very happy playing and not wish to leave the sandpit. It may be felt that, if the pupil is not to be disadvantaged in later life, the accomplishment of some essential skills should not be left to chance. Can we trust that all children will turn to reading and writing when they are ready or should we give them formal teaching?

This then turns the focus onto the teacher. In a child-centred classroom to what extent should teachers intervene and how much can be left to the initiative of the pupil? It is difficult for a teacher to allow experimentation in some areas which may not be seen as socially appropriate. As adults we do more than just discourage young people from trying smoking, drinking alcohol and casual sexual experiences. It is also the case that clear teaching and being 'fed' existing information can save time. The need for every pupil to reinvent the wheel by exploration and experimentation is therefore questionable. Others would claim that self-direction is a more subtle form of control and belongs to the logic of pastoral discipline in which the main desired outcome is the self-regulation of the pupil (Hunter, 1994).

Critics of the 'progressive' approach suggested that the emphasis on individual freedom leads to an increase in permissiveness and a lowering of academic standards. It has been suggested (see Cox and Dyson, 1969a; 1969b) that this is what happened in the 1960s. A period of full employment and increasing affluence led to the indulgence of the individual and the development of a more 'permissive society', which in turn created the social and economic problems of the 1970s. Remember the warnings of Plato and Hobbes?

Ideologies which emphasize knowledge

Ideologies labelled variously as classical humanism, conservatism and traditionalism are placed here by Morrison and Ridley (1989). These emphasize the importance of formal knowledge arranged in subjects. In its more classical form there is respect for what is seen as high-status knowledge. Pupils/students need to start by learning basic facts and then progress through increasingly complex levels. This is done through formal, traditional, tried and tested methods. Assessment is also formal, indicates success and enables the selection of an elite. Discipline is an important part of the academic process. The learner is under close supervision in the early stages and only becomes more autonomous when reaching the higher levels of academic study. Thus, in the classroom in early secondary education the whole class is likely to be involved in the same exercises. Students gain more autonomy as they move from General Certificate of Secondary Education (GCSE) to A level study. There is even more autonomy for an undergraduate at university, while at the postgraduate level students, apart from having higher status, are much more in control of their studies. The pinnacle of independent erudition is deemed to reside with learned academics.

The practicality of subjects is less important than high academic achievement in classical humanism. The public school epitomizes the elitism, discipline and academic standards of this ideology. There is also a strong adherence to the traditional values which have been seen to be those that make a nation great. The criticisms of the more classical forms of humanism concern its elitism and defence of privilege. These may be said to maintain inequality and, in Rousseau's view, would mean the continued use of repressive means to subdue the underprivileged. The belief in tradition leads to lack of adaptability and innovation which is likely to result in economic decline when in competition with modern world economies.

The more liberal form of humanism also stresses knowledge but in a less traditional format. The emphasis is on a core curriculum for all, with elements of choice, as pupils move through the school system. Providing equality of opportunity is seen as important, in addition to maintaining academic standards. A tension is felt between setting by ability to allow the able to progress fully and not appearing to be elitist. This is a dilemma currently faced by Labour politicians when attempting to raise standards in the state system (see Chapter 8).

Ideologies which emphasize society

These are again divided into two by Morrison and Ridley (1989). Ideologies including instrumentalism, revisionism and economic renewal form one group. These ideologies are looking to develop, improve and modernize the economy. The emphasis is on producing workers to enable this to happen. This can mean developing adaptable, thinking, problem-solving, high-quality individuals. The emphasis may also be on the traditional worker qualities of reliability and hard work. Education here has a practical purpose which teaching and assessment should reflect. Competencies become important and the vocational element is stressed. The nature of individualized programmes associated with vocationalism have shades of the student-centred approach but with more external direction.

The second group includes 'democratic socialism' and 'reconstructionism' both of which emphasize the power structures in society. Democratic socialism sees education as important in the creation and protection of equal opportunity for all and the development of all sections of society. The aim is to reform society from within and education must play a significant part in this process. Reconstructionists take this further and point to the possibility of totally reconstructing society through education. Education is seen as a revolutionary force through the enlightenment of the populace and the application of a critical approach to existing structures of social inequality. This is using the education system in the struggle to overthrow existing structures of inequality. Such a revolutionary stance is not generally tolerated by a system it seeks to undermine. There has always been a deep suspicion by the establishment of teachers who may be seen as potential revolutionaries and in a position to influence the vulnerable young. This ideology was a 'popular' part of the left wing political movements of the late 1960s and early 1970s and is shown in works such as *Teaching as a Subversive Activity* by Postman and Weingartner (1969).

The value of typologies

Typologies of ideologies can never be more than generalizations, which at times appear very sweeping, of sets of beliefs which are linked together. They are useful in that they help us to understand the actions of groups of individuals but they are never total explanations because of the existence of variations. This can be seen when looking at the ideologies of education associated with the two major British political parties, Labour and Conservative. There are disagreements between the two and arguments within each. It should also be noted that at times there is agreement between both Labour and Conservatives on certain issues.

Meighan and Siraj-Blatchford (1998) outline 11 significant 'component theories' which when put together make up an educational ideology and identify it from others. Each ideology possesses a theory of:

- discipline and order
- knowledge, its content and structure
- learning and the learner's role
- teaching and the teacher's role
- resources appropriate for teaching
- organization of learning situations
- assessment that learning has taken place
- aims, objectives and outcomes
- parents and the parent's role
- locations appropriate for learning
- power and its distribution (Meighan and Siraj-Blatchford, 1998: 191).

Each ideological grouping outlined by Morrison and Ridley (1989) can be analysed according to Meighan and Siraj-Blatchford's 'component theories', which reveal how sets of beliefs and values, in the forms of ideologies, exist in education. Students take courses, have lessons and are assessed in ways which take a recognizable ideological stance. Different ideologies can coexist at the same time within the same institution, even operating alongside each other. Thus schools emphasize the future employment of pupils as well as academic knowledge. Subjects are taught differently and teachers of the same subject may have very different teaching styles. Although often taught in large classes, pupils are treated as individuals by their teachers as well as being classified into sections within the class.

Marsh (1997) states that the schooling which pupils receive is a result of the decisions and actions of many individuals and groups. These are both professional and lay persons who may be operating at national or local levels as well as within the school. Thus it would be misleading to assume that one dominant ideology has total control. Marsh suggests that it is worth considering the impact of different groups which he identifies as decision-makers, stakeholders and wider influence groups, upon the classroom. This illustrates the many influences on the actual education received by pupils and also the power possessed by those involved in varying capacities. Even when given a formal national curriculum, teachers will decide what each lesson will include. However, they are unlikely to ignore the concerns of stakeholders such as parents, as these are close to their daily activity and can directly affect classroom life. They will also take into account wider influences such as local employers who can offer different kinds of support in lessons and to pupils. Teachers must also pay close attention to the regular school inspections by the Office for Standards in Education (OFSTED) and the increased scrutiny of their work resulting from the publication of league tables of GCSE examinations and National Curriculum test results. Thus teachers are very significant in the education process but they are not, and perhaps never have been, totally autonomous.

Kelly points out that, in examining the development of schooling and the curriculum, one can see the compromise which inevitably results from the constant tensions between competing sets of beliefs:

> which might be broadly polarized as a conflict between the claims of society and those of the individual, the vocational and the liberal, the economic and the humanitarian, a national investment and the right of every child, the instrumental and the intrinsic, what education *is for* and what it *is*, elitism and egalitarianism, and perhaps, in general, between the possible and the desirable, between reality and idealism. (1999: 167)

In conclusion we can say that there are various theories concerning human nature and that these provide alternative views of how society can be organized and, in turn, of the purposes of education. The education system reflects the differing values of the society in which it exists as well as helping to shape its future. As Young put it:

> the history, the social divisions and the many competing interests and value systems found in a modern society are expressed in the school curriculum as much as they are in its system of government or its occupational structure.

> Likewise, curriculum debates, implicitly or explicitly, are always debates about alternative views of society and its future. (1998: 9)

Ideologies are central to the development of education which is not an objective enterprise. Questions concerning its nature and purpose are returned to again and again throughout this book. We now turn to the interest education holds for a number of significant disciplines concerned with the study of people and society. The discussion will illustrate how the approaches and theories developed within these disciplines may be used by those students whose main concern is the study of education itself.

Approaches to the study of education

Philosophy

Philosophy is concerned with the very materials of thought, with ideas and their foundations and asks fundamental questions about the nature of things. Some would claim that philosophy deals with the foundations on which all other kinds of knowledge can be constructed. Philosophy often deals with quite everyday things, but makes them seem strange and unfamiliar in order to see them differently. Martin Heidegger (1889–1976), for example, begins his inquiry into the nature of 'metaphysics' with what he calls the 'question of questions': 'Why is there something rather than nothing?' This question may seem moderately interesting to the non-philosopher for a few passing moments but appears somewhat bizarre when represented as *the* single most important issue in the world. Heidegger's particular obsession was with ontology, the branch of philosophy concerned with 'being': identity, difference, knowledge. Heidegger was equally concerned with defining the 'ontological difference', that is, the difference between Being and beings.

Some of the more abstruse concerns of philosophy, like the question of being, can be demonstrated to have a bearing on important questions for education. Part of the value of this kind of question is that it enables thinking to go beyond the limits of commonsense, the everyday perception of how things are. This can be valuable in terms of gaining fresh perspectives on familiar issues as well as enabling a rethink of what seems to be natural and inevitable. So philosophy can help us to see things again, to refresh our sense of what education is or might be.

Philosophy can provide resources also for thinking, reminding us of some of the fundamental issues that are at stake. This seems particularly relevant to questions about knowledge and the curriculum but also can be useful in terms of taking our thinking back to basics, enabling fundamental questions, such as 'What is a school?'

The philosophy of education raises questions about the relations of theory and practice and particularly about the role of theory. Many teachers and other practitioners may be impatient of theory which they see as irrelevant to the concerns of practical education. This blindness to theory or privileging of practice over theory can be both destructive and dangerous. At the same time, theory which has little reference to the real contexts of education may be justly characterized as out of touch, though that does not necessarily render it utterly and completely useless. In fact, all educational practice is rooted in theory or theories even though it may not realize it. The failure to realize the presence of theory in practice may be characterized as a critical kind of blindness. For example, the learning of practical classroom skills cannot be the end point of good educational practice. There must be an exploration that goes beyond that, that confronts the vital questions like: what is it important to know? How does learning take place? Is teaching the same as learning? What are the relations between the two? Should teachers impose their version of culture and language on pupils? What are the ethics of teaching today? Philosophy can provide routes towards developing answers to these questions. It might not provide all the solutions and the practical resolutions but it is essential to have a philosophical attitude towards these questions to avoid rigidity and tunnel vision.

Epistemology would seem to be the branch of philosophy most concerned with education. Epistemology is concerned with questions of knowledge, how we know what we know and how we may orient ourselves to what we do not know. Plato's dialogue *Meno* puts this question. The pursuit of knowledge, according to the logic of this Platonic question, cannot be solely a matter for the individual. The education of the individual is not self-authoring. It cannot be. Education begins with the acquisition of ideas, images, words, grammar, all the already existing technologies of thought. Above all it starts with the acquisition of language which we now know is embedded within cultural knowledge about the world. Education depends on being born into and inducted into a world of knowledge and meaning that pre-exists the individual. While the quest for knowledge is often represented as a solitary journey through various stages, there must already exist a kind of staging of knowledge. We do not each of us have to find out everything for the first time. We draw on existing and established forms of knowledge held by others and this raises the question of authority and power in the process of knowledge acquisition. Children may be encouraged to explore the world around them for themselves. Some models of education emphasize the investigative nature of learning but children must also acquire established skills and knowledge, like reading, for example, which they cannot make up for themselves. This always requires the submission to a prior authority, an order that precedes the individual. The relations between the individual, knowledge, exploration, the social formation, the institutions of education and knowledge, all may come within the scope of philosophy and link philosophy with more seemingly worldly subjects like sociology and cultural studies.

Epistemology may ask questions of knowledge, its sources, its history, its 'provenance', its claims to authority and where these derive from, and may also ask questions about the relations between the knower and the known, between teaching and learning, individuals and institutions. Sooner or later questions about knowledge touch on questions about society, about ethics and about institutions and how they work. Critical epistemology may ask radical questions of the curriculum, probing the rights of subjects to authority, pressing questions about the contents of subjects and their cultural biases, for instance, or presenting alternative views of what knowledge really is.

Ontology is the branch of philosophy concerned with 'being'. Ontology asks questions about what any aspect of education is and how we can define its being. Take the well-known phenomenon of the school, for instance. Is it possible to say what it is? What are its necessary constituent elements? Where does it begin and end? How can we define its physical being, its social being and its educational being? What are the relations between these different but necessarily parallel modes of being? What is 'the school' in this general sense? While it may seem strange to ask these questions of so well-known a phenomenon as the school, this kind of interrogative starting again may give rise to interesting lines of inquiry.

Hermeneutics is the area of philosophy concerned with interpretation and therefore with questioning. A hermeneutic approach might be characterized as one which *begins* with questions, opens up subsequent questions and pursues its line of inquiry in an inquisitive mode to produce interpretations or possible interpretations. In the context of education this might be seen as an obviously useful and pertinent branch of philosophy, since education is necessarily associated with processes of questioning, discovery, further questioning and, in the end, with producing interpretations. Education is often represented as a kind of lifelong quest and the interrogative, interpretive spirit is sometimes seen as a quintessential factor in the process of being inducted into education.

Hermeneutics might also be applied to individual subject areas, to characterize how they work. What, for example, is the characteristic hermeneutic of history? In other words what are the characteristic questions of history and how does history habitually conduct its inquiries to produce its interpretations of historical matter? In history, for example, it might be said that archaeology is characteristic of a historical hermeneutic: discovering archaeological sources, conducting an archaeological inquiry (or 'dig'), gathering the fragments of evidence, weighing their significance, organizing fragments into a coherent pattern, producing a number of hypotheses, reducing the possible interpretations of the evidence and producing an account of the work conducted in the inquiry and its various paths and their different tracks. This might provide a crude abstract of the hermeneutic of historical archaeology. The same kind of questions might be asked of other subject areas, forms of knowledge which operate according to quite different principles and methods, mathematics or geography, for example.

Clearly, the business of interpretation and of setting the limits of inquiry and procedures of inquiry are of vital importance in education and in the study of education. Hermeneutics may open up questions about methods of teaching and learning, about the specific procedures of inquiry in given subject areas and may also indicate the importance of language and of representation in any arena of study, including education.

Phenomenology, as the word itself would suggest, is somehow concerned with 'phenomena' or 'things'. In fact, questions about what things there are in the world, and how we might know them, are a good deal more complicated, and a great deal more interesting, than they might at first appear. Phenomenology may in fact be a radical way of rethinking the very conditions of knowledge of 'things', of ourselves and of being in the world. Phenomenology explores the relations between consciousness and the world, and so deals with fundamental conditions of knowledge. How do we know what we see? How do we know what we see is? What are the relations between what we see and our ideas? And where do these ideas come from? These question touch on issues concerning identity, language, culture and being. For an account of phenomenology as a branch of philosophy see Moran (2000).

A simple way of exploring the business of phenomenology is to consider and abstract from a single case of the relations between subject and object. A subject is a centre of human consciousness, a 'knower', and an object is something that is apprehended by a subject, a 'thing' or something 'known'. To common-sense perception this is a simple matter. A house is a house pure and simple. In our ordinary, everyday experiences we do not question ourselves along the lines: but how do I know it is 'a house'? What makes it a house? Is it always a house?

We know that schools are perceived quite differently from different perspectives and that it is difficult, therefore, to give a definitive and final version of what a school is. One view will no doubt represent the school as an instrument for learning, as a place for the development of knowledge, skills and understanding. A poor, working-class child in the 1920s might have seen the school in totally different terms as a place of imposed discipline where rules of conduct were enforced, where ideas about the Empire were promoted and where certain practices were maintained under a strictly disciplinarian regime. These differences of perception can be multiplied and will often conflict with one another. Who is to say in the end what the school *is*: instrument of learning or enforced disciplinary regime? The question of the identity of the school is complicated by the fact that the school will have many different aspects.

It may be felt that ethics is at the centre of education, that education is itself an ethical practice. Public discourses increasingly refer to rights of education as natural, recognizing both the rights of children and the rights of parents. At the same time, education is also often seen in contemporary political discourses as a duty, as a duty of the state to make adequate and proper provision. Education is also felt in media discourses, particularly, to be concerned with the communication of values and codes of conduct. In contemporary terms there is a significant tension between the idea of education as an ethical practice concerned with the cultivation of values and the production of active, empowered citizens, and with education as providing the appropriate kinds of knowledge and skills for national economic success. This tension marks the difference between an essentially ethical view of education and a utilitarian view discussed earlier in relation to the perspectives of Rousseau and Hobbes. Philosophy can illuminate these differences and examine their implications for policy and for practice.

Ideas about the world, what and how it is, have an important bearing on conceptions of the good society. Clearly this has an important bearing on education. Many features of contemporary schooling are founded on some kind of social theory informed by ethical issues. Philosophy may not seem relevant to detailed, immediate practical questions of politics, but philosophical thinking may, and does, inform policy. Philosophy has a range of resources and positions for thinking about education (see Barrow and Woods, 1988, for instance). Twentieth-century thought has been especially productive in revealing the interplay between language and philosophy, and to some extent, psychology, sociology and history too.

Sociology

Sociology seeks to produce knowledge about the nature of societies and to provide frameworks for understanding social life and social practices. Sociological researches may be concerned with any number of particular phenomena. Durkheim's (1858–1917) famous research into suicide, for instance, is concerned above all with suicide as an occasion for examining social processes and forces (Durkheim, 1970). At one level, sociology must be highly abstract, general and theoretical. It deals with models of society, attempting to provide working descriptions of the many complex and different phenomena. While some theorists have worked with an overarching theory of society others have argued that this is not possible, that societies are composed of quite discrete departments of existence and that grand social theories run the risk of doing violence to the complexities of industrial and post-industrial societies. Sociology has always been concerned to account for the very nature of social life.

Macro-level research is concerned with such large-scale theories and explanations for behaviour. For example, the functionalist view is that social institutions operate to maintain the whole society. Hence early attempts which describe schools as functioning for the benefit of society (Davis and Moore, 1967) and also accounts of the roles of teachers and pupils (Banks, 1968). The conflict perspective suggests that societies are always riven with antagonism and attempts to show how education is part of the process whereby the ruling classes maintain their position (Bowles and Gintis, 1976). These macro theories emphasize how individuals are 'shaped' by social forces more powerful than themselves. The micro approach of the interactionists is more concerned with how individuals operate within society. They are interested in how students develop self-images through the operation of processes such as labelling and how this in turn influences their future behaviour (Hargreaves, 1967; Hargreaves et al., 1975). This approach emphasizes how social life is constantly being constructed and reconstructed by the actors themselves who make rational decisions according to their interpretations of circumstances. More recently the influence has been felt of 'postmodern' theories that challenge some of the established theoretical positions and that propose new ways of looking at the social world. Postmodern perspectives have been controversial for some. They offer perspectives and ideas that are not always very comforting and suggest that old ideas about history, society and knowledge are drastically out of place in the new postmodern world order. They challenge some of the most deep-seated ideas of the modern period, including the ideas of progress, of 'humanity', of objective knowledge, and they have even problematized the very idea of truth (Lyotard, 1986).

None of these positions has entirely displaced any of the others. While they conflict in quite fundamental ways with one another, there are important ways in which they speak to one another and give rise to new positions (Kumar, 1995). The major division in sociology between theories that emphasize structure and theories that emphasize social interaction has frequently been challenged by influential sociologists from Max Weber (1864–1920) to Anthony Giddens (1993). C. Wright Mills (1959) referred to the attempt to see social structures at work in the lives of individuals as 'the sociological imagination', breaking down conceptual barriers between the private and the social.

Highly sophisticated techniques for gathering and processing data have been developed in sociology. Some of these practices aspire to be scientific in style, dealing in 'hard facts', statistics and quantifiable phenomena. Some sociologists have developed more interpretive research methodologies for dealing with less tangible material, like attitudes, beliefs, ways of feeling and seeing. Ethnography is a research strategy which has been drawn from anthropology to explore social practices, institutions and environments 'from the inside' to understand how people operate within them (see Hammersley and Atkinson, 1995). In education, sociological research has covered a massive range of topics from large-scale studies of educational attainment through generations (Glass, 1954), to small-scale researches into classroom practices and how they are experienced and perceived by the different actors involved in them (Hammersley and Woods, 1984).

Education, of one kind or another, is at the centre of any society. Values, customs and practices are transmitted from generation to generation through some form of education. Processes of socialization, of being inducted into values, customs and practices, are necessarily to do with education. The rise of sociology as a discipline coincides with the development of the importance of the education system in western societies. It is hardly surprising then that education should be seen as a fundamental aspect of sociology, in some ways as a key to the understanding of social processes and values. The school as we know it is a central institution in social life invested with considerable legal and social power. The familiarity of the school for us, a taken for granted feature of social life, should not diminish our sense of the remarkable fact of the school's emergence as a key institution for social management and development in modern (post-1870) societies. In western societies, all children will spend large amounts of their time going through the intricate processes of schooling, learning codes of conduct, values, ideas, different skills and generally being inducted into society. Modern societies are very much schooled societies. Social roles and values are acquired through processes of schooling. Schools work in particular ways to produce age stratification and many would argue to enhance and emphasize social class stratification (Hamilton, 1989).

Sociologists became increasingly conscious of the question of the school and inequality. After the Second World War, as education was being associated with the welfare state and a new social order that offered access to higher education and social advancement to all sectors of society, it became increasingly clear that the dream of social transformation through schooling was not being realized (Halsey and Anderson, 1961). Social class differences were found to be important factors influencing educational success and failure (Douglas, 1964; Jackson and Marsden, 1962). Other kinds of social difference, gender, race and ethnicity in particular, were also found to be significant (Deem, 1984; Klein, 1993; Spender, 1982). In recent years the attention of many sociologists has turned to the policy-making process itself and the power and influence of different socio-political groups (Ball, 1994).

Though it is an academic study, sociological theory and research has, to some extent, been influential in informing governmental policy and has entered into the practices and ideas of teachers. Some of the major policy shifts in education in the second half of the twentieth century in the UK, for instance, were influenced by sociological researches, and their ideas remain powerful for many working in schools and other sectors of education. Education is clearly of great interest to sociologists and provides a rich context for sociological research. The individual and society, socialization, inequality, institutions, values and norms all constitute major themes and concerns.

History

What special kinds of understanding of education can be divined from its history? Any attempt to account for education in the here and now, to describe its structure and its particular concrete reality, can be enhanced by reference to its history, how it came to be what it is (Hunter, 1994).

The present can be seen as the movement from the past to the future. What is here *now* is the product of the past. The history of the education system as we know it, state-funded education from 1870, provides one very powerful way of understanding why things in education are as they are. It is possible to trace the processes whereby the present order of things has become established. It is possible to see the large phases through which education has passed to achieve its current status and form. It is possible to detect the ideas and policies that motivated educational change and the development of practices that now have the status of common-sense wisdom and are accepted as necessary elements (Donald, 1992).

This book will explore briefly the period leading up to the development of state education as we know it. It will also make frequent reference to the post Second World War history of education and especially to recent developments since the mid-1980s that have had an influence on what schools are and how they work, and which have influenced the curriculum, access to higher education and ideas about academic and vocational education. This is done in the belief that the present is marked with the traces of the movements of the past.

There is a history of the school, too, and a history of the classroom. Classroom practice as we know it in schools today has evolved in history. It came into being through different processes and movements. In current practice we can see traces of ideas, movements and habits of past times. The classroom itself is the product of a complex history, just as teaching and the teacher are. The modern, contemporary school may be regarded as an archaeological site that bears the traces of previous eras of the school. Some of these will be faintly present, like early twentieth-century discourses of nationalism, traces of which are visible in the modern National Curriculum and its ideas of a 'national heritage'. Some will be obvious and blatantly visible, like 'moral' school assemblies that have a deep tradition in the history of schooling. Knowledge of former eras and practice can illuminate the present and can also provide a kind of vantage point from which to view and review present practices. Then again, some historians would claim that the history of education has no need to justify itself in terms of a practical value. It can claim the right to exist simply in so far as it advances knowledge and understanding, whether or not for practical application (Grosvenor, Lawn et al., 1999).

The history of education has been dominated by the period from 1870 to the present with a good deal of emphasis also given to the period leading to 1870. The reasons for this are perhaps obvious given that 1870 is the symbolic 'moment' of a huge transition in education, leading to the present order of things. The history of this modern period in education can be divided roughly into phases:

- 1800–70: towards state education
- 1870–1902: the first stages of elementary schooling
- 1902–44: local government and changing practices of the state
- 1944–65: universal secondary education
- 1965–88: the comprehensive school
- 1988–present day: competition

Each of these phases represents a significant stage in the development of education, though some contemporary historians would be wary of thinking in terms of progressive development. The phases outlined above are not completely discrete, either (see Brooks, 1991). The phase belonging to the comprehensive school does not, for instance, represent the unequivocal triumph of comprehensive schooling. The project of comprehensive education, involving a break-up and reformation of the previous 'tripartite' system, was never in fact complete. Comprehensive schools were not universal, though in some areas they became the dominant form of state provision. During the period 1965–88, selective grammar schools remained powerful magnets in many areas and the private/public school system remained largely untouched by developments in the state sector, leaving the question about inequality and an elite system open and unanswered. Similarly, the reforms of 1988 and beyond have not totally erased the idea of the comprehensive school. Many existing local community schools have striven to maintain a comprehensive provision, keeping faith with the ideals of equality of opportunity which the comprehensive school in its ideal form was considered by many to embody. Some would want to fiercely defend the unrealized comprehensive school as the true object of educational development (Benn and Chitty, 1996).

One problem with describing the history of education in phases is that it implies linearity, or a sequence of interlinking events and developments. Some models of history would challenge the idea of a smooth narrative and would also challenge the centrality given to matters of education policy, claiming that the big narrative accounts necessarily omit the countless other stories, struggles and events. They might also complain that linear policy history actually deals with only a small and not necessarily overarchingly important segment of the history of education. Contemporary history of education may review the history of the school as an institution (Copeland, 1999) by asking what were the effects on the populations of schooling, how can these effects be gauged, what of the untold stories of countless thousands who passed through schooling and whose lives were marked with its traces? An ethnography of classroom practices, looking back at former practices, conducting interviews with former pupils and teachers, and so on would furnish a very different kind of history from that which charts changes in legislation and in the formal arrangements of schooling.

Similarly, important areas of educational history have been opened up by a cultural-studies oriented approach where questions might be asked about specific histories in the field of education. The role of women in the management of early board schools, for instance, is one instance of a study concerned to uncover the unwritten gender politics of a small but significant segment of the history of education. Exploring the practices of schooling after the First World War in the cultivation and promotion of ideas of the nation and empire, for instance, might necessitate doing some archaeological or genealogical researches into textbooks, recorded events, ethnographic work with the elderly and so on. Recent historical studies include accounts of the education experiences of refugee populations in England and Wales, studies conducted of teachers' roles in resistance in Europe during the Second World War, analyses of early school photographs and studies of the cultural and social implications of school architecture. Thus different historical studies provide different perspectives on the complex interactions of policy, institutions, practices, individuals and social groups within the field of education. Overarching histories of education may still provide useful accounts of larger movements, surface trends and changing legislative frameworks for education.

The contemporary history of education may witness further developments in terms of its relations with cultural studies and other fields of knowledge. The rediscovery of unspoken, unwritten histories remains an important and potentially very rich area for development. The impact of post-structuralist theories and postmodern theories of social and historical processes also signals a review of hitherto existing histories and tendencies in the history of education. The work of Foucault (1980), for instance, has been deeply influential in terms of generating rethought accounts of the role of schooling in contemporary societies and has had a profound influence on the interpretation of the emergence of state education. Similarly post-structuralist theories of meaning and interpretation can influence how history is conceived of as well as how specific historical researches may be conducted and how specific histories may be produced through a rethinking of symbols, texts and narrative.

It seems self-evident, perhaps, that the study of history should be central to education studies, though little attention is given to the history of education in the training of teachers. Understanding the processes, pressures, events, stages, linkages, ruptures and so on that give rise to the contemporary scene must be useful and productive for students of education and for the development of reflective and aware teachers. Similarly, studying even remote examples may provide useful points of reference to review and rethink contemporary dominant practices.

Psychology

Psychology is a relatively new science, having its early roots in the philosophy of mind, of science and of language. It draws from physiology, neuroscience, artificial intelligence, linguistics, anthropology and cultural studies. Psychology is concerned with how humans process information, how they react to situations and other people, how they feel, behave and think. Each of these aspects of psychological study is of great interest within education. Thus, in Chapter 4, although the core of our examination will lie within *cognitive psychology* (the processes of thinking, knowing, remembering and problem-solving), this cannot be in isolation from aspects of *social psychology* (the processes of relating to others, learning through interaction, and the influence of the perceived views of others on behaviour, motivation and self-esteem).

Psychology would seem to be fundamental to the study of education and to the development of educational practices. Understanding the very specific mental processes of teaching and learning is relevant to both students of education and to intending teachers. The study of psychology, however, like history, sociology and philosophy, is largely omitted from current postgraduate teacher education courses. In the context of the contemporary school the educational psychologist usually has a responsibility for dealing with special cases and with definitions of children deemed to have special needs, rather than informing the work and ethos of the school as a whole. Many would see this lack of psychological knowledge in teaching and learning institutions as critical.

Educational psychology is particularly concerned with questions about what makes learning happen: what are the factors involved in human learning? How do children learn? What kind of environment is most conducive to learning? How can schools promote maximum learning for all their pupils, given all their differences? The psychology of education, then, necessarily has relations and connections with other disciplines including sociology and linguistics, for instance, and may be influential in terms of promoting certain models of teaching and learning and certain kinds of school design.

While the psychology of education is concerned with ideas about the mental processes of learning, it is also concerned with big questions about the influence of heredity and the environment on individuals and has its own contribution to make to studies of underachievement just as sociology has. Some of the most influential reports on education, leading to some fairly seismic shifts in the practices of schooling, have been seriously influenced by psychology. The 1967 Plowden Report (CACE, 1967) on primary schooling, for example, promoted a certain view of learning that became deeply influential in the primary sector and that gave rise to, or at least accompanied, changes in school design which involved large shifts in practice. The Bullock Report of 1975 was influenced in its model of teaching and learning by J.S. Bruner. The influence of Lev Vygotsky could also be felt in the document though it was processed in a particular way through the work of James Britton (see Chapter 4 for a brief account of the work of Bruner and Vygotsky). The Bullock Report had a serious influence on the practices of English teaching as well as impacting upon other subjects with its emphasis on active learning and small group talk in the classroom.

Explanations of how learning and development works, and what might be the impediments to development, derive from a number of perspectives. During the first part of the twentieth century psychology was dominated by behaviourist explanations of learning where the emphasis was very much on how external stimuli led to learned responses (Skinner, 1957; Watson, 1913a; 1913b). Those who emphasized the internal cognitive processes at work in learning and development were dissatisfied with the partial nature of this approach. The work of Piaget (1932; 1954) saw development being structured by pre-given periods of maturation that tended to follow a universal structure in human individuals. This structuralist approach was very influential from the middle of the last century but many of its original claims about the limitations imposed by maturational patterns have since been challenged (Donaldson, 1978). Piaget was interested in the mental structures through which the learner's experience led to concept development. The information-processing school of the latter half of the century developed systematic explanations for concept formation, exploring the processes of attention, perception and memory involved (see Chapter 4).

One of the most influential contemporary set of ideas around learning and development is the movement associated with the Russian psychologist, Vygotsky, which provides a challenge to Piaget's theory of an internal, structural developmental pattern. The major theme of Vygotsky's theoretical framework is that social interaction plays a fundamental role in the development of cognition. Vygotsky states:

> Every function in the child's cultural development appears twice: first, on the social level, and later, on the individual level; first, between people (interpsychological) and then inside the child (intrapsychological). This applies equally to voluntary attention, to logical memory, and to the formation of concepts. All the higher functions originate as actual relationships between individuals. (1978: 57)

Vygotsky's position highlights the social dimension of learning and puts a powerful emphasis on the symbolic and linguistic components of early learning interactions. The range of skill that can be developed with adult guidance or peer collaboration exceeds what can be attained alone.

Theories of personality development are relevant to an examination of individual factors affecting educational attainment. Individuals daily make judgments about the character traits and social responses of themselves and each other. We 'size each other up', making an assessment about how to behave based on how we think the other person may react. In the classroom or lecture theatre this can often be seen in sharp relief in interactions between pupils or between tutors and students. It is important then for those in education to have some understanding of the individual nature of personality functioning. Psychological research also suggests that underlying personality dimensions may determine learning behaviour and that this manifests itself in learners' cognitive styles, approaches to learning and motivation levels (Riding and Rayner, 1998).

Dominant ideas of the last century about intellectual power, or intelligence, have been seriously challenged by a number of newer approaches including Sternberg's (1985) and Gardner's (1993) ideas about different types of intelligence. An emphasis is increasingly placed on the advantages of learners being self-determining and metacogni-tively aware (Montgomery, 1996). Teachers are also more alert to the impact of social and emotional factors and feelings of self-worth on individual achievement.

Some researchers are revealing the potential of literature as a psycho-logical tool, with culture considered to be the foundation of human experience and language, writing and different literary forms providing the cultural-psychological tools by which psychological processes are mastered. 'Ontologically, such psychology should be grounded in cul-ture (versus nature), epistomologically it should be concerned with interpretation (versus prediction), and methodologically it should be oriented towards semiotics (versus physics)' (Kozulin, 1998: 134). The power of literary text analysis to challenge the dependence of cognitive development on decontextualized mental operations is very new but worthy of attention.

The psychology of education then deals with fundamental issues in teaching and learning that touch on ideas, in turn, about the curriculum, the school, about teaching and learning relations, about culture, lan-guage and environment. At the centre of the psychology of education is the idea of person transformation, the very powerful notion that the everyday phenomenon of teaching and learning is actually about chang-ing the substance of individuals and groups of individuals. Given the fact that education remains at the centre of the modern state, this idea itself warrants amazement and takes us back perhaps to the fundamental philosophical question about the 'being' of education: what is education?

Conclusion

Some would argue that too much time is spent looking at questions concerning the nature and purposes of education. There is a tendency to criticise and decry theorising by academics as being removed from the 'real' issues of education. There is perhaps a wish to stop talking and get on with it. This of course assumes agreement as to what 'it' is. Her Majesty's former Chief Inspector for Education, Chris Woodhead, wrote in his annual report for 1998/99:

> we know what constitutes good teaching and we know what needs to be done
> to tackle weaknesses: we must strengthen subject knowledge, raise expecta-
> tions, and hone the pedagogic skills upon which the craft of the classroom
> depends . . . Why, then, is so much time and energy wasted in research that
> complicates what ought to be straightforward . . . If standards are to continue

to rise we need decisive management action, locally and nationally that con-
centrates attention on the two imperatives that really matter: the drive to
improve teaching and strengthen leadership . . . The challenge now is to
expose the emptiness of education theorizing that obfuscates the classroom
realities that really matter. (OFSTED, 2000: 21)

Woodhead's apparent rejection of alternatives could be interpreted as
an attempt to close down debate and to silence dissenting viewpoints.
Education, not least because of its ideological basis, will always be
important in the political arena and for those who study politics and
policy: 'Although many people still take the view that "education
should be kept out of politics", questions about the social, economic
and cultural purposes of education have always been the subject of contentious political debate' (Carr and Hartnett, 1996: 17). Thus the study
of education draws from many disciplines all of which are interested in
people and society. It is important to be aware of this multidisciplinary
character and to acknowledge the complexity of educational issues.

Education is a central part of any society. It is to do with helping to
shape the future in terms of developing individuals and the promotion
of ideas. Politicians, parents, teachers, employers, taxpayers and pupils
all have their own views of the purposes of education and what it
should involve. The interaction of these sometimes competing interests
renders education a fascinating area for study.

Student activities

1 In order of priority compile a list of the ten most important things a
   school should educate its pupils in. Compare your list with those of
   other students in the group. To what extent are ideologies apparent
   in these lists?
2 Choose three significant learning experiences that you remember
   from lessons when you were at school. These may have been isolated
   incidents or they may have occurred regularly over a period of time.
   How do these relate to the ideologies of education considered earlier
   in this chapter? Compare your analysis with others in your group.

Recommended reading

Meighan, R. and Siraj-Blatchford, I. (1998) *A Sociology of Educating*, London: Cassell.
A good book to read after this one. An interesting account of the different aspects

of the educational experience and the sociological perspective on education. An easy to follow discussion of ideologies provides an excellent typology to use in analysis. As the title suggests, this book is also useful reading on how social factors influence success in education.

Morrison, K. and Ridley, K. (1989) 'Ideological contexts for curriculum planning', in M. Preedy (ed.), *Approaches to Curriculum Management*, Milton Keynes: Open University Press. This is an excellent overview of educational ideologies. It illustrates how ideologies underpin curriculum development and also provides a useful analytical framework.

Carr, W. and Hartnett, A. (1996) *Education and the Struggle for Democracy: The Politics of Educational Ideas*, Buckingham; Open University Press. This is a very well written account of the development of the education system and how this is linked to the main political ideologies. An excellent discussion of the underpinning ideologies of education. Though more advanced it tackles important educational ideas and theory which students must confront.

Kelly, A.V. (1999) *The Curriculum: Theory and Practice*, 4th edn, London: Paul Chapman Publishing.This is a significant academic analysis of curriculum development and the underpinning ideologies. Suitable for the more advanced student, this is a detailed and challenging volume.

2

Researching Education

In this chapter we aim to show the importance of research in developing an understanding of the field of education. The relationship between research paradigms and notions of reality are explored. This chapter discusses how the beliefs inherent in the different paradigms inform the whole research process from the selection of issues regarded as worthy of research, the purposes of the research and questions of validity, to the status of different forms of data and the relevance of different methods of data collection. Qualitative and quantitative methods of data collection are briefly outlined and related to the discussion of paradigms. Research is presented as an integral part of the process of education itself and, as such, is argued to be central to individual and professional development. Action research and school-effectiveness research are critiqued in terms of both their methodological features and their contribution to the study of education.

What is research?

Chapter 1 established that education is a broad area of study involving a number of disciplines. Research within these disciplines may provide discrete lessons for the student of education or it may overlap and interweave in a complex manner. The questions which interest education researchers often relate to these specific disciplines. For example, some are interested in the individual, how learning takes place and the cognitive processes involved, while others may wish to examine social issues such as the ways in which race, gender and class continue to be significant in terms of 'success' in education. Yet others decide to examine the policies of successive governments and the influence these have had on practice in different sectors of education. The skills to investigate and gather information in pursuit of these research foci require a working knowledge of the research process. This chapter will consider research in relation to the study of education. It should be read in conjunction with specific methodological texts for practical details of how to construct research projects and devise particular research instruments.

Formal research may seem daunting to the novice but we are already used to gathering data in many ways on a daily basis. The methods we typically use to find things out include observing situations or particular events, listening to the radio, asking different people, looking things up in books or surfing the World Wide Web. All of this normal activity is data collection. We do it to make sense of the world in which we operate. The goal may be simple and straightforward such as to find out what the weather will be like next day. It may involve gathering data from several sources which is perhaps typical of a school homework task where pupils are required to find something out about their neighbourhood. They may need to use newspapers, ask some local people or find a map. Another data gathering task is when we carefully question several friends to find some interesting, perhaps controversial, information, for instance, what happened at a social event we missed. We realize, of course, the subtle differences that asking such friends individually, or in certain combinations, would make to the information gleaned. As new information becomes available to us in our daily lives we are constantly checking, modifying, refining and developing what we know. Local opinion, regional newspapers and international news are all useful but for different interests and purposes. Clearly then, different methods of gathering information are appropriate to different situations.

It is also apparent that the skills of the researcher are very significant to the achievable outcomes and that these skills improve with practice. We are all researchers in that we have to make sense of our world. Our personal research methods are in permanent use. We become skilled at analysing and evaluating data, making decisions as to its validity or truthfulness. Our skills usually depend on previous experience. Some information received carries more weight than alternative sources of evidence. Within conversations do we believe a particular person's account more than someone else's? When watching something happening we probably ask ourselves if this is what usually happens. Are the people involved putting on an act or perhaps showing off? Do we believe the headlines of certain Sunday newspapers or are they exaggerated? We are aware that information gathered may vary and even conflict. So we may expect to hear rather different accounts, for instance, of how efficient the local bus service is when listening to a driver or a passenger in the rush hour. Using both accounts will help provide a broader understanding of the situation.

Information is received from a wide range of sources. Some of this is even portrayed as research findings. In a typical evening's television viewing, for example, information about political conflict and war, economic developments, garden design, possible holiday destinations and the benefits of particular washing powders, may be presented to us. We evaluate and store or disregard all information presented to us. It is presented to help inform our opinions and make decisions about, for example, smoking or non-smoking, drug and alcohol use or which trainers to buy. We accept some data more readily than others and though we enjoy certain adverts, such as for a particular deodorant, we do remain sceptical of its claims for increasing our sexual magnetism. Presentation impacts differently on people and is a major concern of the advertiser. This is worth remembering when we begin to look at how academic or formal research is presented. This chapter will thus suggest that we must consider many ways of looking at things and maintain a healthily critical approach to all research findings. No research into aspects of education, no matter how detailed, extensive and apparently objective, can tell the whole story. All research is positioned.

Formal research

What does the term 'research' mean when used in relation to academic study? Let us begin by considering some definitions of research:

> All types of research should be 'planned, cautious,systematic, and reliable ways of finding out or deepening understanding'. (Blaxter et al. 1996: 5)

> We use the term research here to describe what we might call 'systematic inquiry': inquiry that is characterized by a certain amount of rigour and governed by sets of principles and guidelines for procedures. (Hitchcock and Hughes, 1993: 3)

> Research in education is a disciplined attempt to address or solve problems through the collection and analysis of primary data for the purpose of description, explanation, generalization and prediction. (Anderson, 1998: 6)

Verma and Mallick suggest that research has attained a high degree of respectability and that educators, politicians, business people and others turn to researchers when seeking information on which to base decisions. Most advanced societies have evolved a research-oriented culture, or are in the process of moving in that direction. They suggest that some essential characteristics of research may be summarized as:

- Research is an organized and deliberate effort to collect new information or to utilize existing knowledge for a new purpose.
- Research seeks to answer worthwhile and fundamental questions, by utilizing valid and reliable techniques.
- Research is logical and objective, using the most appropriate test/s to justify the methods employed, data collected, and the conclusions drawn.
- The final outcome of research contributes to the gaining of new knowledge and a better appreciation of the issues involved (Verma and Mallick, 1999: 3).

Research then, in the academic use of the term, would appear to be the systematic gathering, presenting and analysing of data. Actually, some research is more systematic than others. Some research is more formalized than others. The process is often presented as mysterious to 'outsiders', making researchers seem special, to be held in awe. Perhaps we need to 'demystify' the process in the rest of this chapter.

Much academic research takes the information-gathering practices which we all use daily. Watching other people becomes observation, asking questions becomes interviewing. If the questions are written down they are called questionnaires. The difference is that these information-gathering practices are carried out in a more conscious manner. They become more structured, rigorous and deliberate. The findings are recorded systematically and with care. The research methods are formalized for a number of possible motives: to make more 'scientific', to make larger scale, to make more authoritative, to 'prove', to inform action, to take further than individual experiences. Research, however complex or formally presented, is part of the process of knowing and understanding.

Types and purposes of research

Blaxter et al. suggest that there exists a 'baffling' array of types of research. They list pure, applied and strategic research; descriptive, explanatory and evaluation research; market and academic research; exploratory, testing-out and problem-solving research; covert adversarial and collaborative research; basic, applied, instrumental and action research. However, they suggest that a basic shared characteristic of research is the aim to be 'planned, cautious, systematic and reliable ways of finding out or deepening understanding' (Blaxter et al., 1996: 5).

Anderson talks of two different approaches to research in education, the academic research approach and the contract research approach.

> Unlike academic research, contract research places value not on a detached or disinterested quest for truth, but on the need of the sponsor to know. The contract research approach is a utilitarian approach which assumes that useful knowledge is that which influences practice, and the contract researcher is able to serve a client who needs this knowledge to make informed decisions about educational practice, policy or programmes. (1998: 5)

Verma and Mallick developed the following typology of research which highlights 'critical differences between research that is oriented to the development of theory and that designed to deal with practical problems' (1999: 11).

- *Pure or basic research.* Concerned with the development of theory and discovery of fundamental facts to extend the boundaries of knowledge. This is the type of research typified in laboratories and carried out by 'boffin' scientists. It will ultimately benefit society but that is not its initial purpose. It is the pure pursuit of knowledge for its own sake.
- *Applied or field research.* This is the application of new knowledge to everyday problems. Though more practical it usually employs the same methodology as pure research and is just as rigorous.
- *Action research.* This is research of specific practical situations carried out by practitioners. Its purpose is to solve clearly identified problems. As such it is less concerned with theory, according to Verma and Mallick (a point contested by a number of action researchers in education), though methodology should be as rigorous as possible if the issue is to be analysed and solutions identified successfully. This is research carried out by professionals in order to improve their work. As such it is continuous and cyclical.
- *Evaluation research.* This is carried out to assess the effectiveness of specific projects to see if the original aims have been achieved. Certain government-funded projects allocate a proportion of their budgets for evaluation. In the 1980s the Technical Vocational

Education Initiative (TVEI) project allocated 1 per cent of its budget for evaluation. This seems like a small percentage but it amounted to millions of pounds. It is supposed that these evaluations may be useful for deciding future policy. However, some of these evaluations may be seen as political expediency. With TVEI, the government announced an expansion of funding and declared the initial programme successful before the evaluations were published (see Gleeson, 1987, for a critical appraisal of the TVEI project). Several years later the TVEI extension was never renewed and it is suspected that the final evaluations were never read by the politicians who had made the policy.

Research may be presented in a flow diagram as:

Choose research issue ⊳ develop detailed research questions or focus ⊳ design method(s) of data collection ⊳ collect data ⊳ analyse ⊳ present findings

Research appears here as far neater, more orderly and controlled than it actually is. The influence of personal values on the process is also ignored. Every stage in the process can turn out differently if alternative choices are made by the researchers. Just as the whole notion of education is informed by different beliefs and values so too is the way we study and research it. Education researchers have to make decisions throughout the process which will reflect their ideologies and beliefs concerning both education and research.

Research paradigms

This leads us to examine research paradigms. This term describes models of research which reflect general agreement on the nature of the world and how to investigate it. Within a paradigm there would be a general consensus on the research methods which are appropriate and acceptable for gathering data and also those which are not, or are at least less, acceptable. A paradigm then: 'is a network of coherent ideas about the nature of the world and of the functions of researchers which, adhered to by a group of researchers, conditions the patterns of their thinking and underpins their research actions' (Bassey, 1990: 41).

In social sciences research is often divided into two major paradigms, the positivist or quantitative and the interpretivist or qualitative. These are perhaps best seen as characteristics clustering into two general groups rather than as clear extremes.

Positivist paradigm

This paradigm developed in the nineteenth century with the apparent success of the natural, or physical, sciences in advancing human understanding of the world. Scientific advances had led to improvements in many areas of people's lives, notable examples being in the field of health and medicine, and had contributed to increased standards of living (see Hitchcock and Hughes, 1993).

The scientific approach consists of testing a hypothesis (initial idea, unproved theory) by the experimental method. This often involves having two identical groups. The control group remains untouched – nothing is done to it, all factors which could affect it (variables) are kept constant. The other group, the experimental group, is subject to some change in conditions (certain specific variables are altered in a controlled way). Any resulting change between the experimental and the control group must be due to the change in the variables made by the scientist in the experiment. Experiments are able to establish cause-and-effect relationships. Altering a particular variable has a particular, measurable effect.

The findings from experiments in the natural sciences are said to be objective, in other words, the opinions and hopes of the researcher cannot influence the results of a controlled experiment. The outcome of the experiment, if carried out under the same conditions, will always be consistent. Thus natural science is systematic, experiments are repeatable, the results are documented and knowledge of the natural world is incremental, being built up over time (see Cohen et al., 2000). Research in the natural sciences thus has high prestige and the findings are treated with respect. Pure research in the natural sciences, over time, inevitably became an area of applied research, which had the potential to inform future policy. Such a status was regarded as desirable by those interested in the social world and thus an interest grew in developing the social sciences.

The positivist belief is that the approach of the natural sciences could be applied to the social world. It assumes that the social world exists in the same way as does the natural world. Individual behaviour is continually influenced by various pressures upon us. These may be internal pressures, such as biological and psychological, and/or external pressures, such as the norms and values held by the social groups to which we belong. As a result regular and predictable patterns of behaviour can be said to be displayed by individuals and groups in society. In such a way social forces may be seen to exist as both external and internalized constraints. As individuals we operate within these internalized constraints and influences which derive from our interaction with the wider society.

Positivists believe that the structures which create the apparent order in social life can be discovered by research. They contend that society can be investigated in the same objective way as the natural world. The approach is empirical in that it shows something exists through observations, that is, data. Going beyond theory and debate, positivist researchers attempt to show that what is being discussed in the theories actually exists because it has the status of the external, it is not just hypothetical. The purpose is to uncover the 'social facts' which make up our world.

To be objective, the positivist social science researcher would ideally like to conduct experiments, in the same way as the natural scientist. Some educational research is able to use this method, for instance, certain psychological experiments. However, for much social research it is not possible to create experimental and control groups and to alter variables in a controlled way. People need to be studied in their usual environment if they are to act 'naturally'. There are also moral objections to treating people in certain ways, so though it might appear to be interesting to deprive babies of human affection and see how their personalities develop, it would not be allowed in our society.

In order to show relationships between variables researchers frequently use the comparative method. This is where groups are compared and differences are noted. The purpose is to identify significant variables which explain the differences between the groups. The aim ultimately is to show cause-and-effect relationships. This strategy is felt to be more reliable the greater the numbers used in the comparison. Thus the sample size and its representativeness of the whole population being studied are important factors for the positivist. The findings become more significant when the amount of data collected is larger and can be presented in ways that aid categorization and comparison. It is important that the researcher maintains an objective standpoint and keeps personal 'contamination' of the data collection process to a minimum. The most effective positivist research is able to be replicated by others, as with experiments in the natural sciences, or at least compared closely with other similar studies. For these reasons positivist researchers prefer structured methods of data collection which can be carried out on a large scale (macro studies). The data favoured is quantitative, usually presented as statistical tables. This enables others to see how the data has been interpreted and allows for more accurate comparisons. It also attempts to minimize the affect of the particular researcher. The aim is to be able to generalize from the findings.

Certain criticisms have been levelled at the positivist paradigm:

1 Statistics may show trends but they do not explain why people have done or said certain things. They are unable to yield detailed accounts of people's reasons thus the meanings obtained from statistical data remain superficial. Statistics of truancy, absence or examination success may show interesting trends but it is the stories behind them that explain these trends. In this way statistics may be seen as impersonal. Positivist methods may ignore the richness of detailed individual accounts.

2 Statistical correlations should not be confused with causality. There may be statistical relations between social deprivation and lack of educational success but we need to go further than statistical analysis to see if the link is real and to seek explanations.

3 Statistical tables and analysis appear to be objective but the significance of individual researchers in their compilation must not be overlooked. A researcher decides what to look for, designs and asks certain questions yet ignores other possibilities. The statistics have to be collected and the answers interpreted and categorized. It would be dangerous to assume that this whole process is unaffected by human contamination (see Cohen et al, 2000). See Edwards and Usher (2000) for an exposition of strong theoretical grounds for challenging the objectivity and scientific claims of positivist approaches to education research.

Interpretivist paradigm

This is an umbrella term for many social perspectives, notably phenomenology, symbolic interactionism and ethnomethodology (see Cohen et al., 2000, for a brief outline of these perspectives). This paradigm does not see society as having a fixed structure, hidden or not. The social world is created by the interactions of individuals. There are norms and values but these do not exist as clear-cut entities. They are used and changed by people as part of their daily lives. People, termed actors by some interpretivists, interpret events and act in response. Though there are external pressures upon individuals we are not seen to be controlled by some external system. Weber (see Cuff and Payne,

1984) maintained that actions must be seen as meaningful at the level of interaction. By this he meant that action is taken to be deliberate and meaningful to those involved and the interpretivist paradigm seeks to understand the meanings behind these actions.

The interpretivist tries to show how choices are made by actors in social situations within the process of interaction. For the interpretivist there is no single objective reality which exists outside the actor's explanations, just different versions of events. Pupils, the classroom teacher, other teachers at the school, parents, all have a view of 'what goes on' and act according to how they interpret events. The researcher in this paradigm seeks to 'understand' these actions.

Interpretivists prefer 'softer' more 'naturalistic' forms of data collection. While quantitative data, in the form of statistics, is seen as impersonal, qualitative data involves explanations which seek to explain and understand the actions of those being studied. The researcher makes use of individual accounts and biographies, and often includes detailed descriptions to give a 'feeling' for the environment. Methods favoured in interpretivist studies are informal interviews and observations which allow the situation to be as 'normal' as possible (Hitchcock and Hughes, 1993). These methods are often reliant upon the ability of the researcher to be reflexive in the research process.

Interpretivist studies tend to be small scale (micro) aiming for detail and understanding rather than statistical representativeness. While it is not possible to generalize from such studies, their strength lies in the relatability of the findings (see Bassey, 1990). Though researchers within this paradigm do not believe that it is possible to study social life in the same way as a natural science, they do attempt to be as rigorous as possible.

Woods (1999) suggests that the main features of qualitative research are:

- *A focus on natural settings*. 'Qualitative research is concerned with life as it is lived, things as they happen, situations as they are constructed in the day-to-day, moment-to-moment course of events' (1999: 2). Social life is seen as complex with many different layers. The qualitative researcher provides partial accounts, never total. There is no single account of the whole reality. Knowledge through social research is always provisional, to be developed by future research. 'There is no fixed, immutable truth in social science' (1999: 3).
- *An interest in meanings, perspectives and understandings*. The researcher seeks to understand and to portray the participants' perceptions and understandings of the particular situation or event. The researcher

must be reflexive to the meanings which those being studied attach to situations.

- *An emphasis on process.* Interaction is ongoing. The qualitative researcher is interested in how the 'story goes', how those involved act and respond. There is a continuing chain of events which gives insight into how people live. This is more significant than static over-arching models of the positivists.
- *Inductive analysis and grounded theory.* The term 'grounded theory' comes from Glaser and Strauss (1967). In qualitative studies the researchers do not begin hoping to prove or disprove a set hypothesis. They may have ideas on how 'things will go' but the theory comes from the data after the research has begun. It is 'grounded' in the data and the experiences of the researcher rather than being imposed upon the research.

Ethnography

This is a research strategy used by interpretivists which developed from anthropological studies of small-scale societies. Scott (1996) suggests that the spread of this approach can be seen as a reaction to the dominance of positivism in social science. Ethnography is characterized by 'thick' descriptive accounts of the activities of particular groups studied. Accounts focus on the micro, spending much time looking at small groups and particular institutions, such as an aspect of life in one particular school. Fieldwork takes numerous forms and researchers use many sources of data, with particular reliance on 'naturalistic' interpretive methods, such as participant observation and informal interviews. Central to the description and analysis in ethnography are the views and perceptions of the actors. See Hammersley and Atkinson (1995) for an account of methods used in ethnography.

Hitchcock and Hughes note that the term ethnography is difficult to define precisely as it is often used in place of terms such as participant observation, qualitative methodology and case study. They summarized the characteristics of an ethnographic piece of research as:

- the production of descriptive cultural knowledge of a group
- the description of activities in relation to a particular cultural context from the point of view of the members of that group themselves
- the production of a list of features constitutive of membership in a group or culture
- the description and analysis of patterns of social interaction

- the provision as far as possible of 'insider accounts'
- the development of theory (1993: 53).

Approaches to the research process and the type of data considered acceptable very much depend upon how those carrying out the research see the world. Much falls within and between these two paradigms of positivism and interpretivism but sometimes this dichotomy proves to be rather too simplistic. It is worth considering different perspectives on explanations of the social world, for instance, the postmodernist and feminist views of knowledge and research outlined in Chapters 3 and 5.

A comparison of the two paradigms

Positivist	*Interpretivist*
Natural science	Naturalistic
Objective	Ethnographic
Macro	Micro
External structure	Created by actors
One reality	Multiple realities
Quantitative data	Qualitative data
Questionnaires and	Unstructured interviews
structured methods.	and observations.

Research methodologies

There are many ways in which information can be obtained and a list of the most common might include: experimental test scores, interviews, questionnaires, observation – structured or ethnographic – diaries by researchers, diaries by respondents, photographs, video recordings, content analysis (of student work or texts), documents, official records and statistics, and student examination results. Each of these can be subdivided many times to show variations in structure. In deciding which methods to use the researcher will acknowledge the relative data collection time and associated expense of each different method. Some methods may not be possible because of the particular circumstances of the study. For instance, the researcher may not be allowed access to observe certain confidential interviews between the headteacher and parents or other members of staff. Researchers are likely to prefer particular forms of data and thus favour certain research methods over others, depending on the paradigm they are working within. They may have to make difficult compromises but ultimately will have to decide what is appropriate in terms of the type of research they wish to conduct. It may seem sensible to take an eclectic approach. However, this can only be acceptable up to a point. 'Mixing' data can be useful but it may be inappropriate to use quantitative methods when a qualitative approach is what the researcher favours, and vice versa.

Space does not permit a detailed examination of each research method here. Reference to a specialist methodology text is advisable for this.We will now examine briefly three of the more popular methods of gathering data.

Questionnaires

This is a useful method, if carefully planned, for obtaining large numbers of responses relatively quickly and, as such, may be seen as providing quantitative data. It is more difficult to obtain in-depth personal responses by this method and so it is less useful for the qualitative researcher. A questionnaire is simply a list of questions. These can be presented to the respondents in different ways: they may be read out by the researcher who writes the answers, they may be sent by post with a stamped addressed envelope for the reply or they may be given out and collected later by the researcher (Bell, 1999).

Strengths of questionnaires in data collection

1 It is possible to gather large amounts of data relatively quickly.
2 The researcher can compare the responses to particular questions by individuals or between different groups of respondents.
3 The data can be expressed statistically. It is thus possible to make comparisons with other studies.
4 The research may enable overall statements concerning the population to be made, for example, the percentage who left school at 16, the percentage who gained certain qualifications or the numbers who felt that they were bullied at school.

Weaknesses of questionnaires

1 Questions about complex issues are difficult to compose. Respondents may not find it easy to place their responses into specific categories.

2 The short responses required often fail to reflect the varying depth or complexity of people's feelings.
3 It is the researcher who sets the agenda of questionnaires not the respondent. The questions may create attitudes by asking the respondents to comment on things which they may not previously have considered. Alternatively the questions may not give enough emphasis to areas which the respondents see as important.
4 The researcher may attempt to overcome the above problems by adding open-ended questions. Answers to these will need to be codified by the researcher which can lead to the very subjectivity which the questionnaire may well have been chosen to overcome. Munn and Drever (1991) give useful practical advice on questionnaire design.

Interviews

Interviews may take many different forms. They can vary from being highly structured and very formal to being unstructured and so informal as to appear little more than conversations between respondent and researcher (for a detailed overview see Bell, 1999, or Cohen et al., 2000).

In the more structured interview researchers follow a set format with fixed questions. How much they are able to adapt each interview to varying circumstances is decided beforehand, but it may be very little. This approach allows for a team of interviewers to interview a large number of respondents and for the results to be standardized. This is a further development of the questionnaire and is likely to provide quantitative as well as some qualitative data.

Where the researcher prefers the emphasis to be on the respondent's account, a less structured approach is likely to be taken, perhaps relying on a few fixed questions and prompts. The interview may be very informal so it becomes, to all intents and purposes, like a normal conversation. Here the respondents may be very open but the researcher must be very careful not to lead them. These less structured interviews are favoured by the qualitative researcher. The most 'natural' interactions between the researcher and the respondent may take place during participant observation or a chance meeting during a case study (Hitchcock and Hughes, 1993, consider interviews in qualitative research).

Before carrying out interviews several considerations must be made, from the form of the interview and the role of the interviewer to how the data will be recorded and analysed. Crucially the interviewer must determine who to interview. Burgoyne (1994) described this as 'stakeholder analysis'. For example, are the views of the headteacher more significant than those of a Year 7 pupil? Certainly the headteacher has more power within the school but it depends upon what it is being researched. Ball (1990), when looking at the making of national education policy, had to interview those that he felt were most influential in making that policy.

Strengths of interviews in data collection

1 They can be adaptable to different situations and respondents.
2 The interviewer can 'pick up' non-verbal clues which would not be possible from questionnaires, for example, annoyance or pleasure shown by the respondent over certain topics.
3 The researcher can 'follow hunches' and different unexpected lines of enquiry as they come up during the interview. For example, issues of bullying may become apparent that had not been mentioned or suspected before the start of the study.
4 The researcher can obtain detailed qualitative data expressed in the respondent's own words.

Weaknesses of interviews

1 The interviewer may significantly affect the responses. They may influence or lead the respondent.
2 Interviews can take a great deal of time and may be difficult to set up. This will restrict the number it is possible to carry out.
3 The more unstructured they are then the more variation there is between interviews. This makes comparing data more difficult.

Observation

The type of phenomenon to be observed and the perspective of the observer will be key factors in determining the methods of observation selected. The observation may be formal and overt as in many psychological experiments where the researcher notes the reactions of respondents to certain stimulations. Similarly, OFSTED inspectors, though separate at the back of the room with their clipboards, are observing the lesson overtly. Observation may also be formal and covert with those being observed unaware of the observer. Here the 'action' may be observed through closed-circuit television (CCTV) cameras, two-way mirrors, or the observer may just not be noticed in the crowd. The observer may take part in the proceedings with the subjects of the observation sometimes knowing they are a researcher and sometimes not. Teacher researchers may 'help' in another teacher's classroom while unobtrusively observing. Ball (1981) posed as a teacher while collecting data in Beachside Comprehensive.

The techniques employed in collecting of data is very important in this approach. The observer may be noting events as they occur openly or they may have to remember them to be written up as soon as possible afterwards. The more formal the observation the more detailed a tally chart is devised. The Flanders observation schedule, for instance, is very detailed and will yield quantitative data to be analysed. The schedule proposed by the Quality Assurance Agency to observe teaching in higher education has fixed categories that the observer has to write in. With the more informal observations the schedules become looser in outline until, in full participant observation, the observer is making mental notes under broad headings to write up later.

Thus observation may be formal or informal. It may yield certain amounts of quantitative data or it may concentrate on qualitative descriptions. Much depends upon how the observation is designed by the researcher. Ethically the researcher must be sensitive to the situation. It is less appropriate, for instance, to use overt formal observation methods when researching the counselling of pupils than it is in a formal lesson.

Strengths of observation in data collection

1 It is possible to see how people behave in 'natural' situations.
2 The researcher can see whether the subjects in the observation act as they say they do.
3 An observer can gather large amounts of data in a short time.

Weaknesses of observation

1 Gaining access to situations which would be useful to observe can prove difficult. For example, bullying takes place secretively or only when the observer has 'infiltrated' the group; outside observers are not normally allowed into confidential discussions such as teacher appraisal interviews.

2 It is difficult to observe and record at the same time, for example, the Flanders observation analysis used by Ball (1981) in Beachside Comprehensive requires recordings to be taken every 3 seconds.
3 Sometimes it is difficult to categorize behaviour if schedules are being used. It is not always possible to understand actions by observation alone, for example, why a teacher treats children differently. A follow-up interview may be needed. This may actually turn a weakness into a strength by providing a fuller analysis.
4 The observer may affect the situation. Did we behave as usual when the inspector was in the lesson?
5 There are ethical issues of observing people if they do not know that they are being observed. It can be seen as a form of spying.

Any research method can be analysed in similar ways to the three we have outlined. Fundamentally research design is a creative activity in which the researcher crafts an approach which is determined by his/her perspective as well as by the answers to the host of questions raised above. The outcomes of any research are a result of the approach of, and decisions made by, the researcher.

Important research concepts

In any research design issues of reliability and validity are key concerns. However, their importance applies to different degrees depending on the type of research methodology.

Reliability

Reliability concerns the extent to which a research instrument is repeatable. It is an assessment of the consistency of any method: 'In common terms the reliability of a test is the extent to which subsequent administrations would give similar results. A test which is not reliable will give different results every time it is taken.' (Anderson, 1998: 12).

Reliability is of greatest importance to the positivist researcher who wishes to carry out macro research. Here the methods need to be capable of being applied to a large number of respondents in order to generate the data required. To be able to make the desired statistical comparisons the collection of data needs to be consistent, i.e. reliable. The interpretivist researcher, however, is likely to be more concerned with the adaptability of methods used to enable them to elicit qualitative, accurate and detailed accounts from each respondent. Thus the emphasis on reliability varies according to the paradigm of the researcher.

It should be noted that reliability of data does not necessarily mean that it is accurate. For instance, in order to evaluate a particular course a tutor gives a questionnaire to the students. The students are asked to put their names on the top of the questionnaires. They are aware that the tutor will shortly be marking their assignments and this is likely to be on their minds as they fill in their responses to the remaining questions. Not surprisingly this particular tutor always has positive student evaluations. While this method can be said to be reliable, its accuracy in terms of the truthfulness of the student responses is certainly suspect.

Validity

Validity and its measurement play an important part in determining the appropriate methodology to employ. Validity refers to the 'truthfulness', 'correctness' or accuracy of research data. If results are to be considered valid then the research instrument must measure what we claim it to measure. For instance, tests of mathematical ability might actually be producing results which are indicative of the ability to read the questions rather than of mathematical prowess. If our methods are at fault, then the findings will be invalid and the research worthless. In positivism the emphasis is on the accuracy of the method and thus the measure. Cohen et al. point out that: 'In quantitative data validity might be improved through careful sampling, appropriate instrumentation and appropriate statistical treatments of the data' (2000: 105). In an effort to increase validity the emphasis is on standardization of data collection while using as large a sample as possible. The piloting of any method for accuracy is very important.

For interpretivists the emphasis is on the final account: 'In qualitative data validity might be addressed through the honesty, depth, richness and scope of the data achieved, the participants approached, the extent of triangulation and the disinterestedness or objectivity of the researcher' (Cohen et al., 2000: 105). In other words the researcher needs to show on what evidence they base their findings. This can be done in a number of ways such as giving full explanations as to how data was gathered, member checks (Maykut and Morehouse, 1994) whereby research participants are asked if their accounts have been recorded accurately and reducing researcher bias by giving a colleague samples of all data collected to verify the analysis and conclusions drawn by the researcher (as suggested by Miles and Huberman, 1994). See Wolcott (1990) and Woods (1999) for an interesting account of validity in qualitative research.

Triangulation

Triangulation is a navigational term which means to fix one's position from two known bearings. This process is carried out by social science researchers to increase the validity of their research. Denzin (1970) suggested different forms of triangulation, the most common being when several methods are used to gather data on the same issue. Miles and Huberman pointed to triangulation as a way of life. If findings were consciously checked and double checked using different sources of evidence then verification would be built in: 'by seeing or hearing multiple instances of it from different sources, by using different methods and by squaring the finding with others it needs to be squared with' (Miles and Huberman, 1994: 267).

The positivist would hope to show congruency of results from triangulation. The interpretivist would use the different sources of data to give greater depth to their analysis, corroborating or leading to discussion of variation in the findings (Woods, 1999). Thus for Hammersley and Atkinson: 'What is involved in triangulation is not the combination of different kinds of data per se, but rather an attempt to relate different sorts of data in such a way as to counteract various possible threats to the validity of our analysis' (1995: 232).

Certainly both paradigms would suggest the use of triangulation to increase the validity of their findings but would use it in slightly different ways. Cohen et al. (2000) suggest that validity is a matter of degree rather than an obtainable state and that all researchers should strive to minimize invalidity while increasing validity. In order to produce a more thorough and rigorous piece of research several research methods are often used in conjunction with one another. The main methods, in fact, often complement each other. For instance, what has been seen during observations can be raised in interviews by the researcher. This will give an understanding of why something happened as well as a descriptive account.

Case studies

One research strategy which may be thought to increase validity is the case study which: 'uses multiple sources of evidence to analyse or evaluate a specific phenomenon or instance. Most case study research is interpretive and seeks to bring to life a case. It often, but not exclusively, occurs in a natural setting and it may employ qualitative and/or quantitative methods and measures' (Anderson, 1998: 152). This approach is popular in education research where the researcher investigates a specific case or cases. These cases are defined by the researcher and vary in size. Thus the case could be a school, a class or a particular pupil. Blaxter et al. (1996) suggest that in this way the case-study approach is ideally suited to the needs and resources of a small-scale researcher. The researcher aims to study the case in depth and the approach is generally interpretivist. By concentrating on one case, data is collected in several ways, documents, records, interviews and observations being typical. Thus triangulation occurs, increasing validity.

Case studies have been criticized by positivist approaches for lack of representativeness of the wider population and the inability to generalize from the few cases. However, proponents claim the strength of the case-study approach is the in-depth analysis and the understanding gained. For these researchers, the strength of the research approach lies in the 'relatability' of the findings (Bassey, 1990). By this Bassey suggests that, although each case may be unique, there are sufficient similarities to make the findings from one study useful when seeking to understand others.

Case studies often provide fascinating reading due to the richness of the data. Examples of the use of case studies in education research include the work of Lacey (1970) and Ball (1981), both of whom explored particular schools, Willis (1979) who studied a group of teenage boys within a school, and Bartlett (1998a) who studied the changing arrangements for teacher appraisal in three schools.

Research methodology: conclusions

- There are many research methods which can be used to collect data. Even within particular method types there is enormous variation.
- The researcher may use or adapt an existing research instrument. In many cases the researcher designs his/her own instrument.
- Researchers make decisions concerning the methodology to be used in the light of the type of data they require.
- Practical constraints such as time, money and the nature of the respondent group, will be significant factors to be taken into account when designing the research.

- The data collected will be a reflection of the decisions made by, and the skills of, the researcher.
- Researchers aim to be as rigorous as possible but inevitably their beliefs and assumptions can affect research.
- Large-scale research projects are not necessarily better than small-scale projects.
- The researcher needs to address ethical issues including the confidentiality of data collected and gaining the consent of those appropriate.

The design of a piece of research is thus highly significant to the data obtained. Some central influences on this design are the perspective of the researcher, the decisions made due to the nature of the group to be studied and the resources available to carry out the research. We will now consider, briefly, two significant research 'movements' in education.

Action research

Background

The action research 'movement' in education evolved, largely, from the work of Lawrence Stenhouse at the Schools Council (1967–72). His belief was that for curriculum development to be effective it needed to have teachers at its centre. He saw it as essential that teachers were encouraged to reflect upon practice, share experiences and evaluate their work in order to improve. For Stenhouse, teachers needed to view themselves as researchers. Each classroom was seen as a laboratory and each teacher a member of a scientific community.

He had a faith in the power of teachers and in their professional desire to improve education for their pupils and society. Teachers were the best judges of teaching and by working in research communities they would be able to reflect upon and improve their practice. Other interested members of the community, such as parents and employers, would in turn be drawn into this research process. Social democratic ideology ran through this work of the Schools Council. Curriculum reform was visualized as happening at the grass-roots level and involving all those with a stake in education. Reflection and improvement of practice was regarded as a means of empowering practitioners and, therefore, central to the professional development of teachers.

In looking at all types of professional activity, Schon (1983) felt that there had been, in the 1960s and 1970s, a crisis of confidence in professional knowledge expressed by both clients and the professionals themselves. He suggested a change of approach for the modern professional away from the reliance on a traditional model of technical rationality, based upon specialized scientific knowedge, to what he termed 'reflection in action'. The modern practitioner, according to Schon (1983), constantly questions and reflects upon practice. This involves the professional regarding his/her work from the point of view of the client or as an outsider. The purpose of this is to understand all aspects of the process resulting in a greater professional insight. This whole procedure involving evaluation, criticism and ultimately self-development, requires openness and trust between those involved. Discussion of practice is shared with both clients and colleagues. In this way modern professional communities reflect upon, discuss and learn from each other's work. The reflective practitioner approach developed by Schon (1983) stressed the importance of self-criticism as part of improvement. This developmental approach to professionalism emphasized action research.

Hoyle (1980), while considering the professional nature of teaching, differentiated between two sorts of teachers. He regarded restricted professionals as conscientious practitioners. They work hard, prepare their lessons and care about their pupils. However, they are limited in outlook, failing to think beyond their classroom or school. They do not consider the broader picture concerning the purposes of education as relevant to them. They are basically concerned with the practical and not with the wider theoretical aspects of their profession. Extended professionals seek to improve by learning from other teachers and professional development activities. They constantly question and try to link theory to practice. In this way they are continually developing as teachers and placing their classroom work in a wider educational context. Hoyle argued that extended professionals show, in their search for fulfilment, the greater potential. He advocated that this model of professionalism should be the aim of all teachers. It is these teachers who are likely to be involved in action research as a 'natural' part of their professional development.

Action research also grew out of a disillusionment with academic research into education which had developed within the traditional positivist and interpretivist paradigms (see Carr and Kemmis, 1986; McNiff, 1988). This had been of little use to those working in education. It had taken a disengaged stance and offered no help in terms of the practice of teaching. Much influential academic research had promoted a view that either innate factors (Jensen, 1973) or wider social circumstances (Douglas, 1964) largely determined overall educational achievement. It was as though schools did not make a difference to pupil attainment, and the influence of wider social forces or natural ability were seen as the key factors. If anything, schools only reinforced these existing inequalities. They seemed to be processing agencies in which teachers were seen to play an often unwitting part (see Bowles and Gintis, 1976). Little encouragement was given by such research to those working in education. Certainly there was no guidance in how to change or improve things.

In the mid-1970s growing economic problems led to an increased scrutiny of education. Spending needed to be justified and schools to be seen to make a difference. Research was desired which would be of use in improving the education of pupils. It is interesting to note that, while much academic research and writing was proposing that schools made little difference, education was being held by politicians to be at least partly to blame for the national economic decline. McNiff (1988) spoke of a wish to create a study of education which was grounded in practice and developed by those involved. Thus teachers were to develop their research skills to evaluate their practice. The process needed to be as rigorous as possible if it was to create effective change. A critical approach was needed.

Injunctions to become more critical meant far more than simply evaluating practice (Carr and Kemmis, 1986). The development of critical theory was seen as a questioning of the whole purpose and techniques employed by teachers. It involved asking fundamental questions about why things are done in a certain way and why other processes are not used. This would encourage further research, experimentation and, ultimately, change. Carr and Kemmis (1986) saw this as a unifying ideology of action research which would lead to the evolution of a scientific study of education. There would be a linking of theory and practice alongside the development of research for action.

The reflexivity of action research would be heightened as practitioners developed their research skills but more significantly as communities of researchers in schools examined and discussed each other's findings, what Elliott (1993) termed 'discoursive consciousness'. This process would involve others and develop a wider understanding of the nature of education as part of the social democratic process.

Definitions of action research

What then is action research? Some definitions will help to show what the process involves:

> Action research is simply a form of self-reflective enquiry undertaken by participants in social situations in order to improve the rationality and justice of their own practices, their understanding of these practices, and the situations in which these practices are carried out . . . a self-reflective spiral of cycles of planning, acting, observing and reflecting is central to the action research approach. (Carr and Kemmis, 1986: 162)

Action research is 'the study of a social situation with a view to improving the quality of action within it' (Elliott, 1991: 69).

Action research is done by practitioners, those working in the field, to improve what they do. It is about reflecting upon practice and identifying a need for change (the research part), carrying out appropriate changes (the action part), looking at the effects of these changes (the research part), replanning and so on. This is a continuous process in a search for constant improvement (Atweh et al., 1998). Thus action research is cyclical.

Kemmis and Wilkinson stress the participatory nature of action research. They see action research itself as a social and educational process which is part of the development of a professional community:

> At its best it is a collaborative social process of learning, realized by groups of people who join together in changing the practices through which they interact in a shared social world – a world in which, for better or for worse, we live with the consequences of each others actions. (Kemmis and Wilkinson, 1998: 23)

Thus it involves participants in examining what they do to question their rationales and 'normal' ways of seeing their world, to actively make changes which will benefit the situation in some way. This is a collaborative process in which all teachers are involved and is never ending.

Altrichter et al. identify six features of action research:

- Carried out by people directly concerned with the social situation. Though initially teachers this will inevitably draw in others to the research process.
- Starts from practical questions.
- Must fit in with the values of the school and the working conditions of the teachers.
- Methods of data collection are tailored to suit the circumstances.
- Constant effort to link reflection and practice.
- Each research project is designed for specific set of circumstances and so is unique. (Altrichter et al. 1993).

Action research, then, is curriculum development at the classroom level. It is concerned with how to improve education practice and it is practitioners themselves who carry out the research in examining and developing their teaching. The nature of this form of practitioner research means that it is carried out in the teacher's own place of work and so the case-study approach is the most common. Ideally, an eclectic view of data collection is taken with the researcher using a variety of methods to examine the particular issue. Increased validity is aimed at through a rigorous approach to the research coupled with triangulation, and openness at all stages of the process. Though it is not possible to generalize from the findings of such small-scale research its strength, according to Bassey (1990), lies in its relatability to similar situations. Usually the emphasis for these researchers is on a qualitative approach, which will yield a greater understanding of the issue under investigation, ultimately to improve their practice both in the immediate context of the research and through the process of collaborative dissemination.

It should be noted that there are, however, different interpretations of what action research actually involves (Bryant, 1996). For many of the proponents of the late 1970s and early 1980s it provided a whole philosophy of the future development and control of education linked to the social democratic movement in the wider society. Thus according to Carr and Kemmis:

> educational action research as critical educational science is concerned with the question of the control of education, and it comes out on the side of the control of education by self-critical communities of researchers, including teachers, students, parents, educational administrators and others. Creating the conditions under which these participants can take collaborative responsibility for the development and reform of education is the task of a critical educational science. Educational action research offers a means by which this can be achieved. (1986: 211)

However, for others it remained at the level of problem-solving for teachers. They were not concerned to develop a new educational science nor did they take a critical stance on the basic values and actions in their practice.

The demise of action research?

Many critics saw action research as too micro in scale and isolated throughout the late 1980s and 1990s when teachers were subject to increasing pressure and a rising number of directives from central government. Thus, as teachers appeared to be losing control over the curriculum, action research seemed increasingly irrelevant in the face of wider political pressures. The assumption that teachers had the power to change their practice rather than being constrained by wider pressures now appeared rather naive (Avis, 1994). The underpinning social democratic ideology, being promoted in the curriculum developments of the 1960s, 1970s and even the early 1980s, was not embraced by all and by the mid-1990s Carr (1995) felt that action research still lacked a coherent rationale.

Thus it has never been quite clear if action research was a social movement evolving through the professional practice of self-reflection and development or if it was just a way of solving problems using research methods. It is perhaps best to see different levels of involvement by practitioners. Certainly, the increasing central control and development of the market in education over the last 20 years does not fit the image of the extended professional within a social democratic framework.

Action research seemed increasingly out of place in the Conservative administrations from 1979 until 1997, but the climate has changed somewhat in the 'New Labour' administration. There is talk of partnerships in education with all stakeholders working together to raise standards. There is also a redeveloping of the professional nature of teaching. The Labour government appears to recognize the importance of teachers developing their classroom skills and how this can be achieved through reflective practice. There is once again the promotion of teachers researching into their own classroom practice. However, the focus of this research is firmly in the classroom and on raising (largely measurable) standards. Funding made available through the Teacher Training Agency (TTA) and the Department for Education and Employment (DfEE) does not encourage wider questioning of the purposes of education or where these standards have come from. As such this research may do little to create communities of teacher researchers and the professional development will remain largely restrictive (Bottery and Wright, 1999). This is after all a 'new' version of social democracy.

The school effectiveness research movement

Research with a specific emphasis on school effectiveness began to develop in the late 1970s, gaining in momentum throughout the 1980s and 1990s. In a similar way to action research, the school effectiveness movement grew partly in response to the education research of the 1960s and early 1970s. This was when: 'education researchers and policy makers held a rather pessimistic view concerning the possible influence of school based factors over and above the well known influence of school input factors like the pupil's socioeconomic status and ability' (Creemers, 1994: 10).

The perception at the time was that schools were unable to compensate for inequalities in the wider society (Bernstein, 1970). This position began to be challenged in the late 1970s by studies which claimed that schools did make a difference to pupil outcomes. A very significant study in Britain at this time was *Fifteen Thousand Hours: Secondary Schools and their Effects on Children* (Rutter et al., 1979), so named after the number of hours a pupil spent in compulsory schooling. This study considered the 'effectiveness' of 12 inner-city secondary schools in achieving certain indicators of success such as pupil attendance, behaviour and academic attainment. Even when differential social background was taken into consideration it appeared that some schools 'performed' better than others.

As Mortimore (1997) explains, researchers measuring school effectiveness aim to compare one school with another. Data is usually collected on the behaviour and performance of pupils at various stages in their schooling, and schools with significant differences in their impact on student outcomes can then be noted. Researchers: 'have then sought to relate the indicators of school effectiveness to information collected about the detailed life of the school. By examining the positive correlations they have endeavoured to identify the kinds of behaviour – of staff and students – typically associated with the more effective outcomes' (Mortimore, 1997: 478).

Criteria for judging school effectiveness

Various lists of criteria have been developed by school effectiveness researchers. Rutter et al. (1979) considered what they termed 'school ethos' to be important and identified a number of significant factors which contributed to the making of this. Mortimore identified a number of characteristics of effective primary schools in both academic and social aspects (Reynolds et al., 1994). Since then Creemers (1994) has identified a five-factor model which pulled together the most identified factors of effective schools by international studies over a period of 25 years. These are:

- strong educational leadership
- high expectations of student achievement

- an emphasis on basic skills
- a safe and orderly climate
- frequent evaluation of pupils' progress.

Notwithstanding imperfections in the methodology, Sammons (cited in Elliott, 1998) listed 11 key characteristics of effective schools from the literature:

1 Professional leadership – firm and purposeful, participative approach, the leading professional.
2 Shared vision and goals – unity of purpose, consistency of practice, collegiality and cooperation.
3 A learning environment – an orderly atmosphere, an attractive learning environment.
4 Concentration on teaching and learning – maximization of learning time, academic emphasis, focus on achievement.
5 Purposeful teaching – efficient organization, clarity of purpose, structured lessons, adaptive practice.
6 High expectations all round – communicating expectations, providing intellectual challenge.
7 Positive reinforcement – clear and fair discipline, feedback.
8 Monitoring progress – monitoring pupil performance, evaluating school performance.
9 Pupil rights and responsibilities – raising self-esteem, positions of responsibility, control of work.
10 Home–school partnership – parental involvement in their children's learning.
11 A learning organization – school-based staff development.

The DfEE recently commissioned major school effectiveness research by HayMcBer. Interviews were conducted with nearly 200 teachers and 120 of them were observed teaching. Five thousand questionnaires, completed by teachers, pupils and others, were also analysed. A summary of the report can be found at www.dfee.gov.uk/teaching reforms/mcber. Three groups of factors were found to affect pupil progress: a teacher's 'professional characteristics', 'teaching skills' and 'classroom climate' (Barnard, 2000; Slater 2000: 22).

Methodological issues in school effectiveness research

Reynolds et al. (1994) note certain strengths in the British school effectiveness tradition. Research at the school level is already well developed with multiple levels of analysis currently being developed. There is also extensive use of multiple measures of school outcomes which cover social as well as academic measures of effectiveness. Mortimore (1997) suggests that as expertise in this field has developed, increasingly sophisticated statistical multilevelling techniques have been employed to identify differences in pupil outcomes, while making allowances for factors such as gender, race and socio-economic status. However, school effectiveness researchers have themselves acknowledged certain problems with their methodology which may, in hindsight, impact upon their early findings.

Reynolds et al. (1994) explain that certain earlier 'simplistic assumptions' are now open to question. The effect of schools on pupil outcomes in relation to wider social factors does not appear to be as great as first supposed by school effectiveness researchers. The influence of the school, as opposed to the individual classroom effects, is now also open to debate as it appears that the differences reported between schools may to a large extent be the result of actual classroom differences rather than whole-school factors. It was originally assumed that the differences between schools were consistent over a long term of five to seven years. It would now appear that school performance can alter quite radically over just two or three years. There can also be very different outcomes for particular groups of pupils within one school.

There are still problems with relying on statistical correlations even if the techniques have been refined. The relationship between the significant factors is still unclear. The correlations alone are unable to show whether relationships are actually causal and, if they are, which variable is the dependent one. Thus pupils who are successful may enable purposeful teaching rather than vice versa. As Creemers (1994) notes, 'frequent evaluation' and 'orderly climate' may be seen as aspects of strong instructional leadership or independent factors in themselves. High scores in some of the indicators could also be caused by other factors not considered by this statistical analysis.

As with other forms of positivist investigation, problematic issues for the school effectiveness researchers centre on methodology and the accuracy of the statistical methods which they use. Their aim is to continue to develop more sophisticated models which will be able to deal with increasingly complex relationships of variables. Thus accepting that existing research does have its faults, Creemers feels that school effectiveness research is leading us in the right direction:

We can conclude that the school effectiveness movement was a breakthrough with respect to rejecting the idea that schools and classrooms did not matter. In fact, within the school effectiveness movement, the goals and objectives of education were reformulated to focus upon the way in which the school contributes to academic, social and emotional growth of pupils. (1994: 13)

Criticisms of school effectiveness research

A number of criticisms have been levelled at the methodology of the school effectiveness researchers. Many of the indicators leading to school effectiveness appear to be rather simplistic and though presented as statements that most would agree with, such as 'a positive climate' or 'good environment', they remain difficult to define or quantify. For instance, is there agreement as to what constitutes 'purposeful leadership'? If so, how purposeful does it have to be before it becomes overpowering? What is meant by 'involvement of teachers'? Does just being there constitute involvement or does it also require talking to pupils, telling pupils off, helping pupils, discussing work with other teachers? What would actually constitute a teacher not being involved in some way? Thus many of the characteristics and some of the outcomes of school effectiveness are not susceptible to accurate measurement. When findings are presented in statistical form, any discussion as to how they were compiled and the part researcher interpretation played in this process is avoided.

A number of writers (see Elliott, 1998; Willmott, 1999) have questioned the positivist nature of the school effectiveness research and how their findings are presented. They suggest that the items listed appear to be shaped by a particular ideology. This ideology emphasizes the transmission of systematically organized academic knowledge and the 'traditional' values of social order. Elliott characterized the school effectiveness research paradigm as having: 'a mechanistic methodology, an instrumentalist view of educational processes, and the belief that educational outcomes can and should be described independently of such processes' (1998: 78). He suggests that anyone who subscribes to the ideology will inevitably produce such a list as characterizing effective schooling. For politicians and policy-makers the statistics appear to be objective evidence, or at least are treated as such, for their convenience. The HayMcBer findings, for instance, are being used by the DfEE in its establishment of criteria for the performance management of teachers and schools.

The whole nature of what constitutes effective schooling remains an issue for debate. Elliott argues that by presenting their findings in an objective way, by concentrating on issues of methodology and the need to develop even more sophisticated models, the school effectiveness researchers are able to avoid alternative viewpoints on the purposes of education and thus alternative visions of 'effective schools'. Elliott says that their findings are:

> highly questionable, and that they are best viewed as ideological legitimations of a socially coercive view of schooling. [*They*] rule out an alternative vision of schooling as an educational process . . . What is at issue between school effectiveness researchers and their critics are fundamental questions about the nature of education and its central values. (1998: 79)

Inspection as research

Elliott (1998) suggests that this school effectiveness research is useful to those who share the ideology, which appears to be the case with both the previous Conservative government and the current Labour administration.

The Conservative government (1979–97) developed the market in education (see Chapter 6). This was based upon the notion of consumer choice being used to regulate and raise standards. The need for consumers to have information on which to base their choice of school led to the compilation of league tables of institutions based on various indicators of success, most notably examination passes and average grades. The Conservatives developed a system of regular inspections of schools, and later other education institutions, by OFSTED. These inspections were to monitor and report upon standards to the Secretary of State for Education, and also to provide information to the general public through publication of the reports. The Labour government has increased the use of target-setting and benchmarking against which to measure improvements in standards (see Chapter 6).

The OFSTED methodology is based on systematic observations of teaching, interviews, analysis of secondary data such as pupils' work, schools' written policies, assessment results and pupil records. A school's performance is now compared with that of other schools operating in similar circumstances. Benchmarks are established through a (performance and assessment, PANDA) report, produced for each school by OFSTED. Inspection reports are treated as research which teachers and trainees are expected to refer to in order to inform their own practice. The approach by OFSTED appears to be positivist with inspections being very mechanistic in how they are carried out. Elliott's criticisms of school effectiveness research also apply here in that OFSTED is using a particular ideology of education and a specific view of what makes for effective schools. As noted in Chapter 1, the Chief Inspector of Schools asserted in his 1998/99 report (OFSTED, 2000) that what constitutes good teaching is well known, as are the means of tackling the weaknesses.

The importance of freedom in research

There has recently been a resurgence of criticism of academic educational research. Hargreaves (1996) found much of it far removed from practice and suggested that it needed to become more professionally focused. Similarly, Tooley and Darby (1998) in a report for OFSTED suggested that much research published in academic journals was irrelevant. Estelle Morris, the Minister of State for Education (cited in Reid, 1999), argued for teaching to become a more 'evidence-based profession' while David Blunkett, as Secretary of State for Education, has called for more relevant research on how to improve pupil performance. These may be reasonable criticisms and calls for change. However, they could also be ways of certain powerful groups discouraging research and associated questioning which does not fit their own educational ideologies.

Mortimore, in his presidential address to the British Educational Research Association (BERA), suggested that while attempting to produce research of the highest quality we should maintain the breadth of research into education:

> We must do what we have been trained to do
>
> * ask difficult questions
> * demand evidence, rather than anecdote, for answers
> * generate, through our research, new knowledge
> * formulate new theories
> * speak up for what we believe is right.
>
> A democratic society expects – and deserves – nothing less. (2000: 6)

Conclusions

The research process is complex yet, like the questions involving the purposes of education, is often presented as falling within two perspectives, positivism and interpretivism. The positivist believes in the need for scientific research, the purpose being to uncover facts to permit an explanation of reality. The focus is on large-scale quantitative methods, carried out in an objective manner. The interpretivist, on the other hand, sees multiple realities which are created by the actors themselves. Interpretivists prefer small-scale qualitative methods involving 'rich' accounts and description to the impersonal statistics of the positivists.

The ideological underpinning of data collection becomes apparent when particular groups of researchers, or 'schools of research', are analysed. Ideologies of education link in a complex way with the types of research carried out. Thus action research, developed by practitioners, emphasizes qualitative methodologies, seeking to understand what is happening in order to change and improve it. Education is characterized as a constantly developing process.

School effectiveness research is also concerned with improving education but takes a much more positivist approach. The aim is to collect quantitative data in an objective manner so that comparisons can be made using a large number of statistics. By using various statistical techniques, factors which influence outcomes can be isolated and measured. Findings can be used to alter the practice of teachers. The emphasis on objectivity fits with a view of education as a product which can be measured.

Thus there are differing approaches in education research because beliefs and values both predicate and are a part of the research process.

Student activities

1 Design a small-scale research project using the following headings:

   (a) Issue or area to be researched
   (b) Research questions
   (c) Data collection methods.

2 Choose a piece of research and analyse it. Make particular reference to:

   (a) the paradigm of the research
   (b) methods of data collection used – appropriateness, strengths, weaknesses
   (c) validity and reliability
   (d) relationship of findings to the data
   (e) presentation of findings.

Recommended reading

Every degree course has some form of methodology section concerning the partic-ular area of study. Education and the social sciences are no exception and as a result there are a multitude of high-quality texts available.

Blaxter, L. Hughes, C. and Tight, M. (1996) *How to Research*, Buckingham: Open University Press. This is an excellent book for students new to research. It is clearly written and jargon-free. It introduces the student to research and takes them through the process of designing and carrying out a research project. The text is clearly divided to give the student easier access to different aspects of the research process. It makes good use of tables for clarity and has many very useful practical exercises. As the title suggests, this book aims to show the novice how to research. In an effort to 'keep the process straightforward' this book does tend to neglect the controversial nature of research of which any student needs to be aware.

Bell, J. (1999) *Doing Your Research Project: A Guide for First-Time Researchers in Education and Social Science*, Buckingham: Open University Press. This book has been recommended for initial research methods courses for a number of years. It is a well-written, easy to understand, guide on how to carry out a research pro-ject. In this respect it is ideal for undergraduates preparing for a research disser-tation.

Cohen, L., Manion, L. and Morrison, K. (2000) *Research Methods in Education*, 5th edn, London: Routledge. This volume is also highly recommended by many tutors of research methods courses. While giving a clear account of different research methods, it also considers the underpinning philosophy of research in detail. It gives a useful outline of different research paradigms and considers the whole nature of research in relation to notions of truth and reality. As such it is more academically advanced than the other two texts.

3

Knowledge, Beliefs and the Curriculum

Chapter 3 considers the meaning of the term 'curriculum' and goes on to examine the curriculum structures of pedagogy, content and assessment. There is an epistemological analysis which considers differing views of the nature and organization of knowledge. These views are significant in that they are closely linked to perceptions of the world. Thus understandings of knowledge, education and the processes of research are closely related. The significance of beliefs about the purposes and nature of education in the creation and development of any curriculum is illustrated with reference to the history and development of the National Curriculum.

Introduction

The idea of the curriculum is one of those fundamental constructs that have an embedded and taken for granted status. One of the functions of education study and analysis is to open up these central, and apparently given, ideas and to make them available to rethinking. If we start to ask basic questions about them their apparent unity and simplicity dissolves and we can begin to probe them more critically (Foucault, 1988b). The curriculum has a powerful legal basis and represents an important social requirement, which is regulated and kept under strict control by various institutions. Changing the curriculum is a difficult, long-winded and bureaucratic process. All of this indicates that the curriculum and the view of knowledge and learning it embodies are regarded as important matters for governments and for the processes of governance that occur in the various institutions of education – schools, colleges and universities.

The regular and regulated curriculum with which we are familiar embodies a set of ideas and practices that have evolved; it is deeply institutionalized. It lies beyond the direct control of individuals and actualizes ideas and practices that are deeply 'sedimented'. They have moved into what appears to be the natural order of things. Different subjects on the curriculum have their own different histories, the traces of which can be seen in their present forms. Subjects have a 'life of their own' that is expressed in textbooks, in traditions of practice and is written into the very language of professional discourses (Ball, 1993). Subjects are 'authorized' and gain legitimacy, so they accrue institutions and embedded practices around themselves. Examination authorities such as the (English) Qualifications and Curriculum Authority (QCA) significantly influence the form and shape of curriculum subjects and the subject practices of teachers. Teachers, and therefore teaching, can be differently oriented in terms of their subject and general professional practices according to their own preferences, the culture of the department and the general ethos of the school (Jones, 1990). This represents a significant power of control but at the same time, individual teachers are constrained by their role in the school and required to behave in certain ways and to subscribe to certain values. There is always a tension between a teacher's capacity to act on individual conscience and the imperative to represent enforced or agreed general principles (Bernstein, 1971).

What is the curriculum?

In *Pedagogy, Symbolic Control and Identity* Basil Bernstein (1995) considers the organization of knowledge in the medieval period. He gives an account of two different and specialized types of knowledge in the medieval university. Mental knowledge is classified, Bernstein explains, into two different systems: the trivium and the quadrivium. Briefly, the trivium is concerned with logic, grammar and rhetoric; the quadrivium is concerned with astronomy, music, geometry and arithmetic. The trivium is studied first and the quadrivium follows. The quadrivium cannot be studied without the trivium. In effect, what Bernstein is describing is how knowledge came to be divided up in the medieval period in Europe and organized into a system. Bernstein goes on to examine the changing classifications of knowledge that occur in the modern period between the nineteenth and the twentieth centuries. Here he writes about singular forms of knowledge giving the examples of physics, chemistry, sociology and psychology, and how they come to be reorganized into new formations: medicine, architecture, engineering, information science, or education, for example. In these knowledge regions, different singulars may come together and mingle to produce quite new forms and orders of knowledge (Bernstein, 1995).

What Bernstein is describing here is the historically changing patterns of knowledge and the curriculum. In the example of the medieval university curriculum that he examines, knowledge is divided into different spheres, one concerned with language and the other with what were considered to be fundamental ways of knowing the world. The curriculum determines what significant knowledge is and divides it up into different categories. The medieval university curriculum differs from the contemporary school curriculum, but in it we can see a similar concern to define specific areas of knowledge as being significant. The medieval curriculum, as Bernstein describes it, defines significant knowledge, but it also defines what it considers to be appropriate technologies for thinking.

According to Jenkins and Shipman: 'A curriculum is the formation and implementation of an educational proposal to be taught and learned within the school or other institution and for which that institution accepts responsibility at three levels: its rationale, its actual implementation and its effects' (1976: 26).

Lawrence Stenhouse expressed his idea of curriculum differently, as: 'An attempt to communicate the essential principles and features of an educational proposal in such a form that it is open to critical scrutiny and capable of effective translation into practice' (1975: 53).

The study of the curriculum is concerned with definitions of knowledge and with systems of teaching and learning. Her Majesty's Inspectorate (HMI) offered a brief definition of the curriculum in 1985:

> A school's curriculum consists of all those activities designed or encouraged within its organizational framework to promote the intellectual personal social and physical development of its pupils. It includes not only the formal programme of lessons, but also the 'informal' programme of so-called extracurricular activities as well as all those features which produce the school's 'ethos', such as the quality of relationships, the concern for equality of opportunity, the values exemplified in the way the school sets about its task and the way it is organized and managed. Teaching and learning styles strongly influence the curriculum and in practice they cannot be separated from it. (DES, 1985a: 11)

The curriculum is often referred to as though it were a collection of subjects that appear on the timetable of schools, but another way of looking at the curriculum is as all the experiences that the school provides. This would include the 'hidden curriculum' or the *informal* curriculum, both of these terms signifying the non-official learning that goes on in schools. The hidden curriculum refers to the messages implied by school rituals: learning how to be obedient, how to cope with long periods of boredom and inactivity, and learning to remain silent in certain formal social contexts (see Bowles and Gintis, 1976). The informal curriculum refers to all the 'unofficial' learning that might occur among pupils, all the social exchanges that might take place and how this constitutes another form of knowledge quite distinct from the school's official version (see, for example, Willis, 1979).

A whole curriculum will be a particular way of organizing these different elements. What is taught, how it is put into a particular arrangement of learning experiences, the kind of teaching methods used to 'deliver' the curriculum and how the learning of pupils is assessed: all these things are factors in what the curriculum is. This means that the curriculum is a complex and multifaceted 'thing' rather than just a collection of different subjects.

The curriculum is not a given but is a selection from a range of possible choices and it will therefore always represent a particular view of knowledge and learning (Hartley, 1997). The curriculum will define what is important in terms of knowledge and learning (Goodson, 1994; Helsby, 1999). Moreover, the curriculum is made. It is a social construction that sits at the very heart of the education system and gives shape and form to much of what happens in schools.

Curriculum: content, pedagogy and assessment

The term 'curriculum' is often used broadly to refer to the range of subjects taught. There are several aspects of curriculum, however, that can be identified as follows:

- Curriculum *content* and form specifies what should be taught to learners and how this is organized, for example in subject modules.
- Curriculum *pedagogy* indicates how content is delivered, taught or communicated.
- Curriculum *assessment* indicates what aspects of learning are to be formally tested or measured and how this is to be done.

In any attempt to define curriculum, there are a number of fundamental considerations to bear in mind. In the threefold nature of the curriculum – content, delivery and assessment – all of these components may vary significantly though they are closely related. In other words, the content and its organization will influence the forms of teaching and learning that prevail. Assessment is the third variable in this structure and in recent times we have seen how a model of curriculum, the National Curriculum in England and Wales, has been shaped by a particular notion of cumulative, progressive assessment.

Content

Many questions can be asked when considering what should be the content of a curriculum. What kinds of knowledge should be taught? What values do they represent? How useful are they? How relevant is this knowledge? Is it worth being inducted, for example, into the kind of thinking processes required to be able to produce the proof of Pythagoras's theorem? Relevance, of course, is not the only criterion for establishing the value of knowledge.

There may be powerful cultural reasons for learning Pythagoras' theorem. Some would say that the kind of knowledge it represents has important cultural kudos, even though its practical or use value might be limited. Others might claim that, like Latin, it is good mental exercise, so again it is irrelevant whether or not it is pertinent to the needs and demands of everyday life. Yet others might add that it also requires the application of discipline, that all such knowledge is disciplinary, that it involves the learning and application of rules and that the training involved in declining Latin nouns is transferable to any kind of learning whether academic or worldly. It is about a training of the person in the acceptance of authority and is a way of averting more creative/constructive kinds of learning. Others might say that the kind of learning embodied in the declining of Latin nouns is actually about joining a learned caste, becoming a member of an elite social group who may recognize one another and relate to one another through their common heritage of 'useless' but socially powerful knowledge. Reasons for reading Shakespeare's *Titus Andronicus* or Henry James's *The Golden Bowl* may be deeply obscure in pragmatic terms. Nevertheless, the kind of 'knowledge' embodied in these texts represents an authoritative, social and cultural acquisition which in certain circles can be very powerful. Such questions about the established nature of knowledge and knowledge as something socially constructed and reproduced are central to any serious attempt to analyze the curriculum (Storey, 1993).

The characteristic content of the school curriculum is defined in terms of subject knowledge but also in terms of the kinds of thinking and related skills – linguistic competence, for example – that might be deemed to be appropriate for learning. Subject organization implies different and discrete areas of knowledge. The 1988 Education Reform Act had specified ten subjects for the National Curriculum (based largely on the development of the school curriculum up to that point in history). It named three core subjects (English, mathematics and science) and seven as foundation subjects (history, geography, technology, music, art, physical education and, at secondary level, a modern foreign language). This selection of subjects indicates a particular view of knowledge and learning. The terms 'core' and 'foundation' suggest a hierarchy of knowledge with all the concomitant tensions which that implies (Skilbeck, 1994).

Other kinds of curriculum content are conceivable. They may not be subject based, but instead organized around key experiences. Several commentators on the modern school curriculum have looked at the idea of moving away from strict subject boundaries and have advocated that learning, teaching and assessment be structured around critical themes where a number of different conventional subject areas can meet (Bentley, 1998; Lawton, 1999; Ranson, 1994; Young, 1998).

The official curriculum can also be considered as a public statement about what is significant knowledge. In the curriculum, ideas about knowledge are not just expressed. They carry considerable legal, social and moral force. The curriculum says, in effect: 'This is knowledge. This is the kind of knowledge that really counts, it may determine your social future, your capacity to earn, your right to participate in social institutions at various levels.' To control the curriculum is to exert considerable power. Hence, we might assume, the desire of governments to intervene in the nature of the school curriculum.

Pedagogy

Pedagogy, or the science of teaching, is concerned with the methods of teaching and learning. It involves structural features such as the learning environment, the classroom and a mode of practice, for example, a teacher giving instructions or asking questions. Pedagogical ideas are developed from theories about how people learn. Different and contradictory accounts of how learning takes place exist and conflict with one another. Psychometric notions of ability, for example, that were popular in the 1950s, see human capacity for learning as fixed in individuals. Stones (1979), on the other hand, proposes that human learning capacity is generally the same for all individuals and claims that general principles can be established to maximize learning within given contexts, like schools, for instance (Simon and Taylor, 1981). See Chapter 4 for a more detailed discussion of intelligence and learning.

There are many different traditions of learning. In Europe, for example, there is much more emphasis on pedagogy as a distinctive branch of educational knowledge. Pestalozzi, Montessori and Frenais have been associated with different versions of pedagogy. The challenge to institutions of learning to construct an effective and inclusive pedagogy was made by J.S. Bruner in 1972 when he claimed that any aspect of any subject could be made accessible and taught to anybody at any age. The post-Plowden Report (CACE, 1967) emphasis on child-centred learning stressed creativity, spontaneity and individuality in an effort to draw out what was there already in the child. More recently, interest among theorists of pedagogy has turned to socio-cultural activity, using theory that derives from Vygotsky (Engestrom, 1993). These theorists see individual learning as structured mental development. Learning is always a development of the self, it is always social and cultural. This implies a different way of organizing the experiences of learning from that of child-centred approaches. Vygotskyans tend to believe that teaching must take the child forward, must be concerned with new concepts, new hierarchies of ideas and ever more complex forms of mental operation (see Chapter 4 for an elaboration of Vygotsky's ideas).

Methods of teaching and learning also give rise to questions about autonomy and authority. We might consider what are the 'best', most productive, most relevant and most socially desirable forms of practice. How much should teaching and learning within a curriculum be concerned to cultivate the development of autonomy, initiative, critical awareness and other qualities that might be thought of as central aspects of citizenship? The business of teaching and learning in relation to the curriculum engages with fundamental and far-reaching questions about the nature of education and the relations between education and society (see Chapter 1).

Assessment

Although perhaps frequently associated with tests, examinations, grades and certificates, many educators would assert that assessment must be about promoting and enhancing opportunities for learning. One of the main issues concerning assessment in education hinges on the question of its objectivity (Brown, 1990). To what extent can assessment provide reliable evidence? This question can be critical when assessing pupils and students within a selection procedure where social destinies may be affected by the result. One attempt to redefine assessment more positively sought to integrate it within the practice of the curriculum. 'Assessment in education is the process of gathering, interpreting, recording and using information about pupils' responses to an educational task' (Harlen et al., 1994: 273).

Examinations and other formal assessments carry with them many technical problems. Other skills and capacities than those that can be assessed by written examination may be important. To what extent can examinations or tests guarantee parity of experience, reliability and validity? To what extent can tests and examinations be geared towards positive recognition of achievement? Are they instead condemned to making negative judgements with everything below a grade 'A' falling short of the ideal? United States research has indicated problems with the accuracy of formal and public assessments (Brown, 1990). Even the most objective tests can assess only limited knowledge and skills because of their decontextualized nature.

As a reaction to the predominance in public education of narrow forms of assessment, there have been proposals to rethink the role of assessment in the curriculum along the following lines:

- Assessment should be integrated with learning experiences and should move beyond selection and distinction; assessment should always be directed towards fostering learning and enhancing teaching and should be used for formative purposes.
- Assessment should address a range of attributes – personal, social and communicative – and take into consideration the particular context of learning.
- Assessment should be developed along descriptive and positive lines, recording achievements rather than measuring absences, gaps and shortcomings.
- Assessment should undergo a devolution of responsibilities such that pupils participate in the process as much as teachers.
- Certification should be fully extended into lifelong learning rather than restricted to particular age-related segments of the population (Harlen et al., 1994: 275).

Assessment has many functions, not always clearly formulated and not always integrated into processes of teaching and learning. A distinction can be drawn between two forms of assessment – formative and summative. Formative assessment is contrasted with, and complementary to, summative assessment which makes judgements about individuals' achievements in relation to established standards and norms. Formative assessment is used to gauge progression in skills, concepts and knowledge in order to provide direct feedback to learners on their progress, development and quality of learning. Formative assessment data can be gathered in a number of relevant contexts and is usually criterion referenced, in other words it describes achievements in relation to specified criteria. These are shared between pupil and teacher. Formative assessment provides a basis for deciding on future learning and for developing a record of progress. Summative assessment, like formative assessment, is concerned with individuals but its prime purpose is to summarize information on achievement (DES/WO, 1989). Assessment may also be used to certify what individuals have achieved and to confirm their credentials publicly. Assessment provides information about institutional performances, implying judgements about the effective (or otherwise) 'delivery' of the curriculum in public evaluative exercises for the purposes of quality control.

Assessment issues in relation to the curriculum are many, complex and varied. Assessment has important public functions and can dominate curriculum processes and practices. The curriculum may be assessment driven and may therefore lose sight of its broader objectives. When assessment is multifunctional it can also be contradictory and there may be clashes and compromises between its different functions. Supporting learning is not necessarily always compatible with providing qualifications nor with the selection function of assessment.

Curriculum paradigms

In Chapter 1 we considered the notion of ideology in relation to education. The curriculum is always structured in relation to particular ideologies, powerful thought systems that shape what kind of knowledge is contained in the curriculum, how it is delivered, assessed and so on. In modern state education systems, the curriculum is likely to derive from a complex amalgam of different ideologies rather than from a completely consistent, clearly defined paradigm. This can be seen in the current National Curriculum, for example, where different kinds of knowledge sit side by side, the theoretical with the practical, the critical with the instrumental, where pupils are required to show analytical thinking and awareness, and where they are also required to accept culturally biased forms of knowledge (Lowe, 1997).

You will recognize the following curriculum paradigms as related to the ideologies discussed in Chapter 1.

Functional

The functional or technical paradigm resonates with the functionalist and instrumental ideologies. It is based on the codes, practices and beliefs that informed early interventions into the education of the new urban 'masses'. These codes were designed to train large numbers of people for their roles or duties within a fairly strict hierarchical view of society. They were designed to produce skilled workers who would also be literate and numerate and who would be able to conduct themselves as productive citizens contributing positively to the economy and regulating themselves in relation to the values of society. This functional view of the curriculum remains influential and informs the kind of thinking that can frequently be seen in public discourses about education and the economy. According to this view, teachers and schools should faithfully reproduce the curriculum as a distinct body of knowledge and skills. Curriculum development is likely to be seen more as a matter for the state and for central planning than for individual educators, or local groups of schools (see Lundgren, 1983; Tyler, 1949; Wheeler, 1967).

Transactional

The transactional or process paradigm is based on liberal ideas about human beings, life and society, and sits within a liberal humanist ideology. This paradigm is less interested in inherited forms of knowledge and their boundaries, and is more concerned with the production of knowledge. Teachers and learners engage in asking questions and making judgements about values, issues and common concerns, and are fundamentally involved in problem-solving. This model proposes a more active engagement with learning. It is concerned with attitudes and values and seeks to break down the conventional barriers between knowledge and learners (Pring, 1989; Skilbeck, 1984; Macdonald and Walker, 1971).

Critical

The critical or emancipatory paradigm is more directly oppositional and reflects a reconstructionist ideology. It seeks to challenge the given forms of knowledge by encouraging learners to develop their own critical faculties, to re-examine current forms of knowledge and to challenge their authority. The curriculum is seen as a site for contest rather than as something given and complete in itself (Aronowitz and Giroux, 1986; Habermas, 1972; Kemmis and Fitzclarence, 1986; Parker, 1997).

The curriculum and socialization: the state, knowledge and control

The idea that education is a human right is a relatively recent historical idea (Porter, 1999). It can be traced through the rise of nation states in the eighteenth and nineteenth centuries. Legislation appeared through the nineteenth century to control the employment of children, to protect children from sexual abuse and from exploitation as cheap labour. This process has been described by some as the construction or invention of childhood (Aries, 1962). Along with the intervention of the state into questions of the rights of children came an increasing concern with the idea of education as being appropriate for all levels of society and especially appropriate for the young. Given that, during the nineteenth century, education was to be experienced by total populations, these questions took on, and still retain, very considerable force and significance (Green, 1990).

Sociologists frequently represent schools as institutions of socialization (Althusser, 1984). They are at the centre of modern societies and are part of their established processes of transmitting values. In schools, pupils are trained to listen, to follow rules and to be well behaved and self-managing. Socialization refers to the various means and processes whereby values, social practices and ways of thinking and seeing are transmitted from generation to generation. Although at times socialization is represented as a one-way process, as something 'society' does to the unsuspecting young, it will always be dynamic. Pupils in schools, for example, do not always accept the socializing processes that are imposed upon them. Any teacher can relate to the difficulties that can be experienced in the socialization process with pupils who are intent on resistance. And a key feature of modern sociology has been to identify how groups of pupils may actively resist the values of the school that are being thrust upon them.

Some would say that the school system as we know it came into being to ensure that whole populations could be socialized in regular and predictable ways, could be inducted into a common culture and a common set of beliefs and values. Many would claim that the socializing function takes priority over the more 'common-sense' function of the school to purvey knowledge, literacy and numeracy. But, of course, the two processes, socialization and learning, are not separable. All the learning that takes place in the context of the school is involved in the transmission of values and beliefs about the way the world is. The acquisition and development of literacy is not, and cannot be, a neutral process. You always have to learn to read something and, whatever it is, it will convey, and be organized by, beliefs and values.

What is taught in the institutions of socialization will reflect the beliefs and values of any society or of particular positions and groups within that society. Catholic schools, for example, will be likely to promote a generally Catholic view of the world and will probably attempt to instil Catholic virtues and values in its subjects. But does this necessarily pervade the whole of schooling? To what extent do schools represent the cultural values of the society in which they operate? Can they represent the cultural values of all members of the society in which they operate? Are they doomed to represent and maintain dominant values? Can knowledge be free of specific cultural values? Very important questions are thus thrown up about how schools, and the processes of schooling, interact with their communities and the sometimes very different groups that form them (Bentley, 1998; Ranson, 1994).

The classroom is above all a site of practice. Every working day the teacher enters the classroom and engages with pupils in specific learning activities. At the beginning of each day statements will be made that express ideas about behaviour and learning. Work will be set and activities will be organized that represent the world and learning in a certain kind of way. The classroom is the place where the curriculum is enacted and the teacher mediates by translating it into accessible, meaningful segments and experiences for pupils. In this process values are always being expressed both in terms of the knowledge promoted and the conditions in which learning takes place. Even the most ordinary of school activities, lining up outside in the playground, for example, before entering the school, express ideas and beliefs about order, about the school, about authority and about social relations, and will impact on the total learning experience of pupils.

That education is always necessarily concerned with beliefs and values will appear to some as a truth universally acknowledged. For others, it will be imperative that education is seen to be about the imparting of pure knowledge and understanding, that beliefs and values threaten to contaminate the impartiality of true, objective knowledge with their own particular interests. In contemporary terms this conflict can be seen in certain disputes in the USA over the rights and wrongs of teaching apparently anti-religious accounts of the origins of the universe. Recently developed ways of looking at knowledge, postmodernism, for instance, would tend to stress its relativity and would insist that there can be no knowledge without the presence of beliefs and values.

Education then is more than the transmission of knowledge. It also involves the promotion of culture and morality. Education institutions work towards representing a view of the world through the curriculum that embodies a version of significant knowledge, values and beliefs of society. This may mean looking again at the history of modern education, the history of ideas and the philosophy that informed its growth. Rethinking the curriculum may mean revisiting some of the big words and ideas of our times like knowledge, power, society and culture. The connection between these things is one reason why modern nation states increasingly put education at the centre of their political policies (Porter, 1999).

Epistemology: the theory of knowledge

Ideas about knowledge tend to be deeply embedded in 'ideology', in institutions, in particular discourses and in particular social practices; they are rarely the creations of isolated individuals. Our knowledge of the world is the product of a complex network of factors: family background, formative experiences, cultural identity, social class, gender and language are all contributory to our sense of who we are but also our sense of what the world is like and what constitutes significant knowledge. Different ways of life and belief systems will inevitably produce different knowledge and different orientations towards it.

Knowledge comes not just as a body of 'facts' about the world. It comes packaged in a certain style. Official knowledge as expressed, for example, in the school curriculum may clash with alternative forms of knowledge that may belong to the lifestyles and belief systems of different cultural groups (Eagleton, 2000; Williams, 1983). In recent times the awareness of cultural difference and of its impact on schooling has increased. In the USA this has produced some quite fierce debate about the language of schooling and the cultural exclusion of African-American children in particular (Delpit, 1995; Smitherman, 2000).

The legacy of enlightenment epistemology

Enlightenment or modernist epistemology can be characterized by a certain kind of faith in progress. It is associated with the rise of scientific knowledge. After the domination of knowledge by religion through the medieval and even into the Renaissance period, a spirit of freethinking seemed to liberate knowledge but also to give it a rootedness of another kind. Enlightenment epistemology belongs to the history of the past 500 years or so, the post-Renaissance period in Europe. The emergence of the idea of science dates from this period with 'man' at the centre of things. There was also a resurgence of philosophy and the development of ideas that refer back to the classical period of Greek philosophy in the fifth century BC.

During the classical period of the enlightenment one of the big questions that beset western thought and philosophy was the question of certainty and knowledge. Descartes (1596–1650) is most frequently cited as the first thinker of the modern period to confront the question of knowledge and consciousness, responding to the question: how can I be sure that I know what I know? Descartes could only be certain of anything because he could be certain of himself as a thinking subject. For Descartes it is self-consciousness that guarantees knowledge. Immanuel Kant (1724–1804) was fascinated by the critique of knowledge proffered by the sceptics of the eighteenth century who pursued a line of thinking that meant that certainty about anything could not be guaranteed. His philosophy is an elaborate attempt to confront that uncertainty and scepticism with a thoroughly logical account of human understanding and knowledge. Kant's ideas, though radical at the time of their introduction into European thought, are now so deeply embedded that they can be said to be fundamental to western thinking. Kant had faith in the intuitive self-reflective rationality of consciousness. Rationality was seen as the very stuff of thought. The enlightenment idea of knowledge developed by Kant achieves its zenith perhaps in the thought of Hegel (1770–1831), the philosopher of 'dialectics' who in turn deeply influenced Marx's progressive version of history. Hegel saw history as a kind of self-managing logic of progress. Through conflicts of difference, new forms of being and knowledge come into existence which are themselves transformed and surpassed by others. This is the logic inherent in the world. For Hegel, history must follow a law of progression. It is in the nature of things to do so. This idea of necessary progression applies to knowledge and thought as well as to history. In other fields of knowledge a similar rationalism came to dominate thinking. Copernicus produced a model of the universe itself that challenged the idea of the centrality of the Earth but that proposed strict and proper laws of conduct for celestial bodies. The universe itself was being brought within the sphere of rational human knowledge. Darwin detected progress in the order of beings in nature. There was a law of natural selection and the history of biology was the history of a necessary progress.

Enlightenment thinking brought its own problems. Karl Marx (1818–83) took Hegel's dialectic into the political sphere and produced a new 'epistemology', or form of knowledge, based on revolutionary action. Nietzsche (1844–1900) saw that God was no longer there at the centre of things and so announced the death of God! If there was no God, then in what could human knowledge and understanding trust? Its own rational premises? Did this mean then, as Marx would have it, that religion, one of the main forms of knowledge of human history, was no more than a kind of 'drug' to keep the masses in their place or, as Sigmund Freud (1856–1939) would later describe it, nothing more than an 'illusion', the product of unconscious fears and desires? If God was really dead, then it seemed there could be no ultimate grounding for belief or conduct. Nietzsche himself saw this as potentially a great liberation. Existentialists felt it implied great responsibility for the individual to define and live by their own ethics of action. The events of twentieth-century history, with its high-tech total warfare and its various genocides, have prompted greater uncertainties about human progress, about the history of knowledge and about enlightenment values. From the post-colonial histories of the twentieth century have emerged powerful voices and movements to challenge the domination of western enlightenment. Nietzsche, Marx and Freud are often cited as the thinkers who instigated the demise of enlightenment thought, Nietzsche by emphasizing the correlation between truth and power, Marx by proposing a class-based rethinking of history and Freud by introducing the element of the unconscious into subjectivity, meaning that the self-present subject, the very centre of enlightenment epistemology, was nothing more than a self-deluding ruse.

Knowledge – absolute or provisional?

We may tend to think that knowledge is not tied to beliefs and values, and that the square on the hypotenuse is really, in some incontestable way, the sum of the square on the two opposite sides. It has been proven to be the case and it would seem very strange now to argue that the world is really flat, after all. Its roundness has been long established. It is the case, though, that knowledge, no matter how well established scientifically, cannot be totally fixed and absolute. It is always, in some way, relative and contingent, even though for the practical purposes of living we must behave as though certain knowledge is simply true and reliable.

But knowledge changes with time and culture. Different peoples hold different views of the world. We know, for example, pretty confidently, that in order for the sun to continue to appear day after day and to give life to things that we need for our continuing earthly existence, it is not necessary to perform regular human sacrifices. But the ancient Aztecs did not share our scepticism. They believed precisely that it was the case. In addition, they had plenty of empirical evidence to prove that it was so. After all, it always worked. We may now have established beyond doubt that the shedding of human blood is not an essential pre-requisite for the maintenance of solar energy on Earth. For the Aztecs, though, it was as absolute and complete a truth as any idea we might now claim universal truth and validity for.

Another way of illustrating the sometimes impossible collision of ideas about knowledge that inhabit different life worlds can be illustrated in the case of Australian aborigines and their systematic methods of accounting for history and time. When the English first went to Australia, the aborigines proved a deeply mysterious phenomenon. So perturbed were the English by their apparent difference that they regarded them as not human. They had none or hardly any of the characteristics that the white Europeans could recognize as human. This was not, as the dominant idea of the time would have it, because the aborigines were somehow so primitive and basic as to be nearer to animals. It was because the two peoples inhabited totally different 'life-worlds'. The difference had dramatic and tragic consequences for aboriginal Australians whose world was largely destroyed by the invaders. And yet the 'invaders' would hardly have described themselves in those terms. Australia was defined as 'terra nullus', a place of nothing without identity and the Australian peoples, for all their differences and their many different types of knowledge, were not regarded as having a world picture at all. The point of this digression is to indicate how fundamental knowledge about truth and reality may differ in ways which are of great significance and that even the most commonplace forms of knowledge, like knowledge about time, about history and so on, can be seen from utterly different perspectives.

Scientific knowledge is just as provisional a form of knowledge. Clearly there are degrees of provisionality here. We would be deeply unhappy if we thought, for example, that the science of aerodynamics relating to flight engine technology was a kind of open-ended affair dependent upon opinion and belief. But even this kind of hard scientific technical knowledge rests on premises about matter, about physics and so on, that are changing all the time. Thankfully the form of practical knowledge that enables aeroplanes to be effectively managed through take-off, flight and landing is secure (although conditions do change above the speed of sound). Aero-physics is changing constantly and revisions are being made to knowledge in this area, hence new technologies of flight have come into being over the past 100 years. We may, for good reasons, think of medicine as a well-established and highly funded field of contemporary research and knowledge. At the same time, we are all aware of the developmental nature of medical knowledge, new discoveries and technologies of treatment emerging all the time. Scientists frequently argue about the precise nature of the tiniest particles of matter and whether they are particles or waves of energy, just as historians argue about the precise methods for the dating of archaeological evidence. Thus scientific, medical truth is not absolute at any time, but it is often represented as such or at least as unquestionably authoritative.

Organizing knowledge as subjects

The idea of the curriculum as the organization of knowledge into separate subject areas has developed powerfully through state education systems (Bowles and Gintis, 1976; Bourdieu and Passeron, 1977).

It was Paul Hirst, as recently as the 1970s, who believed that the curriculum could be related to universal 'forms of knowledge', distinct areas which have their own concepts. These must be testable against experience and they each have particular criteria for establishing this relation with reality. Hirst (1975) divided knowledge into the following forms: mathematics, physical sciences, human sciences, history, religion, literature and the fine arts, philosophy and moral knowledge. It is this view of knowledge which structures the present-day curriculum in schools and which still exerts powerful influence over subject divisions in other academic institutions like sixth form colleges and universities, for instance.

Knowledge is deemed to inhere in specific subjects which may relate to one another but which also have their own discrete and different sets of ideas, practices and contents. These are not just collections of facts but include ways of looking at things and modes of understanding. Each follows its own rules and practices, being a separate language-game or discourse, though all fall within the general cultural and linguistic environment of the school. The National Curriculum in England and Wales, for example, defines and divides the curriculum in terms of different subjects. Some subjects, however, are defined in the National

Curriculum as being more central and more essential than others. So English, mathematics and science all have core status and are the central concerns of state schooling. In some subject areas there have been disagreements between different individuals, bodies and institutions about what the proper contents of the subject should be. In subjects such as history, English and music, for example, the content may appear to be more contentious and open to debate. In these subject areas questions about subjectivity, perspective and ideology may appear to be more relevant and critical (Burden and Williams, 1998; Cox, 1991; 1995).

Hirst's view is thoroughly liberal, functionalist and uncritical. It accepts the dominant conception of knowledge that is embodied in the history of curriculum since 1902. The (quite plausible) idea that knowledge is a contested field of human life, that there could be different types of knowledge and that the curriculum might simply reflect an ideological history is not entertained in Hirst's account. Against the idea that knowledge is fixed, complete and knowable is the idea of knowledge as constructed through social activity. Different social practices, engaged in by different groups of people, will necessarily give rise to different forms of knowledge and different forms of knowing. A number of commentators on education have sought to produce an alternative idea of knowledge and have interpreted the conventional curriculum of schooling accordingly. Among these Young's *Knowledge and Control* (1971) began to open up questions about curriculum knowledge. More recently Henri Giroux and others have challenged the forms of knowledge and pedagogy installed in contemporary state and national curricula as limited and excluding (Aronowitz and Giroux, 1986). Twentieth-century tendencies in philosophy would generally argue against Hirst's position. The confidence that knowledge can be limited, defined and parcelled has been seriously challenged. Foucault (1977b) sees knowledge systems as shifting according to the dominant 'episteme' or regime of truth. These systems are not progressive and may differ radically from one historical period to another. This works against the confident assumption of accumulating human knowledge and argues for ideas about knowledge that are more open to the excluded and different.

Postmodern versions of, and post-colonial perspectives on, knowledge

Postmodern views of the curriculum characterize it much more as a provisional social construct rather than as the expression of functional and intrinsically important knowledge. In the postmodern world, knowledge is at the centre and controlling it is a means to exercise power. Knowledge in this view is always contested and what we take for progress, the steady march of science for instance, towards more inclusive and more powerful explanations of the world, is really the victory of one set of ideas and one kind of knowledge over others (Harvey, 1991; Lyotard, 1986).

Knowledge requires authority in the modern nation state. Its characteristic education systems depend on the exertion of various kinds of authority. Institutions are endowed with the power to grant social status on individuals, to award them credentials and to authorize ideas and practices with the status of socially significant knowledge. Individuals receive acknowledgement of their accumulated knowledge status through accreditation systems that validate their knowledge at different levels, thus producing a knowledge hierarchy.

In contemporary global conditions, knowledge is rapidly changing shape and form, largely under the influence of new, electronic forms of storage and distribution. Some knowledge becomes commercially very significant and its circulation increases via new technologies. Knowledge becomes more fragmented and more specialized. It changes shape, new forms rising rapidly under the principle of hybridity – where different forms of knowledge meet and produce a new form (as with cultural studies, for instance). The conventional institutions of knowledge – schools, colleges and universities – become subject to the logic of performativity, required to be more cost-effective and more productive and measured against performative criteria (Lyotard, 1986).

A number of intellectuals have come to prominence in recent times to challenge the forms and assumptions of western knowledge. These positions tend to see western knowledge as taking itself as knowledge in total and as representing anything outside itself as a kind of aberration or non-knowledge. Edward Said (1978), for example, has challenged the way that western writings and knowledge have represented 'the east' as something 'other', alien and exotic and have diminished thereby the claims to legitimacy of other kinds and traditions of knowledge. Similar positions have been elaborated in intricate and persuasive detail by Gayatri Spivak (1990) and Aijaz Ahmad (1992) both of whom, like Said, have used the west's own recent traditions of critique to challenge the authority of dominant systems of knowledge and power. In a powerful case study Gauri Viswanathan (1989) gives an account of the imperialist significance of literary study and the practices of English teaching in nineteenth-century India under British rule.

Post-colonial thinking requires that ethnicity as a radical form of difference be rethought in terms of knowledge, values, beliefs and culture. Cultural differences give rise to different ways of looking at things, different ways of seeing and even of being in the world. In contemporary urban centres different cultures meet, mingle and collide. Education is one form of cultural practice that individuals and populations must negotiate in a world of mingling forms and identities (Sahin, 2000).

As we have seen, some thinkers within the functionalist tradition have espoused the singular view that the conventional curriculum of schooling (as in the case of the National Curriculum in England and Wales and shortly to apply to Australia, New Zealand and South Africa) follows the shape and logic of knowledge itself. Against this position is the idea that the curriculum is actually shaped by a number of forces, many of them having little or nothing to do with education or knowledge. We have seen it claimed, from a critical sociological position, that the curriculum embodies what has been set as knowledge by powerful groups in society. It has also been argued that knowledge is actually always a contested field, that the value of what is learned is of less importance than the social authority that learning in institutions carries with it. It has been suggested that discourses of knowledge are historically 'contingent', that they appear and hold authority according to the social pressures that give them legitimacy rather than according to their 'scientific' truth. It has also been powerfully argued that education is really not about the curriculum in the obvious sense, about learning mathematics or punctuation, but that it is precisely about learning to internalize certain social values and beliefs, and that this is its primary if 'hidden' function.

Curriculum: a historical perspective

We saw in Chapter 1 how the history of state education systems can be organized into phases that indicate how the emergence of present ideas has developed. Looking at these historical layers can help to explain some of the tensions and conflicts in contemporary state education.

Elementary education

Education systems evolved out of various needs that came together through the large transformations of society that took place during the eighteenth and nineteenth centuries (Jones, 1977; Mann, 1979). Formal education hitherto had been largely a minority affair for a relatively privileged section of the population. During the early years of the nineteenth century large numbers of children in the new urban centres were working in factories while those remaining in rural areas worked in agriculture or cottage industries of various kinds. By the end of the century most children were attending schools and in some form of full-time education for a significant segment of their early lives. The emergence of state education with the rapid development of the school as a central institution of civil society represented a massive change in the social order. The establishment of elementary schooling was fraught with contentious issues. Religious organizations were keen to ensure that schooling was not to be dominated by rival religious factions. There was a deep-seated resistance among *laissez-faire* liberals, conservatives and working-class activists to the idea of state-funded compulsory education, suspicious of the state's efforts to control education on different grounds.

The early 'poor' schools for urban working-class children were essentially 'drill' schools, concerned with strict training in literacy and numeracy for large numbers of pupils as quickly as possible, given the uncertain nature of the clientele and the uncertain duration of their school life (Donald, 1992; Lowe and Seaborne, 1977). Designed to manage the learning of large numbers via a rank-and-file ordering of all its pupils in a single space, monitorial schooling promoted a monolithic version of learning via repetition. It was the proud boast of these schools that they could effect learning for large numbers of pupils with the presence of a single instructor.

In the early phase of the elementary schools (1870–1900) the curriculum was largely concerned with the teaching of values, virtues, literacy, numeracy, personal hygiene, physical maintenance, domestic skills and rudimentary knowledge about the world and the nation's considerable influence within it. The pioneers of state education had seen the emergent school as the potential instrument of moral transformation, especially important in relation to urban populations that were deemed to be threateningly amoral and disorganized. The school could be a key instrument in the training of populations and in the construction of the idea of community. Early urban state schools can be seen to have this socially symbolic function in their dramatic and often cathedral-like architecture.

The powerful, conservative nineteenth-century idea that education for the working classes was potentially dangerous and might give the proletariat ideas above their station was evident in the limitations of the early elementary school curriculum (Mann, 1979). Early state educators believed that education was necessarily about making the nation cohesive, fostering and cultivating national identity. There was little embarrassment about the political function of that ideological effort. In the 1920s the threat of Bolshevism, which had overthrown the Russian monarchy and set up a powerful communist state with overt internationalist intentions, generated a renewed emphasis on the school as the purveyor of national language and national culture specifically to train the working classes in national allegiance over class conflict (Doyle, 1989; Newbolt, 1921; Sampson, 1952).

As elementary schooling took hold the problem of the curriculum for the maintained sector intensified. There was more time in school to fill and more pressure on the authorities of education to ensure that schooling was meaningful for the various interest groups or stakeholders concerned (Horn, 1989; Hurt, 1979). The Revised Code of 1862 laid down conditions for school managers to claim grants for children attending. To be eligible for these grants children had to attain one of six standards in reading, writing and arithmetic. Each standard in each subject was stated in terms of a precisely defined skill to be demonstrated, rather like contemporary National Curriculum attainment targets. This imposed a concentration on the basics.

In 1904, two years after the Education Act that laid the basis of the compulsory system, the board of education published an elementary code and regulations for secondary schools. The elementary code continued the tradition of the elementary school stressing conduct and discipline with minor emphasis on subject knowledge. The Act itself speaks strongly in terms of 'self-sacrifice', 'respect for duty', 'respect for others', 'instinct for fair play', 'loyalty to one another' and other qualities that emphasize the personal, moral dimension of the curriculum (Jenkins and Shipman, 1976).

More secondary schools emerged after 1904. They mostly tended to borrow the academic curriculum of the private schools which had modified classical curricula. The act specified: English language and literature, at least one language other than English, geography, history, mathematics, science and physical exercises (Jenkins and Shipman, 1976). It added the proviso that girls' schools should include 'housewifery'. The early primary school developed in a learner-centred direction. The Hadow Report of 1926 on primary schooling contained guidelines for the general direction of the primary curriculum: 'Its aim should be to develop in a child the fundamental human powers and to awaken him [sic] to the fundamental interests of a civilized life so far as these powers and interests lie within the compass of childhood' (Jenkins and Shipman, 1976: 29).

The tripartite system

After the First World War, a number of forces and factors combined to pressure for the idea of a type of schooling different from the then well-established elementary school system. At this stage (1918–47) access to proper secondary education for working-class children was strictly limited. The vast majority of children finished their education at 13 or 14. It was only exceptionally that successful working-class children could gain access to full secondary schooling and higher education. As the urban populations threatened to become increasingly self-organized and a force for radical political change, governments became increasingly concerned to counter political ideals with social values and new opportunities realized through the school. Public debates about the need to change education often took the form of a tension or conflict between ideas about the health and wealth of the nation – education as a means towards economic growth, stability and improvement – and education increasingly seen as a social right. Clearly a major shift in the public idea of education was taking place during this period.

At the same time thought was being given to the kind of curricula that were suited to different groups within the population. The Norwood Report of 1943 identified three types of curriculum:

- The first type is academic in orientation and pursues knowledge for its own sake – having an indirect relation to 'considerations of occupation'.
- The second type of curriculum is directed to 'the special data and skills associated with a particular kind of occupation'. This curriculum would always have a limited horizon and would be closely related to industry, trade and commerce 'in all their diversity'.
- The third type of curriculum balances training of mind and body and teaches the humanities, natural science and the arts to a degree which enables them to 'take up the work of life'. While practical in orientation it would appeal to the 'interests' of pupils and would not have as its immediate aim the preparation for particular types of work.

At the same time, the Norwood Committee recommended that consideration be given to general needs that would pertain to all: 'in spite of differences all pupils have common needs and a common destiny;

physical and spiritual and moral ideals are of vital concern to all alike' (Silver, 1973: 82). Explicitly different types of curriculum were deemed to be relevant for these pupils. The civil servants who had forged this new version of the education system drew their authority from the division of humanity expressed in Plato's *Republic*: 'You are all of you in this land brothers. But when god fashioned you, he added gold in the composition of those who are qualified to be rulers; he put silver in the auxiliaries and iron and bronze in the farmers and the rest' (1955: 160).

The moment of the 1944 Education Act, sometimes referred to as the Butler Act after the incumbent Secretary of State for Education, is often represented as *the* defining moment in the history of modern education. Secondary education was to be provided for all according to the age, aptitude and ability of each pupil. This was to be a right for all pupils, rather than being based on ability to pay, as had largely been the case before the Second World War. The act established a nationally funded education system, which was overseen by the Department of Education and Science, and administered by local education authorities (LEAs). The curriculum was to be the responsibility of the individual schools, i.e. the headteachers and teachers. It was in effect a 'national system, locally administered'. The LEAs were to administer the schools in their area. Influenced by thinking at the time that intelligence was relatively fixed and could be measured (see Chapter 4), and being given the legal responsibility to provide a suitable education, the tripartite system of education was developed in many areas. In this system pupils went to a primary school until the age of 11 where they were inducted into the school system and began learning the basic skills of the three 'Rs'. This was seen as an important time when the intelligence and aptitude of the child began to develop. In their final year of primary school, pupils took the 11-plus, an intelligence test designed to show both their ability and aptitude. Based upon the results pupils were sent to one of three types of secondary school.

1 *Secondary grammar school.* These were for the more intelligent pupils with an academic aptitude. The emphasis was on traditional subjects and knowledge. It was expected that these pupils would be suitable for a university education in the future or take a career in the minor professions or the white-collar sector.
2 *Secondary technical school.* These were for pupils with a practical aptitude. Their curriculum would be based on craft and technical skills. It was envisaged that these pupils would be suited to future careers as skilled workers and engineers in industry after taking apprenticeships.

3 *Secondary modern school.* These were for pupils who did not fit either of the above categories and were suited to a more general education to prepare them for their future lives as citizens and (largely unskilled) workers. (See Brooks, 1991 for an account of the development of the tripartite system.)

Comprehensive schooling

Criticisms of the tripartite system began to emerge and pressure to change the system grew throughout the 1960s. Though the three types of school set up in most LEAs were supposed to have 'parity of esteem' this was not the case in practice. Grammar schools were academic and therefore seen as superior. Certainly parents who had career aspirations for their children needed them to take the General Certificate of Education (GCE) O level examinations, an examination in each subject at 16 which preceded the GCSE. It was designed for the top 40 per cent of pupils and led on to A levels taken in school sixth forms which only the grammar schools offered. Increasing parental pressure was put on pupils, especially middle-class pupils, to gain a place at grammar school. Children were coached for the 11-plus and it was soon realized that this was not an accurate measure of innate ability as had at first been supposed. The whole notion of intelligence being fixed and that pupils could fall into one of three types became highly questionable. Academically able pupils were often also very practical and technically minded. Likewise lack of academic ability was not necessarily made up for in practical aptitude. The pressure to obtain a grammar school place affected the primary school curriculum which was increasingly based on preparation for the 11-plus.

Very few technical schools were built. Those that were came to be seen as for those too bright for secondary modern school but not good enough for grammar school. Secondary modern pupils often felt labelled as failures at 11 as they had, from the time of selection, effectively been rejected as lacking in intelligence. These schools became regarded as 'sink' schools with pupils often seeing little reason to work hard. Some secondary modern schools began to copy the grammar school curriculum by developing examination streams to enable some of their pupils to take GCE O levels. The argument that separate schools were required to provide different curricula for different abilities began to be seriously undermined. There appeared to be a great wastage of talent caused by the poor development of pupils placed in secondary modern schools. This feeling was reflected in the growing unease concerning the validity of the increasingly discredited selection procedure (see Young, 1998). The argument for abolishing the 11-plus grew. This was especially strong among middle-class parents becoming anxious at their children's chances of entering grammar schools.

The move towards the comprehensive school was designed to heal the divisions of the tripartite system, an attempt to provide a form of education that would cater for all. In comprehensive schools entrance is not by ability as pupils are accepted across the whole range. In the first instance these secondary schools were often neighbourhood schools, taking all pupils from a particular geographical area in which they were situated. The 11-plus was abolished in those areas which introduced comprehensive education. This immediately reduced the pressure on pupils in their final year of primary school and also on their parents. Primary schools were now more able to follow the progressive recommendations of the Plowden Report (CACE, 1967). Pupils were no longer clearly stigmatized as failures at 11. They were not divided up into separate schools according to ability and they could not be identified in the street by a secondary or grammar school uniform.

Some of these schools were new and built to cope with expanding numbers of pupils now entering secondary education. They were large and able to offer economies of scale. The raising of the school-leaving age to 16 in 1970 meant that the curriculum had to be rethought to be more inclusive (Jenkins and Shipman, 1976). This led to increased choice and diversity in the curriculum with more extra-curricular facilities available. There were differing ways of organizing the teaching in these schools. Some used setting, some streaming and, increasingly, in the 1970s, classes were of mixed ability. It is interesting to note that primary schools had always been comprehensive schools in the way this term was now being applied to secondary schools. Pupils in primary schools had also usually been taught in mixed ability classes.

Although it was never the case that there existed a single and unitary form of the comprehensive school curriculum, there were a number of tendencies that appeared to make the curriculum more relevant to the newly extended school population (Chitty and Dunford, 1999; Jenkins and Shipman, 1976). This sometimes meant the inclusion of vocational areas of study for the non-academic, but also meant that subject boundaries began to be less rigidly adhered to. Integrated humanities and integrated science courses appeared, for example. New, open forms of assessment came into being through the Certificate of Secondary Education (CSE) examination and began to infiltrate the socially and academically prestigious General Certificate of Education (GCE). In

1985 these two different systems were unified into the General Certificate of Secondary Education (GCSE) and forms of assessment became much more liberal, flexible and open. Continuous assessment through coursework and module tests came to have equal status with end of course examinations.

This historical appraisal reveals huge ideological shifts and conflicts that can still be felt in contemporary values and ideas about education and the proper identity and function of the curriculum (Silver, 1973).We have seen how the nineteenth-century concerns of education for the working classes being dangerous have given way to powerful, often socialist, pressures to make education accessible to the people and to reconstruct the curriculum along more inclusive and liberal lines. The seminal 1944 Act seems to have instigated many of the themes that still haunt debates about education. A central issue remains the provision of differentiated schooling. While liberally providing education for all, the Act ensured that differentiation of provision would be structurally established, a legacy that remains powerful. The contemporary curriculum, with its tensions between academic knowledge and life-skills, liberal conceptions of learning and vocational training, bears something of the unresolved tensions of that history (CCCS, 1981). We turn now to the contemporary scene, starting with the National Curriculum.

The National Curriculum

The Education Reform Act, 1988

The National Curriculum was established by the 1988 Education Reform Act (DES, 1988) which prescribed a compulsory curriculum for all maintained schools in England and Wales. This new curriculum was to occupy most if not all of pupils' time and was to sit within the 'whole curriculum', an overarching vehicle responsible for the 'spiritual, moral, cultural, mental and physical development of pupils at the school and of society' (section 1 of the Act). Within the whole curriculum were specified 'themes, skills and dimensions' which schools should cater for in a cross-curricular manner. These included equal opportunities, economic and European awareness, environmental education, citizenship and so on (DES, 1989). The guidance for elements of the whole curriculum had only advisory rather than statutory status. Consequently these important elements slipped down the agenda under the weight of the statutory requirements of the centrally determined National

Curriculum. The 1988 Act made religious education compulsory but stated that daily worship should normally be 'broadly Christian' in character. Religious education is not part of the National Curriculum, though, and its syllabus is a matter for local agreement. It is not determined by central government and parents may withdraw their children from it. The curriculum specifications of the 1988 Education Act were amplified by the 1993 Education Act. Under this legislation sex education (including education about HIV and AIDS) has a similar status to religious education, though only in secondary schools. It is compulsory for schools to provide it, but it is outside the National Curriculum and parents may request that their children be withdrawn from it. Sex education, the Act specifies, should have regard for moral matters and should give due consideration to the value of family life.

The Education Reform Act was probably the most important piece of legislation in education in England and Wales since 1944 (Chitty, 1992; Ranson, 1994). The 1993 'sister' Education Act enhanced central curriculum control with the establishment of OFSTED, charged with reporting on the delivery of the National Curriculum in state schools and with conducting extensive inspections of all schools once every four years. The National Curriculum met with protests at its inception – significant objections were raised on the grounds that the curriculum was being taken, in effect, from the hands of teachers and other education professionals and given to central-government appointed bodies.

This 1988 Act changed the nature of the curriculum and its fundamental authority. The curriculum was now to be determined by law, no longer left to the professional educators, the universities, schools and colleges, and examination institutions. The act emphasized the need for the curriculum to be broad, balanced, relevant and accessible to all (DES, 1989). Clause 2 of the Act states that the aim of this curriculum is to prescribe a number of school subjects and to specify in relation to each:

- knowledge, skills and understandings which pupils of different abilities and maturities are expected to have
- matters, skills and processes which are required to be taught to pupils of different abilities and maturities
- arrangements for assessing pupils.

Background to the National Curriculum

Before the 1988 Education Reform Act, central government had no direct hand in controlling or defining the curriculum of schools. The

1944 Education Act specified only religious education as a compulsory subject and even in that case parents had the right to opt out on behalf of their children. Otherwise the curriculum was left to the control of local authorities and schools (in association with governing bodies after the 1986 Education Act). The school curriculum was not a free for all before the 1988 Act. In reality the curriculum was subject to many constraints and shaping factors that tended to ensure a kind of uniformity across schools and across the country, including examination practices, school culture and well-established professional habits.

We have seen that prior to comprehensivization, secondary modern schools had a practical and vocational orientation while grammar schools had a more academic curriculum, dominated by a conventional array of subjects up to 16+ including English, mathematics, modern foreign languages, the sciences and the humanities. Comprehensive reorganization led largely to the emulation of this grammar school curriculum throughout secondary schools. During the 1980s the secondary school curriculum in England and Wales had been broadly divided up into English (13 per cent), mathematics (13 per cent), science (16 per cent), design and technology (4 per cent), foreign language (5 per cent), history and geography (10 per cent), art, music, drama and design (7 per cent), physical education (8 per cent) with the remaining 10 per cent taken up by other subjects (DES, 1987). Talk of the 'entitlement curriculum' (HMI, 1994) which would provide a broad and balanced diet for all pupils, had existed for some time, since the emergence in 1977 of HMI papers *Curriculum 11–16*. In primary schools, where there was little concern with external examinations, the curriculum was more open and could be quite varied from school to school both in terms of content and style.

Content of the National Curriculum: subjects

The 1988 Education Act does not specify itself what the National Curriculum should include nor how it should be assessed. It provides a structure in outline and it empowers the Secretary of State for England and Wales to fill the details in 'ministerial orders'. There are now two statutory bodies governing curriculum and assessment: the Qualifications and Curriculum Authority (for England) and the Qualifications, Curriculum and Assessment Authority for Wales (ACCAC – Awdurded Cymwysterau Cwricwlwm ac Asesu Cymru).

The National Curriculum was subject to fairly frequent modification in its early years, but the current ministerial orders have been in place since 1995. With the National Curriculum specifications for subjects came detailed prescriptions for what should be taught and for what should be regarded as the appropriate levels of attainment at the different 'key stages' established by the National Curriculum. These influenced the forms of assessment at Key Stage 4 (KS4) or GCSE level, reducing the coursework and continuous assessment elements in favour of end of course examinations.

The National Curriculum in England is now divided into the following subjects, with the first three designated as 'core' and the rest as foundation subjects: for the first two key stages: English, mathematics, science, information technology, design and technology, history, geography, music, art, physical education, a modern foreign language (and citizenship from 2002).

The specific requirements concerning these subjects vary according to the ages of the pupils. The teaching and assessment of the National Curriculum is divided into four key stages as follows:

- Key Stage 1 – up to age 7 (Years 1 and 2)
- Key Stage 2 – up to age 11 (Years 3–6)
- Key Stage 3 – up to age 14 (Years 7–9)
- Key Stage 4 – up to age 16 (Years 10 and 11).

At Key Stages 1 and 2, English, mathematics and science have to be taught according to the detailed programmes of study specified in the National Curriculum. Design and technology, information technology, history, geography, music, art and physical education are still required to be taught but since September 1998 schools have been given more freedom in their approach to these subjects (DfEE/QCA, 1999). No foreign language is compulsory at this stage. Since September 1998, schools have been required, at Key Stages 1 and 2, to devote an hour each day to literacy and, from September 1999, an hour each day to numeracy.

At Key Stage 3, a modern foreign language is included in the requirements and all 11 subjects have to be taught according to the detailed programmes in the National Curriculum documents. At Key Stage 4, history, geography, music and art are no longer compulsory.

It is interesting to compare National Curriculum subjects with the subject regulations for 1904 and 1935 (Mayes and Moon, 1994: 248):

1904	1935
English language	English language
English literature	English literature
One language	One language

1904	1935
Geography	Geography
History	History
Mathematics	Mathematics
Science	Science
Drawing	Drawing
Due provision for manual work and physical exercise (Housewifery in girls' schools).	Physical exercises and organized games
	Singing
	(Manual instruction for boys, domestic subjects for girls).

The National Curriculum is not intended to take up all of the time pupils are in schools, but there are no statutory regulations about how schools should divide up their time. The Dearing Report of 1993 made some recommendations indicating that English should occupy 14 per cent, mathematics 12 per cent, science 13 per cent, technology and foreign languages, religious education and physical education 5 per cent each, and that the remaining 43 per cent should be discretionary but to include a balance of other specified subjects (Dearing, 1994). (See Andrews, 1996, for a full account of the National Curriculum.)

The structure and assessment of the National Curriculum

It was the assessment framework that gave shape to the National Curriculum, drawing criticism that the assessment tail was wagging the curriculum dog (Gipps and Stobart, 1993). The framework was established by the report of the Task Group on Assessment and Testing led by Paul Black (DES, 1989). It represented a major break with the assessment traditions and ownership of the past as it established national, externally marked tests at ages 7, 11 and 14. The programmes of study for each subject are set out in booklets published by the Department for Education and Employment and the Welsh Office (some together and some separately). Each subject is divided into different attainment targets, as illustrated here for the core subjects of English, mathematics and science:

English	*Mathematics*	*Science*
Speaking and listening	Using and applying mathematics	Experimental and investigative science
Reading	Number	Life processes and
Writing.		living things

English	*Mathematics*	*Science*
	Algebra (KS 3 and 4) Shape, space and measures handling data (KS 2–4).	Materials and their properties Physical processes.

For each attainment target in most subjects nine successive levels of attainment are identified. Each of these has level descriptions. In effect this means that the National Curriculum sets out how pupils should make progress in each subject area from the very beginning of their studies at age 5 to the end of Key Stage 3 at age 14. These levels do not coincide directly with Key Stages as there is recognition that children may differ in their rates of progress. However, it is specified that by the end of each Key Stage, the vast majority of pupils should have levels of attainment within the following ranges:

- End of Key Stage 1 – levels 1–3
- End of Key Stage 2 – levels 2–5
- End of Key Stage 3 – levels 3–7.

There is also a level 8 for 'very able' pupils and a ninth unnumbered level for 'exceptional performance' at Key Stage 3. These levels of achievement do not apply to Key Stage 4. Nor do they apply to art, music or physical education at any stage. These subjects have end of Key Stage *descriptions*, setting out the achievements expected of most pupils at the end of each of the four Key Stages.

Modifications to, and criticisms of, the National Curriculum

So it was that the National Curriculum, a historical milestone in the history of education in England and Wales, came into being. It was probably the most significant feature of a vitally important piece of legislation in terms of the kinds of experiences pupils could expect from schooling. It was attacked in many ways and on many grounds at the time (Lawton and Chitty, 1988). In the years following, the National Curriculum has continued to receive drastically critical treatment from educationalists, many of whom agreed with the principle of a National Curriculum but deplored the process of its installation and development, lamenting the unimaginative form it has taken (Lawton, 1999). Complaints included the absence of a clear educational purpose, its disregard of recent debates about curriculum and the failure to engage in detailed and sustained consultation with teachers and other education professionals. There was early pressure to reconsider the curriculum as originally established; this provoked a review in 1993 by Ron Dearing. This made some relatively small changes to the structure of the National Curriculum but could not achieve the radical rethink that some called for. Nor could it provide the kind of ideological rationale and professional support for the curriculum that it lacked from the outset (Chitty and Dunford, 1999). In the main, subsequent changes have been in the form of cutting subject and content requirements and limiting national assessment to the three core subjects. More recently the Labour government that took office in 1997 has granted power to the managers of Education Action Zones to modify or abandon parts of the National Curriculum.

The original National Curriculum was critiqued on the following grounds: it was too bureaucratic; it centralized control of education; private schools were exempt; the curriculum was felt to be too traditionalist and too conventionally academic in orientation; testing at 7 and 11 was felt to be dangerous in terms of labelling; and the theoretical ideas underpinning the notion of cumulative achievement within all subjects was challenged (Gipps, 1993). It was felt that the National Curriculum worked against the spirit of comprehensive reform that had envisaged the development of a school curriculum based on the idea of a common culture (Lawton, 1975). Some critics have claimed that the National Curriculum favours certain (middle) class groups above others and that it works against the cultural orientations of ethnic minority groups in its historical and cultural biases, in terms of its implicit valuations of languages (negating entirely the many languages of ethnic minority groupings) and its failure to engage with cultural experiences other than mainstream 'canonical' culture (McNeil, 1990). The new emphasis given by the National Curriculum to Christian religious traditions has also been noted as symptomatic of cultural bias (Troyna and Carrington, 1990).

It was in the introduction of national standards that the National Curriculum was felt by some commentators to be most likely to accentuate class differences. The introduction of standardized age-related testing has been represented as meaning that children will be ranked and ordered as never before, and that their value to the school, in the labour market and in the sphere of education will vary accordingly. For some this means that the National Curriculum is a massive machine for differentiating children against fixed norms – a very powerful, pervasive and multivalent form of control. The decision to publish test results exacerbated these fears at a school level on the grounds that it could further disadvantage schools operating in deprived areas. In some schools these league tables of results led to the differentiation of pupil groups. Differentiation can mean that pupils will be segregated from one another (banded or streamed) and that they will follow different educational trajectories leading in the long run to different social destinies. This inevitably works against equality of opportunity but sits well with a differentiated school system with grammar schools, city technology colleges, private schools and grant maintained (now foundation) schools as well as poor schools and wealthy schools (Johnson, 1991; Lawton, 1999).

Curriculum 2000

There has recently been a review of the National Curriculum following the moratorium on change imposed from 1995. Thoroughgoing conceptual changes to the National Curriculum are still not encouraged. A report published in 1998 by the National Advisory Committee on Creative and Cultural Education (NACCCE) in response to the government's own White Paper, *Excellence in Schools* (DfEE, 1997b), called for a systemic approach to creative and cultural education, where these are not simply subjects in the curriculum but functions of education: 'By creative education we mean forms of education that develop young people's capacities for original ideas and action; by cultural education we mean forms of education that enable them to engage positively with the growing complexity and diversity of social values and ways of life' (NACCCE, 1998: 6).

The report was not published quickly by the government and has not met with the acclaim that might have been expected given that its authors were handpicked prestigious people from higher education, schools and the arts. It made very explicit recommendations in relation to the major review of the National Curriculum in 2000; some quite radical actions were 'required' of the DfEE, QCA and OFSTED. For instance, the report called for the distinction between core and foundation subjects to be removed, for the curriculum to make explicit the creative and cultural knowledge, skills and values that young people should acquire and for assessment outcomes to be specified in relation to creative and cultural education. The guidance (DfEE/QCA, 1999) outlining the National Curriculum requirements from 2000 onwards does not appear to take on board any of these recommendations.

Conclusion

The impact of different ideologies and beliefs on the creation, positioning and structure of a curriculum has been illustrated. We have seen that perceptions of the nature of knowledge and what is seen as important to 'know' play a central part in the design of any curriculum. Knowledge can be structured and presented in different ways. In the context of modern schooling, traditional subject knowledge may be seen as important or knowledge may be presented thematically. Thus teaching and learning can take many different forms depending upon the purpose of the curriculum and the beliefs of the teachers. The emphasis may be on practical applications, experimentation, didactic teaching or open learning. Even within a particular course the teaching methods can vary greatly. For instance, students learning a modern foreign language may have a very different experience from peers taking the same subject in the next room. One teacher may emphasize an interactive, oral approach to language development, whereas another may stress writing and rote learning as ways of extending the students' vocabularies.

Assessment is a fundamental element of the curriculum and can take many forms. It may consist of formal written examinations, oral tests or practical tasks. Its purpose might be to test students on completion of a course (summative assessment) or it may be to monitor their progress as they go through the course (formative assessment). These different forms of assessment reflect what those designing and delivering the curriculum see as important in terms of student outcomes. They are tied very much to the purposes of the curriculum and beliefs concerning the nature of education.

The structural features of the curriculum are thus influenced by the purposes and beliefs of the teachers, course designers, examination boards, government ministers and established discourses. The final delivered curriculum is often the result of a complex interaction and power struggle between the various interested parties.

Student activities

1 Look at the DfEE website and find the National Curriculum: http://www.nc.uk.net/. Read the section entitled 'Values, aims and purposes' and identify the key words and any important contrasts that are set up. To what extent do these concepts inform the subject-based curriculum that is available on the same web pages?

2 Consider your own experience of the curriculum. To what extent were aspects of yourself developed positively by the curriculum? Were there aspects of yourself that were not developed positively? Or that were not addressed?

3 Look again at the National Curriculum. Examine the section 'Learning across the National Curriculum'. Comment on this programme, considering why it is there and defining your own thoughts and reactions to it.

4 Some critics, Lawton (1999), for instance, have suggested that the curriculum should be rethought, and that the traditional subject-based curriculum is moribund and anachronistic. What might be included in a radical rethink of the curriculum, in terms of contents, experiences, teaching and learning, and assessment? Is it possible to define a new programme for learning? What would be the basis for this new curriculum and how would it meet the needs of contemporary conditions and people?

Recommended reading

Apple, M. (1996) *Cultural Politics and Education*, Buckingham: Open University Press. An interesting and challenging review of curriculum issues which is extremely relevant to contemporary questions of inclusivity. Apple seeks to rethink the whole project of state-funded education in terms of the driving concerns of democracy and equality. This provides a useful introduction to alternative ways of seeing the everyday and embedded practices of education.

Edwards, R. and Usher, R. (1994) *Postmodernism and Education*, London: Routledge. This contains some very accessible accounts of more recent trends in thinking applied to the field of education. Key areas including curriculum are reinterpreted through post-structuralist and postmodern perspectives that emphasize the importance of culture, systems of thought and institutions. The book provides a resource for producing critiques of key dominant ideas and practices.

Moon, B. (2000) *A Guide to the National Curriculum*, Oxford: Oxford University Press. This book provides an introduction to the historical background, structure, development and implications of the National Curriculum and the changes it has wrought on education in the British context. It provides a critical review of central features of the national curriculum while also being very informative about it.

Ross, A. (2000) *Curriculum: Construction and Critique*, London: Falmer. This book approaches the curriculum from the perspective of different accounts of the purposes of education. It provides a vocabulary for discussing curriculum issues and examines current debates about curriculum while also looking towards likely future developments. It takes a critical position and asks questions about the curriculum from both philosophical and social perspectives.

4

Individual Achievement:
Major Psychological Theories

Chapter 4 focuses on the individual and achievement from a psychological perspective. It examines briefly the influence of philosophy on ideas about how the mind works and explores the concepts of self, intelligence, cognition, personality, creativity, motivation and metacognition. The major perspectives on learning are outlined including behaviourism, Gestalt theory, Piaget's cognitive-developmental theory, the social-constructivist ideas of Vygotsky and others, and the information-processing approach.

Introduction

A focus on the individual points us in the direction of psychological research since it is concerned with individual *cognition*, that is knowing, understanding, remembering, and problem-solving. It is also able to illuminate our understanding of human behaviour, motivation, achievement, personality and self-esteem. Throughout this book we maintain that perspective influences the explanations we develop for phenomena. Psychology is no different so it is important to briefly chart the most significant influences from within philosophy from which different views about the way mental processes work have been derived. In the first part we will also give an overview of the seminal work of the earliest psychologists and of classic twentieth-century psychological research having relevance to education. Leaving a long-established legacy are:

- the debates of seventeenth- and eighteenth-century philosophers about rationalist and empiricist explanations of human understanding

- the earliest psychological investigative approaches of introspection and functionalism
- behaviourist theory with its emphasis on external stimuli for learning
- gestalt theory which developed principles of perception grounded in the brain's search for 'wholeness'
- personality theories – psychoanalytic, psychometric and humanist explanations
- motivation theories – instinct, drive/need and cognitive explanations
- creativity and intelligence theory – the impact and controversy of IQ testing
- cognitive-developmental theory – Piaget's maturational explanation of human development and learning
- cognitive psychology: schemata and concepts; information-processing theory – processes of attention, perception and memory.

The influence of philosophy

The French philosopher Descartes' seventeenth-century notion of the *dualism* of mind and body still prevails as a common-sense explanation of the mechanistic, material body existing in parallel with something quite non-material, the mind. The work of neuroscientists shows us, of course, that the mind is just as material as the body but to think of it so mechanistically does not sit comfortably with most ordinary people. Think, for example, how easily we use expressions like 'in my mind's eye'. Similarly, the seventeenth- and eighteenth-century argument about whether knowledge exists outside of human reasoning and experience is still played out today. *Rationalists*, like Descartes, believed that there is knowledge beyond experience, the existence of God, for example, or of abstract ideas like 'triangle'. *Empiricists*, on the other hand, maintained that all knowledge derives from experience. Thus Locke, a late seventeenth-century English philosopher, believed children were born with a blank slate for a mind on which all learning and experience is imprinted. He advocated individualized instruction and control of self through reward and punishment. In contrast, in the eighteenth-century the Swiss Romantic, Rousseau, believed that talent and genius were inborn along with an innate sense of right and wrong. He advocated a free, unrestrained environment which the child would explore, learning at its own pace. These ideas could be found over a century later within the progressive movement of Montessori education for example.

What follows from these differing perspectives are very different accounts of the way the mind works. Thus empiricists see the mind as an information-processing device which applies processes of attention, sensation, perception and memory to each new stimuli (experience). Conversely, rationalists, and their later incarnation, *nativists*, governed by their belief that some ideas are innate, maintain that the mind is similarly preprogrammed with an inherent structure of concept development and language acquisition (see Wilson, 1999, for further discussion). Researchers within these opposing traditions necessarily take different approaches to psychological study, with empiricists' starting point being objective, experimentally acquired data on human behaviour from which theories about mental processes are developed. Rationalists and nativists will start from their theories of a priori knowledge and innateness of mental structures and explore how these are manifest within human behaviour. Three centuries on, the nature/nurture debate is still alive and well with much research data now available to support both sides of the argument.

Brook (1999) describes Immanuel Kant, the eighteenth-century philosopher, as the single most influential figure of pre-twentieth-century cognitive thinking. A rationalist for most of his life, he was strongly influenced by David Hume, the British empiricist who distinguished between ideas and impressions and gave an early account of concept formation. Kant theorized that mental representation requires concepts *and* sensations. In other words we need information to make judgements about, but we also need to be able to discriminate (Brook, 1999: 427). *Representationalism* held that thoughts are intermediaries between the physical objects or abstract ideas we experience and the internal mental structures of our minds. If you think about 'kindness' you are representing a socialized act that you have experienced using the mental structures of concept formation and discrimination. Much more recently a parallel theory has been developed by Fodor (1975). Fodor espouses a Language of Thought, a mental language through which we are able to think and reason. Kant was the first theorist of the modern era to suggest that the mind was a system of functions, a position which continues to spawn much research.

Early psychological ideas

The earliest psychologists did not emerge until the late nineteenth-century. Darwin's (1859) work on origins of species was influential in establishing child psychology as a scientific discipline. Preyer, a German researcher interested in ontogenesis (the origin and development of individual beings), is sometimes said to be the father of modern psychology. The earliest psychologists used methods of *introspection* – reporting on one's own feelings and thoughts – to find out how minds worked. Wilhelm Wundt established the first psychological experimental laboratory in Leipzig in 1879 where he studied behaviour through experimentation and systematic self-observation methods. He believed that ultimately the only way to systematically study the differences in societies' beliefs, language, personality and social cognition was to detail everything about those societies.

Around the same time William James was working, in America, on the first modern psychology textbook (James, 1890). He was very interested in states of consciousness and took a phenomenological approach to their analysis; in psychology *phenomenology* holds that each person's perception of events or experiences is unique and determines how the person will react, therefore the study of psychology should be these individual perceptions. Like John Dewey, James developed a *pragmatic* or *functionalist* explanation for phenomena, that words and thoughts are only meaningful in relation to the purpose to which they are put. Thus a school is not defined conceptually in terms of its physical properties as a building but in relation to its purpose as a community of learning. Similarly, mental processes were seen as adapting to the function in hand and, as such, functionalists stressed the need to examine mental phenomena within natural contexts. Influenced by Darwin's new theory of adaptive evolution, they also believed that mental processes transcend species such that, for example, the processes involved in moving from one place to another would be fundamentally the same whether within human or animal because their function or goal is identical. This signalled a move away from introspective methods which could not be used to examine the behaviour of other species.

In contrast to functionalism, other early psychologists were interested in the structure rather than the function of mental activity. Ebbinghaus (1885) used introspective methods to study memory systematically; he memorized hundreds of nonsense syllables and then studied the rate of memory loss at recall. He established the importance of *associations* in learning, that is, adding to what is already known. The modern-day version of this is *connectionism* in which a

cognitive architecture of ever-increasing neural connections is proposed as an explanation for thinking and understanding.

Behaviourist theory

Introspection had obvious drawbacks in terms of reliability because of
its first person perspective; nevertheless, the contribution of these early
psychologists was fundamental to the discipline's development.
Approaches concentrating exclusively on observable behaviours
emerged in the early part of this century through the work of the
Russian physiologist, Pavlov (1927) and of Thorndike (1911) in
America. Pavlov trained dogs to salivate through the association of
external stimuli (a buzzer) with food and Thorndike measured how
long it took cats to escape from puzzle boxes, outside of which their
food lay. This behaviourist school of psychology was developed further
by two American psychologists, Watson (1913) and Skinner (1957),
who revealed laws of stimulus–response, conditioning and reinforcement. Watson famously claimed that he could teach a child anything.
These psychologists realized that *classical conditioning*, where new signals are acquired for existing responses, could be contrived to create
associations or 'learning'. An example of this can be presented as:

Unconditioned stimulus	*Unconditioned response*
Teacher instructs pupils to work quietly.	Pupils work quietly on tasks.
Conditioned stimulus with additional stimulus	*Unconditioned response*
Teacher instructs pupils to work quietly while putting her fingers to her lips.	Pupils work quietly on tasks.
Conditioned stimulus	*Conditioned response*
Teacher puts her fingers to her lips.	Pupils work quietly on tasks.

You will probably be able to recall situations in which your behaviour
has been classically conditioned. For people of the author's age, for
example, the sight of a dentist's chair can evoke fretful behaviour!
Sometimes unpleasant experiences become irrationally associated with
particular places, colours, odours or even people. A teacher who is
constantly carping at pupils while teaching them mathematics might
condition pupils to dislike the subject.

Operant conditioning is when rewards and punishments are used within teaching. Instructional programmes and schemes designed to help learners with special educational needs use a simple, incremental design wherein a small step in learning, for example, forming a letter of the alphabet or adding a simple sum, is followed by the positive reinforcement of being correct. Primary schools have for many years adopted the use of stickers, smiley faces and merit stars to reinforce pupil learning. Positive teaching schemes which train teachers to use praise, ignore poor learning behaviour and reward good learning behaviour have been developed by Birmingham psychologists, Wheldall and Merrett (1985). An assertive discipline scheme (Canter and Canter, 1977) has also become very popular in British secondary schools in the last decade. All of these schemes are external to the learner, encouraging and reinforcing learning behaviour, so they do not reveal knowledge of the learner's cognition. Although achieving results in the short term, teachers will be mindful that external reinforcers have a limited life expectancy, for example, with a recalcitrant, self-conscious 14-year-old or a 9-year-old who has received her fiftieth smiley face. The challenge in education is to harness the external reinforcer to an intrinsic desire to learn through a sense of personal achievement. Albert Bandura (1977) thought that reinforcers were not always necessary because children learn from watching or listening to others – *observational learning*. Society encourages parents and teachers to model good behaviour, attitudes and values for children to learn from. The strength of peer modelling has been noted for some time and there is currently concern about a 'laddish' ethos developing among boys which is encouraging them to feel that working hard in school is not 'cool' or masculine (Wragg, 1997).

Stimulus–response theory was predicated on a very simplistic form of *associationism* wherein each response becomes the stimulus for the next thus forming an associative chain. Although attractive, this explanation does not account for the creativity which individuals bring to their thinking. If somebody says the word 'egg' to you, a multiplicity of chaining is possible because you might associate egg with omelettes but also with ornithology. Wilson (1999) contends that the external processes of behaviourism must have corresponding internal processes which generate them and vice versa. In other words, we are not reinforced in a way of behaving unless we have reasoned, even at some basic level, about the consequences of consistently performing that action. In its most extreme form, behaviourism seems not to concern itself with these internal cognitive processes. Noam Chomsky (1965) criticized the principles of behaviourism for their failure to explain complex human behaviour such as language and communication. Chomsky argued that there are pre-existing mental structures including an innate language structure that has a latent grammatical structure which develops as an individual matures. Behaviourism dominated psychology during the first half of the twentieth century and, as we have seen, its influence is still felt; it was not until the 1960s and 1970s that the focus on mental processes begun in the nineteenth century was revived.

Gestalt psychology

An alternative view to behaviourism, 'gestalt' psychology, was developed simultaneously in Germany by Wertheimer (1923), Koffka (1935) and Kohler (1940). They were disdainful of behaviourism and associationism for their treatment of sensory experiences as independent segments of experience. Gestalt psychologists maintained that animals and humans perceive things and events in their most simple, unified form as a coherent whole, 'that the whole is greater than the sum of its parts' (Gavin, 1998: 14). They used perceptual experiments which indicated that people tend to reorganize information to impose order on it, for example, by extracting an image from its background (figure/ground principle), by grouping things together if they are in close proximity (principle of proximity) or by completing missing lines to create a whole picture where, for instance, a triangle shape is drawn with a break on one side (principle of closure). Think about what happens when you look at a sentence which has one word missing – you actually perceive the word to be there in order to allow you to make sense of the sentence. These principles can guide teachers about appropriate ways of presenting information to pupils to aid their understanding. Whereas behaviourists explained that trial and error led to the solving of problems through the development of associations, gestalt psychologists believed that animals and humans developed insight in order to determine the solution. These views were influential within research into the perceptual processes of cognition but were criticized for describing rather than explaining perceptual activity (Taylor and Hayes, 1990).

Social psychologists emphasize the importance of seeing cognition embedded in its context – personal, social and environmental. Personality development, social cognition and motivation have all to be understood if an individual's education is to be maximized.

Personality theory

There are a number of distinct approaches to personality; we will deal with the main three – psychoanalysis, psychometrics and humanism. Looking back briefly to how the Greeks explained personality differences by reference to bodily fluids gives some idea of the diversity of views in this field. The Greeks associated a *melancholic* personality – pessimistic, suspicious, depressed – with black bile; a *sanguine* personality – optimistic, sociable, easygoing – with blood; a *phlegmatic* personality – calm, controlled, lethargic – with phlegm, and a *choleric* personality – active, irritable, egocentric – with yellow bile (Child, 1986). While the association with bodily fluids might be hard for us to accept, we will all recognize the personality descriptors used.

Psychoanalytic theory

Freud's (1901) psychoanalytic theory has influenced psychological study because of his ideas about the unconscious processing of information. Freud denied the supremacy of a single governing self-will and, like early cognitive psychologists, contended that behaviour derives from the interaction of complex internal systems. He proposed that personality development depended on stages of psychosexual development. While many of Freud's ideas have been opposed, the notion of stages of development governing personality was pursued further by Erikson (1980) who proposed eight stages of conflict resolution which people go through during a lifetime. Erikson's stages of psychosocial development explain the way in which an individual's self-concept develops. For instance, adolescents go through a role identity conflict which must be resolved in order to progress healthily to young adulthood. In schools teachers often encounter, and try to deal sensitively with, the identity confusions young people experience. Harter's research (1985) has since indicated the significance of teacher–pupil relationships for pupils' feelings of self-worth in relation to learning competence. These explanations of personality development are known as *idiographic* because they are concerned with how the features of individuals contrive to shape personality behaviour.

Psychometric approaches to personality

In contrast, others, most notably H.J. Eysenck and R.B. Cattell, were interested in *nomothetic* explanations, the comparison of individual features with those of the averages or norms of the rest of the population. This approach had already been used within the psychometric method of intelligence testing. The emphasis of behaviourist approaches on the search for objective evidence also impacted upon the development of personality theories. Thus Eysenck (1947) developed self-report measures which sampled an individual's responses to situations which were said to reveal underlying personality traits. Through factor analysis Eysenck revealed two independent dimensions of personality: extraversion–introversion and neuroticism–stability. In 1976 he added a third dimension, psychoticism–normality. Since these qualities were thought to be normally distributed throughout a population, the average person would score at the midpoint of each dimension. Only exceptionally would an individual be found to be extremely introverted or neurotic and so on but variations would be found along the three dimensions. Behaviour traits were said to be associated with certain personality types, for example, the more extroverted person would present as outgoing, lively and gregarious. Interestingly, Eysenck found the personality types outlined by the Greeks to be fairly accurate. When integrating the characteristics of his two dimensions, it can be seen that a stable extrovert, for example, corresponds well to the description of a sanguine personality (Hayes and Orrell, 1987). The criticisms of Eysenck's approach are first, that in isolating just three personality dimensions there is an oversimplification of a complex phenomenon and, second, that self-report measures are unreliable in that they are affected by mood and context at time of completion.

Eysenck (1967) postulated that the inheritance of features of the nervous system could account for basic personality type differences. He explained that the cortical arousal system required different levels of stimulus in extroverts from that needed by introverts. Similarly, he thought that people who inherited a strong automatic nervous system, the part which deals with stress, were likely to react more to emotional situations, in other words to exhibit more neurotic behaviour. Considering the biological basis of personality in this way can be helpful to teachers in understanding something of why pupils behave or present as they do. Eysenck developed questionnaires for use with adults and separate ones for children. If too much stimulus is known to be counterproductive for introverts or too little stress affects neurotics adversely, teachers can try to create different conditions according to individual personality traits. Obviously this cannot be achieved individually for each person in a class of 30 but the teacher can be sensitive about expecting introverts to thrive on a lot of noise or neurotics to fare well without a certain amount of drama in their lives.

Raymond Cattell (1970) also developed a trait theory of personality, using factor analysis of questionnaires to determine 16 source traits of personality. He developed a test known as the 16PF which is widely used, especially in the selection of people for certain jobs. Often head-teachers and others in education management are given the 16PF at interview to examine whether they exhibit the right profile for the post. The test provides a profile of an individual's personality across the 16 dimensions. These include, for example, expedient–conscientious, timid–venturesome, relaxed–tense. Cattell's theory has been criticized for oversimplification and for ascribing too rigid a set of characteristics which does not fully capture the range of human personality behaviour. Like Eysenck's theory, the issue of whether people give what they feel to be socially acceptable responses and whether different situations or frame of mind would spawn different answers has to be considered when using the test. It is probably safest to take the view that these tests may provide a skeletal guide to personality types but that only a deeper knowledge of the individual concerned will flesh out the story.

Humanist theories of personality

It is helpful to briefly examine studies from social psychology which elaborate the influence of social interaction on personality and behaviour. In 1902 Cooley wrote about the 'looking-glass self' in describing the socially interactive nature of self-perception. The critical role of significant others in this analysis was also a feature of Carl Rogers's (1983) view of personality which was grounded in the notion of the developing self-concept. Rogers believed that every individual has an inbuilt need to reach his/her potential, that is, to *self-actualize*, and an equally important need for approval from others. The centrality of this led Rogers to argue that the personality could not be perceived as separate traits as the psychometric approaches proposed but as a coherent whole (Hayes and Orrell, 1987). In order for self-actualization to be successful the individual has to have experienced unconditional approval, usually from parents, in order not to worry about how his/her views and talents will be regarded and therefore be free to pursue and develop them. Where children have been granted approval which is always conditional on good behaviour, they tend constantly to seek approval from others. This can sometimes manifest as deviant school behaviour as they strive for approval from their peers. It can also appear as setting very high standards for themselves that they almost always cannot reach. The healthy development of the self-concept is therefore fundamentally important and teachers are now taught to appreciate this in their dealings with young people.

Mboya (1995) investigated the relationship between perceived teacher behaviours and adolescents' self-concepts with 874 students from four high schools in Cape Town, South Africa. Perceived teacher support, interest, encouragement and expectations were found to be positively related to adolescent self-concepts. The relative significance of teachers is dependent less on their perceived status than on the organic nature of their relationship with individual pupils. Lawrence (1996) has suggested that teaching is more effective where the teacher is able to establish a close relationship with pupils. A differentiated classroom, where a choice of tasks increases the pupils' ownership and direction of the learning, may enable the pupil to define the parameters of teacher and peer involvement. The extent to which a teacher or peer is significant to the pupil will be a factor in this definition. In a more tightly structured, 'closed' classroom environment which relies on greater teacher input and direction, the pupil's control over who shares in the learning process is restricted. Thus a pupil for whom the teacher is not significant may have little commitment to either the task or the guidance. If significant others affect an individual's learning, framing a context where the pupil can control this would suggest a greater potential for learning, for instance, the organization of group work could, on at least some occasions, pay heed to pupil friendship groups.

Personal construct theory

George Kelly's personal construct theory (Kelly, 1955) does not fit into any of the three traditions described above. His is a phenomenological approach which explains the uniqueness of personality development and learning behaviour by reference to the personal constructs which people use to make sense of new situations, information and so on. Kelly believed that we react not to a stimulus but to what we interpret the stimulus to be (Child, 1997). He developed a technique known as *repertory grid method* which reveals bipolar constructs held by individuals in relation to significant others. Thus an individual may hold a construct such as sensitivity – brashness; another person might see sensitivity juxtaposed with strength (for a full description of the technique and its applications see Ravanette, 1999). Differences in pupils' behaviour and responses would be deemed a product of the various theories they have to explain events, which are in turn a product of their previous experience and analysis of it. Theories or *constructs* are progressively refined as more interactions occur. Sets of constructs held by pupils about learning in a particular subject will therefore differ, as will the teacher's. If the teacher holds a construct which defines reticence of oral response as lack of understanding rather than as uncertainty of the context or shyness, he/she might adapt his/her instruction in a way which is inappropriate to the learner's needs. The pupil's construct of oral response may include a perception that the ownership of the vocabulary lies with the teacher, or it may be shaped by cultural and ethnic reference points at variance with those of the teacher.

Given that there is a limit to which teachers and learners can clarify their constructs within their interactions, it would seem best to foster a learning situation in which the individual constructs of all participants can be accommodated (see Burton and Anthony, 1997, for a case study example). Such a situation would involve pupil-centred learning, peer interaction, individualized learning and self-monitoring. Opportunities for testing and extending these constructs, that is opportunities for learning, might thus be liberated from the framing effect of the teacher's constructs so that pupils, with access to resources and support, could interpret the task and develop their learning according to their own frames of reference. In so doing, they might construe the situation more inventively such that the constructs are altered through what Kelly calls 'constructive alternativism'. (See Crozier, 1997, for an account of personality differences in education.)

Motivation

Healthy self-esteem is fundamental both to pupils' academic performance and to their emotional well-being since it affects motivation. Leo and Galloway (1996: 35) found that recent developments in the study of motivation highlighted a range of cognitive-based processes such as children's attributions for their successes and failures, perceptions of control over their own learning processes, metacognitive processes, self-perceptions of ability and beliefs about the utility of effort (Dweck, 1991; Nicholls, 1989; Weiner, 1979; 1992). Reviewing studies in this area, they warned that:

> the National Curriculum and resultant pedagogic practices could serve to foster debilitating cognitions in primary children about their abilities if, in practice, comparisons among primary children become more salient. School

level practices that emphasise, and focus upon, ability comparisons can inter-
fere with classroom-level practices that foster task-related or mastery goals
(Maehr and Midgley, 1991), thus undermining task-oriented classrooms.
Orienting classrooms and pupils towards individual and not ability evalua-
tions has been claimed to increase and sustain motivation. (Elliott and
Dweck, 1988: 41).

Within education it has traditionally been thought that a certain
amount of competition between individuals increases motivation. The
dangers in such an approach are, however, clear. Inevitably, differences
in ability impact on the outcomes of a competitive learning situation
and, in order for some to win the competition, others have to lose.
Covington (1998) has exposed the detrimental effects of competition
on motivation, pointing to the tendency of learners to avoid the risk of
failure by not attempting things and to the demise of learner integrity
which is encouraged by competitive practices. Neither can a competitive approach to learning be reconciled with some of the current influences on education. The collaborative approaches suggested by social
constructivists, for example, would be antithetical to a competitive
learning environment.

High levels of motivation to learn among students must be the holy
grail as far as teachers are concerned. The differences between teaching a
self-motivated adult and a recalcitrant 15-year-old are well known and
theories of motivation are helpful in explaining these differences. Child
(1997) provides a useful examination of motivation theory, noting the
early twentieth-century instinct theories derivative of Darwin and Freud,
the drive and need theories of the 1930s and 1940s, and the cognitive
theories of the 1950s and 1960s. To these might be added behaviourist
theories since Skinner's ideas about reinforcement of behaviour highlight
the effect of praise and punishment on motivation to learn. Instinct theories emphasized the animal urges and instincts humans are born with,
for example, instinctive fight and flight responses. Drive and need theories differentiate between the basic survival needs of hunger, thirst and
warmth, and the secondary or social needs, such as the need to achieve,
to dominate, to affiliate with others and so on. A very well-known drive
or need theory is Maslow's (1954) hierarchy of needs which explains that
basic needs must be satisfied before the drive for the higher-level needs
of love and belonging, high self-esteem and, finally, *self-actualization* or
the achievement of one's full potential can be aspired to. In some cases
pupils come to school with some of their basic needs not met as they
arrive hungry or poorly clothed. Others may feel unloved. If Maslow is
accurate in saying that these needs must be attended to first before the

child can begin to be interested in any form of self-actualization through learning, teachers need to be very sensitive to individual differences. Given that these needs *are* met, teachers have an important role to play in creating the circumstances which will facilitate self-actualization. Pupils need to feel safe and valued in class, they need to be listened to and empowered to make decisions about their learning.

Cognitive theories give weight to the role of thinking within motivation which it is contended plays a greater part than instinct and need/drive theories allow. They also point to the effect of an imbalance or cognitive dissonance between normal performance and unexpected performance (Festinger, 1957). For example, if a pupil normally passes tests quite easily but one day fails, this could motivate him/her either to try harder to redress the failure or it could lead to avoidance of that particular subject. An example of a cognitive theory is Rotter's (1966) *locus of control* theory in which those with strong internal control believe that it is by their own efforts and talents that they will succeed and those with strong external control believe that any success or progress they make is down to luck or other external factors such as task difficulty. This was developed further by Weiner (1972) into *attribution theory*. As well as attributing their successes and failures to internal or external factors, Weiner argued that learners attribute them to stable causes like ability or unstable causes such as effort. This attribution affects how future tasks are then approached, for example, if a pupil attributes failure to unstable causes or internal locus of control she is more likely to persist in the face of failure (Child, 1997). Conversely, attribution to stable causes and external locus of control will lead to minimal effort because responsibility for the failure is being attributed outside of the learner.

Covington claims that many minority pupils 'exhibit an external locus of control . . . They feel like pawns of fate, buffeted by forces beyond their control' (1998: 63). Most of our readers, as adult self-determining learners, will of course attribute their success or failure within Education Studies to unstable, internal causes such as effort levels! It can be a major challenge, however, to encourage adolescents to take responsibility for their own learning. Child points out the link to McClelland's (1955) theory of *achievement motivation*. Pupils with a high need to achieve usually attribute any failure to internal causes of lack of effort while low-need achievers attribute their failure to external factors. McClelland's work was developed further by Atkinson (1964) and shows the complexity of the dynamic between success, failure and motivation. Repeated failure, unsurprisingly, does not motivate learners to achieve; a mixture of success and failure can be productive; fear of failure is usually destructive because it leads to safer, lower-order tasks being chosen. Covington explains that it is not so much the event of failure that disrupts academic achievement as the meaning ascribed to the failure. 'Thus, rather than minimizing failure, educators should arrange schooling so that falling short of one's goals will be interpreted in ways that promote the will to learn' (1998: 75). A related issue is that of teacher expectancy. Teachers form opinions of pupils which indirectly encourage them to respond in accordance with those expectations. Rosenthal and Jacobson (1968) famously coined this the 'self-fulfilling prophecy'.

Capel (1999: 109–10) provides a useful chart comparing the theories since the 1950s, which we have looked at above. She also includes McGregor's (1960) *Theory x, Theory y* ideas about managers. This is relevant because teachers manage learning and learners. Theory x managers assume the average worker is lazy, lacks ambition, is resistant to change, is self-centred and not very bright, while theory y managers assume the worker is motivated, wants to take responsibility, has potential and works for the corporate good of the institution (Capel, 1999: 109). Relating this to teachers, Capel explains that a theory x teacher externally motivates pupils with controlling actions while theory y teachers encourage intrinsic motivation through self-development. Intrinsic motivation in learners is clearly more productive than extrinsic motivation, not least because it does not require reinforcement through external rewards and punishments. Sometimes, however, teachers will provide these external reinforcers initially with the aim of encouraging task success in learners which will in turn create intrinsic motivation as a product of the pleasure derived from that success. This behaviourist approach to motivating learners can be seen in Wheldall and Merrett's (1985) positive teaching programmes which advocate positive teacher reinforcement for good learning behaviour. Motivation is a complex area of study because it involves personality factors, social and environmental factors, previous experience, the developing self-concept, physical well-being and so on. The interplay of these influences on human behaviour inevitably results in a very individualized picture of learner motivation.

Intelligence and creativity

Individual differences in human competence and performance have always provided a rich research ground for psychologists, the fruits of which are invariably controversial. Francis Galton (1869), a British psychologist of the second half of the nineteenth century, was interested in the hereditariness of genius, advocating the need to measure individual differences. His work laid the foundations of what has developed into probably the most contentious explanation of individual differences, intelligence testing theory, or *psychometrics*, which seeks to measure the ultimate intellectual power an individual has. The first test was devised for the French government by Alfred Binet and Theodore Simon in 1905. It is important to note that right from these early beginnings the intelligence test was devised for the practical purpose of determining how well a child might do in school. Not surprisingly then, the test contained items which resembled school tasks, such as comprehension of facts and relationships, vocabulary measures and mathematical and verbal reasoning (Bee, 2000). Soon afterwards Lewis Terman of Stanford University modified and extended the test, developing the Stanford-Binet which has tests for each age of child and can be used from around age 3. Terman (1924) derived the child's 'intelligence quotient' by dividing the mental age the child had achieved in the test by its chronological age and multiplying this by 100. Nowadays an individual's score is compared with the scores of a huge standardized sample of children of the same age. The average score is still 100, however, with the majority of children scoring between 85 and 115. The very few who achieve very high scores of above 145 are said to be 'gifted' and those with scores below around 55 are said to have moderate to profound 'retardation' (Bee, 1992: 211). A score of 115 was said to be the threshold for passing the 11-plus examination to attend grammar school (Child, 1997).

Intelligence testing is attractive because it enables us to categorize and pigeonhole people and, despite years of critique of its theoretical foundations and its methodological weaknesses, some version of intelligence quotient (IQ) testing is still used in many schools today to indicate potential. One of the major problems is being sure that it tests what it purports to. If school type tasks are included, can training in those tasks help? Does reading ability play a part in the outcome? Do different cultural and linguistic experiences affect an individual's performance on the test? In fact, it is very difficult to isolate underlying competence because the individual's experience, disposition, motivation and health on the day of the test will all impact on the outcome. Thus, to some extent, an IQ test is a test of achievement. Nevertheless, Bee (2000) cites research which indicates a fairly strong correlation between IQ score and school achievement grades. In terms of stability of test results, Bee et al. (1982) found that a typical correlation between a Bayley mental test score of a 12-month-old and the score of the same child at age 4 on the Binet test was only .20 or .30. While this does indicate a significant correlation, it is a long way from a perfect correlation of 1.

At the heart of the controversy over IQ testing is the question of whether it tests some innate, immutable ability. Hebb (1949) distinguished between Intelligence A – innate potential entirely dependent on neurological facilities – and Intelligence B – interaction of Intelligence A with the environmental influences upon an individual. In this analysis Intelligence B can vary while Intelligence A cannot (see Child, 1997). Child notes that neither is directly testable and that the best we can manage is indirect sampling of some aspects of intelligent behaviour using standardized tests.

A number of intelligence theories have been developed during the last century. Charles Spearman (1927) believed two types of intelligence could be identified by IQ tests – g factor (general ability) and s factors (various mental abilities detected in different degrees by different tests). Cyril Burt's *Hierarchical Group-Factor Theory* proposed group factors of intelligence as well as g and s factors because many tests involved a number of skills at the same time, for example, verbal ability together with a specific ability (Child, 1997). General ability was thought to govern a series of abilities such as verbal, spatial, practical and numerical skills which themselves interacted with specific abilities measured by each test item. Thurstone (1938), an American psychologist of the 1930s, felt that g and s abilities should be compounded to give a range of factors known as *primary mental abilities* which provided a broad profile of abilities rather than an overall measure. These included verbal comprehension, number ability, word fluency, perceptual flexibility and speed, inductive reasoning, rote memory and deductive reasoning. Guilford (1950) proposed a model of the intellect which had 120 mental factors derived from three independent aspects of intelligent acts. The individual carries out *operations*, such as remembering or thinking, using *content* like symbols or figures, in order to *produce* outcomes, for example, relations or implications. Albert and Runco (1999) point out that Guilford's seminal work on creativity challenged the simplicity of intelligence testing which sought to locate people along a single dimension. Guilford (1967) suggested that measuring intelligence and creativity was far more complex than this. He posited two forms of thinking: convergent, wherein a single correct answer is sought, and divergent, which produces a whole range of possible answers. Cattell

(1963) defined two types of intelligence. *Fluid* intelligence includes reasoning and memory processes and spatial performance, and Cattel thought it to be hereditary; measures of it vary according to the individual's processing speed at the time of measurement. *Crystallized* intelligence reflects the accumulated products of processing carried out in the past and can be tested by general knowledge and vocabulary questions; Cattell maintained that it is influenced by environment and is therefore likely to increase with education and experience (Salthouse, 1999).

In 1955 Cyril Burt, the British psychologist, claimed to have found high correlations between the IQ scores of 53 sets of identical twins who had been brought up in different environments. These findings were very influential because they seemed to indicate the relative lack of importance of environmental factors to intelligence. The English education system paid great attention to Burt's conclusion that there should be different types of education depending on innate intelligence. His argument supported the separation of children into grammar and secondary modern schools. In 1976, however, Burt's findings were exposed as fraudulent. As Hayes notes, 'this is an important case, because it shows how ready people were to believe that IQ is inherited' (1993: 146). Burt's figures were also used as the basis of further studies, for example, Jensen's (1969) controversial race studies. Jensen argued that intelligence was 80 per cent inherited and 20 per cent environmental. However, as Chapter 5 explains, Labov's work on linguistic/cultural differences in relation to educational achievement debunked the myth of black unintelligence.

Reporting on research studies which throw light on the relative influence of hereditariness and environment, Bee (1992) cites Bouchard and McGue's (1981) studies of the few pairs of identical twins reared apart which found a strong correlation of between .60 and .70 in their IQ scores. However, more detailed analysis of the cases revealed that the less similar the environmental circumstances the less correspondence is found between twins' IQ scores. The nature/nurture argument is more productively approached, then, by examining the interaction of heredity with environment. Weinberg (1989) proposed that genes establish a *reaction range* for IQ which can vary as much as 25 points depending on the environmental conditions the child grows up in. Thus findings that black children score lower on IQ tests than do white children by as much as 15 points can be accounted for within Weinberg's suggestion of an environmentally determined 25 point range. The debate about genetic intelligence was revived in the mid-1990s by the publication of the highly controversial book *The Bell Curve* by Herrnstein and Murray (1994) in which it was reported that African-American children consistently score lower than Euro-American children on IQ tests. Despite the 12-point gap falling within the accepted Weinberg reaction range and despite substantial evidence of differences in the environmental conditions of the two groups, Herrnstein and Murray argued that the findings signified fundamental genetic differences in intelligence. Their claims created a furore and a spate of research studies emerged to categorically refute them (see Cooper, 1999, for an up to date account of the research).

In the second part of this chapter the issue of intelligence is picked up again as the interest in this phenomenon is still intense and newer theoretical positions have been developed.

Cognitive–developmental theory

Piaget's maturational theory

The concept of maturation (genetically programmed sequential pattern of changing physical characteristics) was developed by Arnold Gessell in the USA in the 1920s (Gessell, 1925). The concept of maturation was applied to cognitive growth by Jean Piaget, a Swiss psychologist of the last century, whose work has enjoyed very wide influence within education. Piaget (1932; 1952; 1954) explained cognitive growth as being driven by an internal need to understand the world. He saw intellectual and moral development as sequential with the child moving through stages of thinking. Piaget's theory is one of maturation in which the learner's stage of thinking interacts with his experience of the world in a process of *adaptation*. Piaget used the term *operations* to describe the strategies, skills and mental activities used by the child in interacting with new experience. Thus adding 2 and 2 together, whether mentally or on paper, is an operation. Discoveries are made sequentially, for example, adding and subtracting cannot be learned until objects are seen to be constant. Progress through the sequence of discoveries occurs slowly and at any one age the child has a particular general view of the world, a particular logic or structure that dominates the way he/she explores and manipulates the world. The logic changes as events are encountered which will not fit with the *schemata* (sets of ideas about objects or events) the child has constructed. When major shifts in the structure of the child's thinking occur, a new stage is said to be reached.

Central to Piaget's theory are the concepts of *assimilation*, taking in and adapting experience or objects to one's existing strategies or concepts, and *accommodation*, modifying and adjusting one's strategies or concepts as a result of new experiences or information (see Bee, 2000, for a full outline of Piaget's theory).

Table 4.1 *Piaget's stages of cognitive development*

Stage	Age	Description
Sensorimotor	Birth–2 years	The baby 'understands' the world in terms of what he/she can do with objects and of his/her sensory information. A block is how it tastes, feels to grasp, looks to the eye.
Pre-operational	2–6 years	By about 18–24 months, the child can represent objects to him/herself internally and begins to understand classification of objects into groups and to be able to take others' perspectives. Fantasy play appears, as does primitive logic.
Concrete operational	6–12 years	The child's logic takes a great leap forward with the development of powerful new internal mental operations, such as addition, subtraction, class inclusion, and the like. The child is still tied to specific experience but can do mental manipulations as well as physical ones.
Formal operational	12 years +	The child becomes able to manipulate ideas as well as events or objects in his/her head. He/she can imagine and think about things that he/she has never seen or that have not yet happened; he/she can organize systematically and exhaustively and think deductively. (Bee, 1985, p. 228)

The application of Piaget's theory to education

The neatness of Piaget's theory rendered it appealing to educationalists. The 11-plus test fitted well, for example, with the age at which children were thought to begin abstract or formal operations. Investigative and experiential methods, often referred to as 'discovery learning', were readily inferred because they provided cognitive conflict, the jarring of cognitive structures or schemata to promote new learning. The Plowden Committee which reported in 1967 on primary education was influenced by such maturation theory, advocating child-centred, experiential approaches to learning. It is easy to see, however, that a theory which specifies stages of capability can set up expectations about learning readiness, that children only learn effectively if their educational experiences are suitably matched to their current level of understanding. This can then determine the content and pace of instruction. If a child has not reached the anticipated stage the teaching will be too advanced. If the child has gone beyond it the teaching could constrain potential achievement. In the same way that intelligence testing can establish an arbitrary ceiling on learning, the rigid application of Piaget's theory could also place limits on achievement.

Criticisms of Piaget's work

There are other problems, too, with Piaget's theory. It says nothing about individual differences, social context or modes of learning. The child is viewed as a system of developing logic not as a social, emotional being. The importance of language to thinking, a significant component in any model of human development, is underplayed: other psychologists, such as Vygotsky and Bruner, have demonstrated language and socio-cultural linguistic differences to be fundamental to learning, as we shall see later.

Piaget used clinical, decontextualized methods with a very limited sample of middle-class children including his own children. When experiments have been repeated with account taken of the importance of context, the power of children's thinking has been found to be in advance of Piaget's claims (Donaldson, 1978; Hughes, 1975; McGarrigle and Donaldson, 1974). The success rates among 4–6-year-olds were much better when tasks were not disembedded from the context, were made relevant to children's experience and when the children understood what the experimenter wanted. These findings called into question Piaget's claims about young children's egocentricity, revealing a more precocious ability to decentre (to see things from another's point of view in space and time), and about their ability to 'conserve', understanding, for example, that the volume of a liquid remained the same despite its movement to a differently shaped vessel.

Piaget's theory of stages has been seriously challenged too. Although he concedes that the structures or operations (coordinated principles, rules or strategies that are applied across problems or tasks) do not develop all at once, he does imply that all learning could be approached at the same operational level. However, we know that while, like now, we operate at a formal operational level dealing with abstract ideas, we very often operate in our day-to-day lives at a concrete level, needing actual objects or events to work our logic on, for example, the use of diagrams. Bee (1992) claims that the information we have does not show that children are very consistent in their level of performance across tasks. She cites much research to support her (Bee, 1992: 273).

Piaget's legacy

John Flavell, a one-time student of Piaget, concluded that human cognitive growth is generally not very stage-like (in Bee, 1992). He did, however, attest to the sequential nature of learning, saying 'sequences are the very wire and glue of development. Later cognitive acquisitions build on or are otherwise linked to earlier ones, and in their turn similarly prepare the ground for still later ones' (Flavell, 1982: 18). Within any given task, then, there seem to be predictable sequences shared by most children. The key task for teachers is to examine the progress of individuals in order to determine readiness to deal with increased intellectual demand.

Piaget's work can be said to have influenced the ideas of some other psychologists. Kohlberg (1976) posited links between children's cognitive development and their moral reasoning, proposing a stage model of moral development. Selman (1980) was interested in the way children make relationships, describing a set of stages or levels they go through in forming friendships. The stress on the idea of 'stages' in Piaget's theory has thus been quite far-reaching but a rigidly staged model of development is probably less helpful than the features of development the various stage theories describe.

Cognitive psychology

Despite the pre-eminence of behaviourism in America during the first half of the twentieth century, an interest in cognitive psychology was maintained by European psychologists such as Frederick Bartlett (1932) who developed the notion of schema. The value of Bartlett's work was not recognized until 1975 when Minsky, a computer scientist, read his book and developed from it the notion of frames of knowledge within artificial intelligence (Brewer, 1999). Rumelhart and McClelland (1986) later related these connectionist models of schema and concepts to psychology. The correspondence between how computers and the human mind process information had fascinated researchers since the 1960s when the *information-processing* approach to explaining cognition became the dominant view. Connections had already been drawn between cognitive processes and neural mechanisms, and there was a renewal of interest in the processes of attention, perception and memory which paralleled the huge advances in computer intelligence. As early as 1943 the British psychologist, Kenneth Craik, likened the brain to a computer. Essentially information-processing theorists proposed that sensory experience (sounds, sights, tastes, smells and tangibles) is perceived and selectively attended to, depending on the individual's motivation, other distractions or emotional state, analysed within a short-term memory and stored within a long-term memory. This process is usually presented graphically as:

SENSORY		ANALYSIS		STORAGE
INPUT		in STM		in LTM
(Perception)		(Attention)		(Remembering)

Schema and concept development

Bartlett (1932) introduced the important idea of *schema* to account for the fact that we do not reproduce facts when we recall them, rather we reconstruct them. Schemata are the organizing vehicles which we have built up in our minds from previous experience and knowledge which we then use to analyse new information. If you are presented with a new concept within your studies your tutor will probably attempt to explain it by reference to something you have already studied within that area, thus allowing you to employ the relevant schema. The material held in the long-term memory is stored as 'schemata' ('schema' is the singular) – mental structures abstracted from experience. They comprise sets of expectations which enable us to categorize and understand new stimuli. For example, our schema of higher education includes expectations of students, lecturers, students' union and so on and is refined as we gain more experience and more information is categorized. Everyone's schemata are different, for instance, a teacher's schema of school will include expectations about hierarchies, pupil culture, staffroom behaviour and so on, while the experiences of parents are unlikely to have refined their schema of school to this extent.

A range of work on schema development and concept formation has been conducted over the past half-century. Collins and Quillian (1969) developed the notion that we store concepts hierarchically with general, overarching concepts being subdivided into more specific ones. Thus we hold the concept of animal which we define by a range of criteria such as four legs, no language and so on. As we gain more experience we learn to discriminate between types of animal – we notice that cats are furry and dogs are hairy, cats purr and dogs bark. Animal is a superordinate concept to which dog and cat are subordinate. Other models postulate linkages between concepts which are triggered via a logical association which is not necessarily hierarchical, for instance, brainstorming a topic produces many related ideas. Sometimes this is referred to as concept mapping. Anderson and Bower's (1973) model claimed that knowledge was stored as propositions about the world. Linkages between these propositions would constitute learning. Teachers encourage concept differentiation through comparison of objects or ideas and they usually introduce new ideas by reference to concrete examples. Even adults find new ideas easier to grasp if given concrete examples of them.

Schemata are thought to differ from concepts because they deal with larger phenomena like discourse structure and events which consist of their own particular concepts and interrelations. If you are presented with a bizarre drawing of a familiar object you will employ your schema of that object to make sense of it even though it does not conform entirely to the set of expectations the schema contains. Think, for example, of a bicycle drawn without handlebars and saddle and missing the back wheel. Although unrideable, you would still recognize it as a bicycle! Similarly, when we see clouds which appear to be making recognizable shapes our schema are being involuntarily pressed into service to make sense of the shapes.

Implications of concept development for learning new knowledge

Psychologists interested in education have long argued that new knowledge should be linked to what is already known (Ausubel, 1968). The work of both Gagne (1977) and Ausubel indicated the need for material new to the learner to be structured in a hierarchical way which reflects the inherent conceptual structure of the topic, skill or information in order for assimilation to be effective. Ausubel distinguished between *reception* and *discovery* learning, explaining that most school knowledge is of the former type because there is so much to learn that there is not time for pupils to discover everything anew. However, a certain amount of discovery is involved in learning even prepackaged information because the learner must engage with the material, by reading it or listening to it and then make new connections with existing knowledge. The use of sequential procedures, moving from the general to the specific and the recall of key words and ideas from previous lessons to cue the learner are all strategies which can aid retention and recall.

Chyriwsky (1996) claims that mathematical knowledge should be worked through hierarchically. In mathematics we move from the general concepts of addition, subtraction and multiplication to more specific computations like calculating area, solving equations or estimating probabilities. If the teacher has given instruction based on the inherent hierarchical structure of the material, the assimilation and accommodation of schemata will be achieved at varying levels by learners. It could therefore be profitable to create cognitive environments which stimulate new and unique reconstructions of the taught material by individual learners through the use of open-ended tasks.

The clarification and extension of declarative or factual subject knowledge (facts, vocabulary, formulae) has traditionally taken precedence over the learning of procedural knowledge specific to each subject, for example, the mechanics of performing calculations in mathematics, the process of writing for different genres in English or the steps taken to set up an experiment in science. Latterly, however, procedural knowledge has been recognized as important in school learning; tasks which facilitate the learning of procedural knowledge are likely to be of an investigative applied nature, possibly involving open-ended role-play or problem-solving.

An emphasis on structure and sequence is evidenced in the learning of modern foreign languages (MFL). Mitchell found that foreign language teachers generally adhered 'to a bottom-up language learning theory, with an emphasis on the recognition and acquisitions of discrete vocabulary items, and the subsequent construction of spoken and written sentences' (1994: 56). Knowledge from other subject areas which falls into this category is that of a formulaic nature such as the periodic table from chemistry or logarithms from mathematics. Information of this kind is traditionally learned by rote but knowledge acquired in this way can have limited retention and is a rather uneconomic means of storing information. Material learned meaningfully, where the essence of something read, seen or heard is abstracted from the whole experience, is stored substantively rather than verbatim in the memory. Combining concrete examples with abstract instruction can assist this learning (Anderson et al., 1996), for instance the use of practical or visual 'props' in the teaching of languages or mathematics.

We can employ an example now to illustrate the difference between meaningful and rote learning. If you are asked the four times table you will probably recite 'one four is four, two fours are eight' and so on. You probably will not explain the mathematical principle of multiplication by a factor of four. If, however, we ask you the meaning of the term 'standard deviation', you are unlikely to recite a verbatim answer. Instead, your short-term memory (STM) searches your long-term memory (LTM) for your 'schemata' of statistical terms and relationships. You then articulate your abstracted understanding of the term. The intellectual challenge involved in articulating the second answer is greater although knowing one's tables can be very useful. Rote learning is not inherently meaningful so cannot be stored in LTM with other related information. Rather it must be stored in its full form, taking up a lot of space in the memory. It is analysed only superficially in STM because the pupil does not have to make connections with other pieces of information.

In the context of information-processing theory the teacher's role is to help learners apply their knowledge and skills by finding new ways of recalling previous knowledge, solving problems, formulating hypotheses and so on. Montgomery (1996) says that games and simulations are highly appropriate because they facilitate critical thinking and encourage new connections to be made between areas of subject knowledge or experience.

Unpacking information processing

Perception

Perception is deemed to be the first part in the information-processing mechanism. It is the interpretation by the brain of the signals received by the senses. As we have seen, gestalt psychology had revealed some important principles about perception and much research into visual illusion has helped elucidate our understanding of perceptual processes. Gibson (1979) emphasized the functional aspects of perception through his research into pilots landing aircraft. He identified the perceptual phenomenon of a constant aspect approach where the pilot sees the landing point as motionless with the land around it pulling away from that point. Thus the perceptual process assists the perceptual function to which it is harnessed. Neisser (1976) postulated a perpetual cycle of perception in which what we expect to see affects what we do see. The notion of 'perceptual set' where we can be predisposed to perceive something in a certain way is of particular note to education. A simple illustration of this is when we cannot see the other interpretation within an ambiguous drawing, for example, Rubin's vase/faces. When applied to more complex situations this perceptual set can inhibit or advance learning. Often our emotional state can precipitate perceptual set, for instance if a child associates a certain interpretation of an event with a dissatisfied response from a parent or teacher he/she may be unable to perceive it in that way again. Conversely, a teacher may contrive perceptual set among a class of pupils in order that they are ready to learn a certain topic; if the topic is three-dimensional drawing in the natural environment pupils might be shown in previous lessons a number of artworks in which the three-dimensional perspective is particularly well drawn.

Attention

Broadbent (1958) developed a model of attention which held that stimuli are selectively filtered out because of the limited capacity of the short-term memory to analyse incoming stimuli. The effect of interruption, doing two things simultaneously and dividing one's attention have been the focus of research in this area (see Gavin, 1998). The level of familiarity we have with a task will determine the extent to which we can be interrupted and still perform the task well. If you are a seasoned knitter you will be able to simultaneously engage in quite detailed discussion; not so for the novice! You may well be quite practised in the art of listening to two conversations at once but in fact we do this by tuning in to one or the other at intervals and while attuned to one we can only register very superficial signals from the other.

In learning environments gaining the attention of the learner is very important – huge tracts of guidance have been written for training teachers on this topic! Younger children are more susceptible to distraction; it is fascinating to note just how much more incidental learning they achieve than do adults. This is learning that derives from attending to stimuli to which the teacher has not directed them. You can do a simple experiment to show this. Show a group of 5-year-olds an interesting, lively picture for a couple of minutes and a group of fellow students the same picture for one minute (time varies to account for adult competence). It might be a picture of some animals in a farmyard. Tell them to concentrate on what the animals are doing. Afterwards ask them what the animals were doing and a series of unrelated questions based on other information within the picture, such as:

'What was the farmhouse made of? How many windows did it have? What were the children doing? What colour was the farmer's jumper?' You will probably find the children better able to answer the questions relating to incidental learning than the students. Teachers generally want their pupils to focus on the matter in hand rather than on incidentals, so they have to use cueing signals to direct attention, develop learning materials and tasks that are stimulating and interesting, use strong colours and sounds, and maintain variety of task and approach.

Memory

While Atkinson and Shriffin (1968) contended that incoming sensations were analysed in a short-term memory and the organized or abstracted idea deposited with the relevant schema within the long-term memory, Craik and Lockhart (1972) suggested that it was the level of processing of the stimuli which determined the degree of permanence with which it was stored. Miller (1956) revealed our ability generally to remember chunks of information up to 7, plus or minus 2. Studies have also shown that recalling later items in a list is more difficult when earlier ones have been learned and recall tested. The finding that we tend to recall the first and last sets of items heard when a list is read out is explained by the most recently heard items being retrieved from STM and the least recent items from LTM. The ones in the middle of the list tend to be lost because they have not been processed for storage in LTM and have been subject to decay from STM. These and other findings have obvious implications for teaching and learning: the value of repetition, rehearsal and mnemonic strategies such as acronyms, rhymes or imagery, the danger of studying too much information at once and the need to organize material in a conceptually coherent way which aids retrieval.

Tulving (1972) postulated two types of memory: episodic and semantic. Episodic memory is when we recall actual events and experiences, replaying conversations verbatim or 'seeing' actions that occurred. It often applies to major events, for example, many of you will be able to recall precisely where you were and what you were doing when the news of Princess Diana's death was announced, but we also have episodic memories of non-significant occurrences too, such as feeding the cat or eating a meal. These fade within days as we have more and more experiences of a similar type but the episodic memories of significant events can remain for a very long time. If you talk to old people, although they might have become very forgetful they will often be able to recount vivid descriptions of what they were doing at times of significant events which marked autobiographical, national or international historical turning points even if 50 years ago. Semantic memory stores the abstractions from our experience, so if you read a book you will not recall its contents verbatim but will have a précised account of its meaning within your memory. Sometimes we can retrieve episodic memories which then enable us to retrieve a stored semantic memory. A huge amount has been written about memory which is quite fascinating and of obvious consequence for educational practitioners, but we do not have space to deal with it here (see Baddeley, 1997, or Tulving and Craik, 2000, for comprehensive texts). Ultimately, for the teacher and the learner, strategies for retention and recall are of primary importance.

Conclusion

This chapter has provided an overview of key psychological theories which illuminate our understanding of how educational attainment can differ from individual to individual. The legacy of ideas such as those of Piaget, of the behaviourists and of the cognitive psychologists is powerful and we have seen how their theories have impacted upon pedagogical trends. These psychologists give different explanations of mental ability and individual development. The emphasis of behaviourist theories on external stimuli to learning contrasts sharply with the maturational patterns revealed by Piaget or the information-processing approaches of cognitive psychologists. Certainly there has been heated discussion about how much of an individual's character and ability is due to genetic inheritance (nature) and how much to socialization and environmental factors (nurture). The type of education deemed suitable has depended to a large extent on whether ability was considered to be innate or determined by experience. This rather simplistic dichotomy of nature/nurture has been rendered more complex by psychological studies of the past 30 years which we will look at in Chapter 5. We now focus on how the interaction of these two influences affects learning development.

Student activities

1 Look at some of the experiments which Piaget used (Bee, 2000). Try some of these with a couple of children you know. If possible, choose

children of different ages so you can cover at least two of Piaget's stages. Discuss your results with a tutor or other students. Do you think the experiments are useful? Would you/did you alter them in any way?

2 Refer to a text which describes personality measures (Child, 1997, for instance). Most take the form of some sort of inventory of character-istics against which the subjects rate themselves. You might like to have a go. Discuss with other students the value of such inventories. Are there any problems with self-report measures?

Recommended reading

Bee, H. (2000) *The Developing Child*, 9th edn, London: Allyn and Bacon. An excellent, readable text which covers all aspects of human development. The latest edition of this classic brings the research right up to date.

Child, D. (1997) *Psychology and the Teacher*, 6th edn, London: Cassell. A comprehensive, accessible text covering all aspects of educational psychology.

Bancroft, D., and Carr, R. (1995) *Influencing Children's Development*, Oxford: Blackwell in association with the Open University. An edited collection which looks at practical applications of psychologists' work in relation to specific contexts, for example, computer technology, language impairment, deafness, children as witnesses and child therapies. Particularly useful for those on a multiprofessional course.

5

Education and Psychological Research: Contemporary Influences

In this chapter influential psychological developments of the last 25 years are examined, including constructivist approaches and cognitive processes in science, multiple and emotional intelligences, and situated cognition. The growth of interest in individual learning styles and strategies is explored, so too is the growing body of research into 'brain chemistry'. The chapter concludes by examining the implications for individual attainment of pupil grouping and pedagogical strategies.

Introduction

Psychologists' interest in how the mind works and how education affects individuals is as vibrant now as it has ever been. It might be argued that the theoretical and empirical work described in the last chapter, although revealing a great deal about mental processes, also opened new avenues of enquiry. This chapter will examine psychological research which has become influential during the last 25 years within education, including:

- constructivist theory which urges a focus on pupils' existing conceptions
- social constructivist theory which stresses the importance of social interaction and scaffolded support in the learning process
- metacognitive theory which demonstrates the value of learners understanding and controlling their learning strategies
- learning style theories which imply not better/poorer distinctions between ways of learning but the matching of learning tasks to a preferred processing style

- multiple intelligence theory which suggests a multidimensional rather than a singular intelligence
- emotional intelligence theory which emphasizes the potency of the learner's emotional state
- situated cognition theory which explains all learning as context-bound
- the growing knowledge of brain functioning.

The final part of the chapter examines how perspectives from psychological research facilitate an analysis of the implications of learner grouping and individual attainment.

There is an increasing interest in explanations for pupils' differential success rates in learning which go beyond notions of static intelligence and learning readiness (Sotto, 1994; Stones, 1992). There are also calls for learning opportunities to be differentiated in the classroom, to match work to pupils' needs (Hart, 1996; Jameson et al., 1995). However, justifications for differentiation are seldom made clear, appearing only to be built on implicit assumptions about ability and intelligence. As we have seen, individual differences have traditionally been conceptualized as differences in intelligence as measured by IQ tests. The sterility of this notion as an explanation for pupils' learning is partly revealed by its stasis. Commentary, particularly from the socially aware 1960s and 1970s (Ball, 1982; Hargreaves, 1972; Jackson, 1964), was very sceptical of the ceiling effect on pupil attainment which such a view implies. This is the self-fulfilling prophecy mentioned earlier where pupils meet the expectations set of them and no more. Ironically, the conditions which were said to encourage this ceiling effect, namely setting by ability, are again on the increase because of the current emphasis on conventional, publicly comparable, assessment data. The difference now is that richer explanations of how pupils learn can inform the pedagogy of teachers working with those setted groups. We begin by looking at research which stresses the individualized nature of constructing meaning.

Constructivism

Constructivism is predicated on the idea that people make their own sense of things in a unique way. It attaches great importance to the individualized nature of learners' conceptions. Information-processing theorists would probably attribute the differences between individuals' conceptions to the different ways stimuli are perceived or represented in their minds. But Driver and Bell (1986) have argued that stimuli, or knowledge, are not that straightforward. New information is problematic for the learner, who must examine it in relation to prior conceptions and experiences and see to what extent it fits. Little emphasis is placed on the role of instruction. Rather the teacher must create situations which facilitate individuals constructing their own knowledge. If pupils harbour misconceptions they must be helped to take them apart at the root since long-held conceptions are very difficult to shake off and are resistant to change even when teachers and others explain the error. Constructivism emphasizes the need to give learners responsibility for directing their own learning experiences. It is in the science subject area that constructivist ideas have been most influential. Naylor and Keogh (1999) have developed work in this area. They have devised concept cartoons which strike at the very heart of learners' misconceptions about scientific ideas in an effort to help them rethink the problem.

Social constructivist theories

Vygotsky

Educators have increasingly recognized the importance of the ideas of Lev Vygotsky, the Russian psychologist, during the past 20 years. Vygotsky's work dates from the 1920s and 1930s but did not become available in the west until the 1970s which explains why his publications date from after this time despite his early death from tuberculosis in 1934, aged 38. The sociological ideas of Durkheim, Wundt's emphasis on cultural psychology, gestalt psychology, the early works of Jean Piaget, and the new modernist theories of linguistics and literary theory emerging in the USSR in the 1920s influenced Vygotsky. This eclecticism was denounced as anti-Marxist and Vygotsky's work went into oblivion. After the political rehabilitation of his work in the USSR and its delayed discovery in the west, his seminal work on the relationship between language and thought spawned studies of major importance in the former USSR and in the west. Cole and Scribner's (1974) studies, focusing on Vygotsky's view that children's learning of scientific concepts depends on the interaction between these and the child's own spontaneous everyday concepts, revealed that school-based cognitive skills become more important where there is an increased demand for scholastic-type activities outside school.

Kozulin juxtaposes Piaget's and Vygotsky's theories, explaining their 'common denominators as a child centred approach, an emphasis on action in the formation of thought, and a systematic understanding of psychological functioning' and their biggest difference as their understanding of psychological activity (1998: 34). For Vygotsky (1978), psychological activity has socio-cultural characteristics from the very beginning of development. Theoretical concepts are generative from a range of different stimuli, implying a problem-solving approach for the learner and a facilitator role for the teacher. Whereas Piaget (1959) considered language a tool of thought in the child's developing mind, for Vygotsky language was generated from the need to communicate and was central to the development of thinking. Vygotsky emphasized the functional value of egocentric speech to verbal reasoning and self-regulation, and the importance of socio-cultural factors in its development. In 'inner speech' the sense attached by the individual predominates over meaning but speech forms originating in external dialogues have to be internalized and internal thoughts translated into a form of speech comprehensible for others. Vygotsky likened this to there being two co-authors, where one accommodates his/her thoughts to the pre-existent system of meanings and the other immediately turns them into idiosyncratic senses, in simultaneous outbound and inbound conversations.

In communicative talk then the development is not just in the language contrived to formulate the sentence since the process of combining the words to shape the sentence also shapes the thought itself. Thus Vygotsky's work highlights the importance of talk as a learning tool. Reports of some eminence have reinforced the status of talk in the classroom, highlighting its centrality to learning (Assessment of Performance Unit, 1986; Bullock Report, 1975; Norman, 1992). The encouragement of pupil talk for the learning of both declarative and procedural knowledge is increasingly considered to be of value since it allows learners to refine what they know through the articulation of their thoughts (Withers and Eke, 1995).

The concept of 'psychological tools' was a cornerstone of Vygotsky's theory: 'symbolic artefacts' such as signs, symbols, texts, formulae, and graphic symbolic devices which help learners accomplish their own 'natural' psychological functions of perception, memory, attention and so on. They serve as a 'bridge between individual acts of cognition and the symbolic socio-cultural pre-requisites of these acts' (Kozulin, 1998: 1). Naturally existing signs, such as tracks, are replaced by artificial versions of the same and are dependent on the social environment. Vygotskyan theory holds that intercultural cognitive differences are attributable to the variance in systems of psychological tools and in the methods of their acquisition practised in *different* cultures.

Kozulin explores the work of Feuerstein et al., (1991) who developed Vygotsky's notion of the human mediator in the interaction between child and environment. Charting the philosophical and sociological antecedents of mediated interaction, Kozulin cites Hegel's description of work as a mediated activity and Mead's view that the interaction between the individual and the environment is always mediated by meanings which originate through social relations. For Vygotsky, psychological tools mediate humans' own psychological processes. Feuerstein developed mediated learning experience (MLE) theory working with culturally different groups, culturally deprived individuals and learning-disabled children. Mediated learning experience is achieved by the involvement of an adult between the stimuli of the environment and the child with the intention of modifying 'learner deficiencies'. This appears to be a deficit model of learners but Kozulin claims it can reveal hidden learning potential and can reorient parents and teachers from passive acceptance of children's 'deficiencies' to active modification of them.

Bruner

Jerome Bruner, an American psychologist who has contributed a huge amount in a variety of areas of psychological research since the 1950s, also placed an emphasis on structured intervention within communicative learning models. He formulated a theory of instruction, central to which is the notion of systematic, structured pupil experience via a spiral curriculum where the learner returns to address increasingly complex components of a topic as he/she develops over time. Learners construct new ideas or concepts based upon their current/past knowledge. Thus in Year 5 at primary school tackling the problem of fractions will be approached using many more concrete examples than when it is returned to in Year 7 at secondary school. For Bruner, learning involves the active restructuring of knowledge through experience with the environment. The learner selects and transforms information, constructs hypotheses and makes decisions, relying on an internal and developing cognitive structure to do so. Cognitive structure (schema, mental models) provides meaning and organization to experiences and allows the individual to 'go beyond the information given'.

As far as teaching is concerned, good pedagogy should try to encourage students to discover principles by themselves. The instructor and student should engage in an active dialogue, asking questions, presenting and testing hypotheses. Thus Bruner advocated discovery methods rather than the provision of prepackaged materials. The teacher's job was to guide this discovery through structured support, for example, by asking focused questions or providing appropriate materials.

The influence of social constructivist theories

The pedagogical implications of the work of Vygotsky and Bruner centre on the role of communication and structured intervention in thinking and problem-solving. Essentially, if pupils discuss with others what new ideas mean to them, further thinking is generated with more complex links between ideas afforded. The role of the teacher in facilitating learning situations involving talk is of critical importance. Judicious grouping of pupils for such talk is important. Brown (1994) has espoused the notion of learning communities which operate like research seminar groups. Taking a Vygotskyan approach she has argued that 'students navigate by different routes and at different rates. But the push is towards upper, rather than lower, levels of competence' (Brown, 1994: 7). Homogenous grouping and pairing has been considered to have advantages in fostering learning, particularly in its promotion of argument and sharing of complex ideas (Rogoff, 1990). Research reviewed by Scott-Baumann (1995) indicated that when 10-year-old pupils were paired according to their similar levels of functioning, they worked best and were often faster at solving chemical problems than when they worked alone. A separate study revealed similar findings when pairs of 11–13-year-olds worked on computers. However, both studies indicated that the initial gains in understanding made by pairs were not sustained when pupils were tested individually later. This might suggest that strategies for individual consolidation of learning following pair work need to be encouraged by the teacher.

Bruner's ideas about the power of systematic and well-structured pupil experiences to promote cognitive development are fundamental to such an approach. Maybin et al. (1992) have used Bruner's (1983) ideas of 'scaffolding' in relation to classroom talk. The ideas of pupils emerging through their talk are scaffolded or framed by the teacher putting in 'steps' or questions at appropriate junctures. For example, a group of pupils might be discussing how to solve the problem of building a paper bridge between two desks. The teacher can intervene when he/she hears an idea emerge which will help pupils find the solution, by asking a question which requires the pupils to address that idea explicitly. Bruner argued that the scaffolding provided by the teacher should decrease in direct correspondence to the progress of the learner. Wood (1988) has developed Bruner's ideas, describing five levels of support which become increasingly specific and supportive in relation to the help needed by the pupil:

- general verbal encouragement
- specific verbal instruction
- assistance with pupil's choice of material or strategies
- preparation of material for pupil assembly
- demonstration of task.

Thus, having established the task the pupils are to complete, a teacher might give general verbal encouragement to the whole class, follow this up with specific verbal instruction to groups who need it and perhaps targeting individuals with guidance on strategies for approaching the task. Some pupils will need physical help in performing the task and yet others need to be shown exactly what to do, probably in small stages.

Some researchers favour slight differences between partners in order to encourage cognitive conflict through interaction. However, the research findings are by no means clear so it is not possible to conclude whether pupils matched on the basis of similar or different previous performance is most advantageous; this is likely to vary according to the task and the learners. The issue of how well teachers can determine the prior understanding of their pupils and, in turn, match work to individuals, is itself controversial.

The Vygotskyan notion of 'zones of proximal development' has application here. These zones describe the gap between a pupil's current level of learning and the level he/she could be functioning at given the appropriate learning experience and adult or peer support. Teachers are well aware of the extent to which these zones vary from pupil to pupil even if they do not use Vygotskyan terminology; indeed it is the extent of this variation which constitutes the challenge for the teacher. This challenge can turn to frustration as teachers seek to homogenize these zones in an effort to utilize a directive teaching style. There is often an element of fear of the unknown in moving to a more pupil-centred, discursive pedagogy because a degree of control transfers to the pupils. Pressures of fulfilling the National Curriculum requirements can exacerbate this fear, thus constraining an often genuine desire to incorporate such methodology.

Metacognition

The process of coming to know more about one's own learning strategies, such as strategies for remembering, ways of presenting information when thinking, approaches to problems and so on, is known as metacognition. If pupils are helped by their teachers to become more metacognitively aware, they are more able to take control of their learning. Being metacognitively aware can be likened to having a commentator in the learner's mind who analyses and comments upon the methods he/she is using to learn a new concept or skill while the learning is happening. Flavell claimed that 'a person's awareness of his or her own cognitive machinery is a vital component of intelligence' (1979: 907, in Montgomery, 1996: 15). Learners should be encouraged to explore their own ways of knowing and remembering, to experiment with learning strategies, to appreciate teaching and learning techniques which help them learn best and to monitor their own learning. Anderson et al. (1996) reported that studies show that transfer of learning between tasks is enhanced where the teacher cues learners into the specific skill being learned and encourages them to reflect on its potential for transfer.

Quicke and Winter (1996) found that, in a small-scale study with a mixed ability Year 8 class, engaging pupils in a metacognitive dialogue about 'good' learning enhanced their understanding of learning processes. Kramarski and Mevarech (1997) showed that metacognitive training helped 12–14-year-olds draw better graphs in mathematics. The role of the teacher is to provide the 'scaffolding' for the pupils to think for themselves. Montgomery (1996) described such an approach as 'cognitive process pedagogy' wherein the emphasis is on critical thinking through games and simulations, problem-solving tasks, study skills, collaborative learning and experimental learning. This approach is informed by a view that hierarchically ordered levels of thinking can be determined (and therefore striven for) in children's learning in the way that Benjamin Bloom's (1956) *Taxonomy of Educational Objectives* theorized.

Bruner (1966) argued that difficult ideas should be seen as a challenge and that, if properly presented, can be learnt by most pupils. Adey and colleagues have developed a system of cognitive acceleration in science education (CASE) which challenges pupils to examine the processes they use to solve problems (Adey, 1992). In doing so it is argued that pupils are enhancing their thinking processes. The activities are designed to create 'cognitive conflict', that is, 'a dissonance which occurs when a child is confronted with an event which s/he cannot explain when using his/her current conceptual framework or method of processing data' (Adey, 1992: 138). Pupils are given problem-solving tasks which require them to justify their conclusions. The teacher's role is to carefully question pupils so that each one rethinks the basis for their conclusions. Adey has argued that the activities are appropriate to mixed ability classes because, although undifferentiated, they make intellectual demands at a range of levels. To substantiate this he cited the results of the project as being equally successful with both high and low scorers on initial measures of cognitive development. He claimed that a two-year programme of fortnightly CASE lessons with Year 7 and 8 pupils led to substantial gains for those pupils in science, mathematics and English GCSE results in Year 11. The apparent transfer of higher-order cognitive skills beyond science suggests that a focus on pupils' metacognition is worthwhile. The CASE project is premised, then, on the notion of an underlying set of intellectual processes rather than domain-specific thinking skills. It is argued that, through discussing their views of, and solutions to, problem-solving tasks: 'students become accustomed to reflect on the sort of thinking they have been engaged in, to bring it to the front of their consciousness, and to make of it an explicit tool which is then more likely to be available for use in a new context' (Adey, 1992: 141). Applying a Vygotskyan explanation, Adey has claimed that the encouragement of pupils to describe reasoning patterns using appropriate terminology, even when they do not fully understand the terms, aids their ability to think about how they are thinking because the more the terms are used and discussed with peers, the greater meaning they accrue. The notion of learners having different learning styles creates a further justification for such a strategy.

Learning styles, strategies and approaches

Research into learning styles and strategies has grown apace over the past 40 years and some of the more easily understood categorizations have been popularized within both education and management studies. A currently fashionable way of identifying 'learning style' is to refer to learners' preferences for visual, auditory and kinaesthetic ways of working. Of course, it is not a simple case of identifying one style to the exclusion of the other two because we know that learning requires the use of different strategies according to the task and the context. Curry (1983) developed a model which grouped learning style measures into strata which resemble the layers of an onion, distinguishing between a habitual and involuntary underlying feature of personality, the individual's intellectual approach to assimilating information and their instructional preference or choice of learning environment. Since Curry's model was presented, a great deal more research has been done. It is therefore helpful to define what is meant by the four main areas of research in this field.

1 *Learning or cognitive style*: habitual way of representing and processing information; innate to learner; not susceptible to change.
2 *Learning strategy*: way of approaching and tackling tasks; learned; capable of change.
3 *Learning approaches*: motivation for and attitude towards learning; largely stable but can change according to task or purpose.
4 *Learning preferences*: environmental preferences for learning, such as place, light, atmosphere.

The important principle which characterizes each of these research areas is that learning is not better or worse depending on style, strategy, approach or preference but is *different*. Whereas intelligence theory sets a limit on the capacity to learn, these theories describe the differences between learners' preferred or involuntary styles. This implies that a match between a learner's preference and the learning task will remove any such limits on learning potential.

Learning or cognitive styles

Individual differences are thought to underlie a whole range of more readily observable differences. Learners bring to their studies a stable, involuntary mode of representing information during their thinking. Riding (1991) has proposed that two overarching dimensions can be identified which subsume the various constructs of previous researchers. These are *wholist-analytic style* – whether an individual tends to process information in wholes or parts – and *verbal-imagery style* – whether an individual represents information during thinking verbally or in mental pictures. Riding (1996) advocated advance organizers for wholists since they have difficulty seeing the structure and sections of learning material. A topic map indicating the hierarchically related separate areas would help them divide it into its parts. However, the wholist would have trouble disembedding particular information from tables and densely packed diagrams. For analytics an overview after the information has been presented would help learners to create an integrated picture of the topic. Analytics tend to focus on one part at a time, sometimes overemphasizing an element of the whole. They are therefore likely to need help in seeing links and relationships between the parts of a topic and in establishing the appropriate balance between the significance of the parts. An overview in the form of a concept map would be highly relevant, as would tabulated information.

The predominant coding style of verbalizers suits them for tasks involving texts and definitions so verbal versions of pictorial and diagrammatic material are helpful to them. The greater use now of technology in schools means that it should also be possible, during teacher exposition and questioning, to use interactive techniques involving computers, cassette recorders and video equipment. Since imagers are found to achieve best on material which can be visualized in mental pictures, and which does not contain many acoustically complex and unfamiliar terms, it is suggested that verbal material should be converted into pictorial form for them. Imagers would also benefit from concrete analogies of abstract ideas. As they are superior to verbalizers on spatial and directional information, mapping tasks could be encouraged across subjects. Teacher exposition and questioning could be punctuated with pictures and artefacts or presented using computer graphics and video material. Motivationally wholist-verbalizers will probably be less willing to focus for long periods on material or tasks which are not particularly stimulating, whereas imagers may well persevere with it. They are also likely to be happier working in groups while imagers usually prefer to work alone. Riding and Burton (1998) found that teachers rated the behaviour of wholist boys in Years 10 and 11 as significantly less good than that of analytic boys. They pointed out that a wholist style tends to be associated with a more sociable, outgoing personality which may, among some adolescent boys, present to teachers as deviant behaviour. For a full account of style constructs which can be grouped with Riding's dimensions, see Riding and Cheema (1991.)

Integrating assessment of wholist-analytic and verbal-imagery dimensions

Riding (1991) developed a computer-presented test which directly assesses both ends of the wholist-analytic and verbal-imagery dimensions. The Cognitive Styles Analysis (CSA) comprises three subtests and uses response time to determine the subject's position on each dimension. The validity of the instrument is supported by the finding of significant relationships between style and a range of school learning performance (see Riding and Rayner, 1998). For pupils who exhibit learning difficulties a mismatch between their preferred learning styles and the learning tasks can affect their achievement more than a mismatch would for competent learners.

Learning strategies

Kolb's work (1976; 1985) describes two dimensions: perceiving and processing. The dimensions are bipolar with abstract and concrete thinking at the ends of the perceiving dimension and doing (active) and watching (reflective) at the ends of the processing dimension. Kolb said that these dimensions interact so that four types of learner can be identified: 'divergers' who perceive information concretely and process it reflectively, needing to be personally involved in the task; 'convergers' who perceive information abstractly and process it reflectively, taking detailed, sequential steps; 'assimilators' who perceive information abstractly and process it actively, needing to be set pragmatic problem-solving activities; 'accommodators' who perceive information concretely and process it actively, taking risks, experimenting and needing flexibility in learning tasks. Kolb developed the notion of experiential learning as a cyclical sequence through the four areas of learning mode implied by the interaction of the two dimensions. His descriptions of learning styles are therefore not to be seen as static, but modifiable by the learner's training in the four sequences of the cycle. Learners will have a predilection for one of the stages, thus giving rise to the four styles. McCarthy has pointed out that if learners are provided with experiences which ensure their use of stages in the cycle, in addition to their preferred one, their learning strategies may be extended (McCarthy, 1987).

Kolb's work influenced both workplace management training (Honey and Mumford, 1986) and has found favour, to a growing extent, in educational settings. The Technical, Vocational and Educational Initiative (TVEI) funded by the Department for Employment (DFE) in the mid-1980s was very influential in developing 'flexible learning'; this used Kolb's work as its theoretical underpinning (Harris and Bell, 1990). Gibbs's (1992) work on adult learning has also been influenced by Kolb. In further education, projects looking at the application of Kolb's learning styles to flexible, support-based pedagogy have been developed (Fielding, 1994).

Learning approaches

Biggs's (1978; 1987a; 1987b) work on approaches to study has been developed from Marton and Saljo's (1976) studies of 'deep' and 'surface' approaches to learning and Entwistle's (1981) work on learning orientations. Entwistle described four orientations to learning, 'meaning', 'reproducing', 'achieving' and 'holistic'. It was suggested that combinations of these orientations with extrinsic factors, such as the desire to pass examinations or a keen interest in a subject, generate certain approaches to study which employ different levels of thinking from 'deep' to 'surface'. Approaches to learning are thus a function of both motive and strategy and motives influence learning strategies (Biggs, 1993). An instrumental or surface motive engenders reproducing or rote-learning strategies. An intrinsic desire to learn is associated with deep motive and the use of learning strategies which emphasize understanding and meaning. An achieving motive might result from the need to pass examinations; from this can come strategies which stress time management and efficient organization.

Students whose motives and strategies are compatible with the learning tasks are likely to perform well. Conversely, someone with a deep approach will be constrained by too superficial a task and a student who has an achieving motive will probably flounder if long-term, vague objectives are set. Ausubel (1985) has shown that the need to compete in public examinations can lead to the adoption of rote-learning techniques resulting in temporary, peripheral learning. The type of learning orientation which has been encouraged in the USA, and the UK by the increased emphasis on performance testing and school comparability, is that of the achieving type (Darling-Hammond, 1994; Madeus, 1994). This militates against deep approaches which require learners to enjoy few time constraints and full learner autonomy. Clearly the short-term practices of schools to improve results serve to cultivate, at best, an achieving orientation and, at worst, a surface orientation to learning.

Learning preferences

The *Productivity Environmental Preference Survey* (PEPS) (Price et al., 1991) derives from the work of Dunn et al. (1979; 1989) and is widely used in the USA to measure the 'learning styles' of adults. Learners are thought to possess biologically based physical and environmental learning preferences which combine with emotional traits, sociological preferences and psychological inclinations to make up an individual style profile. Measures include preferences relating to sound, light, temperature, seating design, motivation, structure, persistence, responsibility, sociological needs, physical needs (auditory, visual, kinaesthetic and tactile), best time of day for learning, mobility, intake of food and drink, processing styles, impulsivity/reflectivity and hemispheric dominance (see the later section on the brain).

The Learning Style Inventory (Dunn et al., 1989), from which the PEPS was derived, uses similar factors to determine the preferences of younger learners. Dunn (1991) argued that instruction should be arranged which accommodates learners' preferences. The implications of this for a school classroom are quite profound since the potential range of factors a teacher would have to consider for a class of 30 pupils is enormous. The measure is clearly better suited to adult self-use and, apart from possible application with small groups or with sixth form students, it is not easy to see how teachers could reconcile the extent of instructional matching which it implies with curriculum requirements within a school's resource base.

Cross-cultural studies into learning styles, strategies and approaches

Woodrow (1997) has suggested that the style differences observed in different cultural groups are a function of environmental and cultural factors. Purdie and Hattie (1996) have compared the learning strategies employed by 16–18-year-old students in Australia and Japan, using the Self-Regulated Learning Interview Schedule of Zimmerman and Martinez-Pons (1986; 1988; 1990). They found that the range of strategies used by three culturally diverse groups was the same but that the pattern of use differed for each group. Significantly, the range of strategies used was broadest among high achievers irrespective of cultural group. This might suggest that, where learners are free to determine their own strategy use, high achievers are those who have used their habitual style traits without any mediation of culturally bound learning strategies. The Japanese students made far greater use of memorization by rote than the Australian students, as did the Japanese students who had studied in Australia. Effort and willpower were seen to be closely associated with this use of strategy in a bid to succeed. The cultural determinant of this can be said to lie in the Japanese view that repetition is a route to understanding (Hess and Azuma, 1991). Kember and Gow (1990) have reported the same tendency among the Chinese, and Lim (1994) among the students of Singapore. More recently two separate studies concerned with cross-cultural validation of Biggs's Study Process Questionnaire (Kong and Hau, 1996; Wong et al., 1996) have revealed links between an achieving orientation and a deep approach to learning among Chinese secondary age pupils. Salili's (1996) investigation of achievement motivation among British and Chinese students, using McClelland's (1985) thematic apperception test (TAT), revealed the same tendency.

Implications of research into learning styles, strategies, approaches and preferences for education

Rayner and Riding have argued that a pupil's style profile will be 'a key consideration in curriculum design, assessment-based teaching and differentiated learning' (1997: 24), recognizing, however, that such a profile needs to be manageable, accessible and geared to the real world of teaching. It is not necessary, even if it were possible within the constraints of organizing and delivering a diverse curriculum, to know an individual's profile on the full range of style and strategy measures. Given that, unlike measurements of ability, learning styles, strategies and approaches are differentiated not by value but by function, acquiring a more definitive knowledge of individual style is less important than providing a diverse range of classroom approaches, resources, teaching styles and assessment media such that every learner has maximum access to the learning.

Situated cognition

'Situatedness', the study of cognition within its natural context, grew out of dissatisfaction with the 'disembodied' approach of traditional cognitive psychology. Both information-processing and constructivist approaches essentially depicted knowledge as an object located within learners who are isolated from one another. They emphasized rational, individual, abstract thought processes, the study of which could reveal universal principles generalizable to all individuals in any circumstances. In contrast, situated cognition theory (Greeno et al., 1993; Lave and Wenger, 1991; Suchmann, 1987) stresses that learning cannot be studied in isolation from its context without destroying its defining properties. Situated learning casts the individual learner as a subsystem to a series of increasingly complex systems (classroom, school, neighbourhood, culture and humanity) wherein learning exists as a part of those contexts. This placement of learners within more complex systems is not new, having been described by Bronfenbrenner in his ecological model of human development. Bronfenbrenner (1979) conceptualized human development as 'the process of understanding and restructuring our ecological environment at successively greater levels of complexity' (Smith and Cowie, 1988: 10). His theory postulated four nested systems of development in context (Figure 5.1):

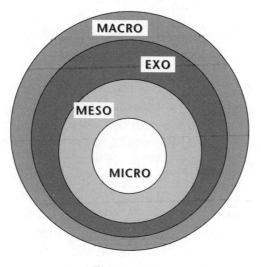

Figure 5.1

- Microsystem: the home, the classroom, friendships.
- Mesosystem: links between microsystems, for example, no breakfast at home can lead to poor work at school.
- Exosystem: links between microsystems and settings in which the child does not participate but is affected by, for example, mother's stressful work environment may provoke intolerance with the child.
- Macrosystem: the ideology and organizations of society or subculture in which the child lives, such as unemployment levels, social taboos.

Bronfenbrenner's model of ecological systems and subsystems helps explain the interconnectedness of environmental factors which impact on a child's learning, illustrating, for example, the effect of the inter-play between a child's health, the state of the parents' relationship and a decision at national level to make budgetary cuts in education. The impact of this 'development in context' on the growth and measure-ment of intelligence cannot be ignored. Baltes (1996) has emphasized the life-span nature of development and the importance of historical influences stressing that age-related trends are but one of three impor-tant influences each determined by an interaction of biological and environmental factors:

- *Normative age-graded influences*: for example, the advent of puberty (biological genesis) or starting school at 5 (environmental genesis).
- *Normative history-graded influences*: for example, the Ethiopian famine (biological impact) or China's one-child policy (environmental genesis).
- *Non-normative life events*: for example, an accident causing brain damage (biological impact), divorce or job loss (environmental genesis).

Situated cognition theory goes further than Bronfenbrenner's and Baltes's analyses, espousing a collective knowledge which is embodied in 'the ongoing, ever-evolving interaction' between people (Davis and Sumara, 1997: 115) in real-life situations in the work or marketplace, social or educational settings. Whereas a cognitive approach to investigating adult performance in mental arithmetic showed poor results as it was in a laboratory setting, Lave (1988) argued that asking the same questions in the context of grocery shopping in the supermarket produces more realistic results (Seifert, 1999). Think, for example, of how quickly darts players sum their scores in the pub!

Situated explanations of cognition generally dispute the transference of knowledge between learning activities because the situative perspective does not allow that knowledge can exist as a 'substance' within the learner (Greeno, 1997). Instead, 'generality of knowing' is preferred as a phrase to describe a learner's 'participation in interactions with other people and with material and representational systems' (Greeno, 1997: 11). The situative perspective further claims that context-bound learning is more effective than the abstract representation of phenomena which constitutes much classroom teaching. Greeno calls for school learning to become more beneficial beyond the classroom, 'providing students with general resources for reasoning both in and with the concepts of subject-matter domains' (1997: 14). In recent years, the English school curriculum has increasingly adopted the use of 'authentic' learning activities which seek to replicate real-life situations. However, the idea that transference of learning is not possible is not generally embraced by teachers.

Clear parallels can be drawn with the work of Vygotsky, given his emphasis on interaction promoting cognition. However, some forms of situated cognition theory deny the possibility of individual cognition, suggesting instead that all learning is embedded within its interactive context and that there is therefore only collective cognition. It is difficult to see how cognition can be said not to be occurring in an individual's mind irrespective of any form of group cognition. Nevertheless, it is now widely accepted that much value comes from emphasizing collaborative classroom activity. Cooperative group approaches to teaching and learning in which no one person has the monopoly on the direction of the learning are inferred by the situative perspective. Greeno has called for the arrangement of 'complex, social activities' with an emphasis on enquiry where pupils are given opportunities to formulate and evaluate 'problems, questions, conjectures, conclusions, arguments and examples' (1997: 10).

In acknowledging that the social world of the classroom is a crucial stage for learning, it is possible to consider the two ostensibly competing perspectives on learning – the situated cognitive and the traditionally cognitive – coexisting as explanations of the learning process. The former could be said to be descriptive of the social contexts and interactions within which individual cognition, as explained from a cognitive perspective, occurs. Both are useful in their inferences for pedagogy. The cognitive perspective can be used to explain phenomena about individual pupils' learning, personalities and behaviour implied by the analysis of empirical data. However, learning environments are quite clearly social, interactive contexts which can profitably be analysed from a situative perspective. Researchers, for example, usually describe the socio-political context and the educational, interactional settings within which the research takes place. Without the latter, the former would be unbound by context and, as such, difficult to make sense of. However, whereas it is usually argued that empirical validity and generalizability can be claimed for the theoretical frameworks and constructs investigated within a traditional cognitive approach, for example, the construct of learning style, intelligence or creativity, Anderson et al. (1997) have suggested that this is not the case for the situative perspective because the basis of the analysis is not amenable to empirical testing, arising as it does from collectively constructed understandings which are bound by time and context and therefore not replicable.

The brain

More is being learnt all the time about the way the brain functions and this helps to elucidate our understanding of mental processes. Neuroscientists revealed many years ago the physiology of mental functioning. The Spanish neuroscientist Cajal studied the central nervous system, revealing the function of nerve cells (neurones) in

transmitting information to and from the cerebral cortex (DeFilipe and Jones, 1991). The gaps between the neurones (synapses) are traversed and new connections made when thinking occurs. Readers will also be aware of the research into hemispheric specificity which indicates that the left side of the brain deals more with language and logic and the right side with spatial and visual awareness. It is also claimed that we can infer from electrical activity in the brain, measured using an EEG (electroencephalogram) while someone is asked to perform a variety of tasks, the different parts of the brain associated with the various processes of perception, attention, remembering, retrieval and language comprehension (Fodor, 1983; Hillyard, 1993). This theory contrasts with the ideas of developmental psychologists and information-processing theorists who argue that mental processes are domain–general not domain-specific. More recently, however, doubts about this modularity or localization of brain functioning have been expressed (Fodor, 2000). Fodor now queries his own claims for modularity and is sceptical about how much is actually known for certain about brain functioning. Interest in how the brain works in relation to consciousness has been revived by the recent publication and televising of Susan Greenfield's book, *Brain Story* (Greenfield, 2000). Greenfield casts doubt on the modularity theory, suggesting instead 'neuronal assemblies' in which millions of brain cells compete to create elements of consciousness. She does not provide robust evidence for this theory though. Thus, psychologists are still trying to find an answer to the 'hard problem' of how subjective thought and streams of consciousness are derived from brain matter. In the meantime there is currently a trend for the ever-growing army of educational consultants to cull the most persuasive bits of neuro-scientific theory for application within the classroom (see, for example, Alastair Smith's, 1996, *Accelerated Learning in the Classroom*).

Work on brain functioning has impacted on education in a less superficial way, however, because of what it can tell us about specific learning disorders such as dyslexia, a reading disorder thought to derive from sensory-perceptual processing delays which impede the brain's phonological representation. Dyslexia is thought to affect 4–5 per cent of the school-age population, a not insignificant percentage. Problems about its definition and prevalence (more boys are reported to suffer from the condition but this may be because girls' better behaviour hides the problem) still abound but explaining the condition using 'brain science' has reduced the stigma which attached to it when the cause was attributed to lower intelligence.

Different views of intelligence

Multiple intelligences

Debate about whether a single intelligence can be identified or whether intellectual power is better characterized as multiple intelligences exercises contemporary theorists. Those who favour an information-processing explanation of human understanding, Robert Sternberg in the USA, for example, describe intelligence in relation to its cognitive components. Thus Sternberg (1985) proposed a triarchic model of intelligence comprising three major aspects which interact with one another: analytical, creative and practical thinking. Analytical or *componential* intelligence is what is normally measured on IQ and achievement tests – planning, organizing and remembering facts then applying them to new situations. Creative or *experiential* intelligence is the ability to see new connections between things and to develop original ideas. Practical or *contextual* intelligence is the ability to read situations and people, and manipulate them to best advantage. Neither experiential nor practical intelligence are measured in IQ tests according to Sternberg.

Howard Gardner (1983; 1995) also shuns a unitary explanation of intelligence, developing instead his theory of multiple intelligences (MI). Eight distinct intelligences are said to exist independently of one another: linguistic, spatial, logical-mathematical, musical, bodily-kinaesthetic, interpersonal, intrapersonal and naturalist. Gardner explains that individuals have different entry points to learning depending on the strength of their various intelligences. Sternberg (1999) points out that, although Gardner cites evidence to support his theory, he has not carried out research directly to test his model. We are all aware of our particular talents or tendencies so it is easy to see how Gardner's model could gain currency at a common-sense level. Indeed the school curriculum and Hirst's (1975) forms of knowledge use similar categorization. However, if one sees cognition as the processing of information using fairly universal sets of mental strategies it is difficult to conceive of separate, discrete intelligences. Gardner's work has become very popular in educational circles, possibly because it offers an alternative to the view of intelligence as unitary and fairly stable, encouraging instead a focus on developing particular individual capabilities to their highest potential.

Silver et al. (1997) advocate a synthesis of Gardner's MI theory with their own learning style theory, arguing that the former offers ideas about the content and context of learning while the latter elucidates the generalized processes of learning within which can be observed individual differences. Their integrated model of style and MI suggests how different combinations might translate into vocations, for example, logical-mathematical intelligence within a person with a mastery learning style might lead to a job as an accountant or bookkeeper. Where it combines with an interpersonal learning style it is suggested the vocation might be a tradesperson or homemaker. There can be dangers in being overly enthusiastic about a theory or theories since a sceptic might argue that the integration of a different model of learning style with MI theory could elicit a whole range of other vocational trends. The value of learning style theory, MI theory and other ideas we have looked at in this chapter is that they provide us with more questions with which to probe human behaviour and different ways of understanding it. Theoretical and empirical categorizations help us to make sense of our observations but attempting to characterize different types of learning or vocation too precisely can obscure our focus on the individual differences between people which make them unique.

Emotional intelligence

A recent construct within the field of intelligence research is that of *emotional intelligence* (Goleman, 1995; Salovey and Mayer, 1990). While there is debate about the existence of discrete brain structures (the limbic system) for emotional experience and behaviour, there can be no doubt that an individual's emotional state and ability to deal with their feelings can impact on their educational performance. Traditionally this 'affective' domain of experience has been little more than acknowledged by educators with their main focus being on the 'cognitive' domain. It is now receiving more attention as a result of Goleman's popular work. He has related the ability to control impulses, motivate oneself and regulate moods to improved thinking and learning.

Much research effort has also been put into understanding genius, giftedness and creativity in relation to normal intelligence. Sternberg and O'Hara (1999) have reviewed research into the relationship between intelligence and creativity, concluding that psychologists have still not reached a consensus about the relation between creativity and intelligence nor even a shared understanding of what these two constructs are. The very uncertainty of their work, however, should itself raise a critical awareness among educators of the complexity of their sometimes taken-for-granted assumptions about the measurement and fostering of 'ability' within learners.

Individual differences in learner attainment and pupil grouping

A broad overview of psychological research provides us with a set of perspectives with which to analyse issues about how pupils and other learners are grouped and how learner attainment is conceptualized.

Streamed groups

In 1964 a seminal study was produced by Brian Jackson, who wrote from the heart as an experienced teacher, disenchanted with an education system which he had taken for granted but later found to be wanting. His investigation into the effects of streaming children into groups, on the basis of mathematical or literacy competence, within primary schools was highly influential. It came at a time politically and economically ripe for consciousness to be raised about perceived social and educational injustices. Jackson found that 'A'-stream teachers were more experienced and better qualified, that children with autumn birthdays were overrepresented in 'A' streams, that working-class children were underestimated and relegated to the 'C' stream where they stayed and that over a third of parents had no idea what streaming meant.

Jackson adopted a teaching approach, as a result of his findings, that put no ceiling on his expectations of pupils which, in turn, liberated them from simply meeting specified goals. He also developed teaching resources which caught the interest and met the needs of his pupils. What Jackson was breaking down was the much discussed 'self-fulfilling prophecy' wherein teachers' expectations of pupils were said to limit their achievement. There was serious worry about this phenomenon when the Plowden Report (CACE, 1967) confirmed that, at as young an age as 7, a child's life chances were fixed because there was seldom any transfer between streams. This phenomenon may have drawn a spurious legitimacy from stage theories of development such as Piagetian theory (1970). Widely adopted as applicable to an educational context, they did tend to spawn ideas about learning readiness which suggested that it was not sensible to expect certain capabilities from children until they were maturationally ready. Teachers may have considered that the concept of learning readiness could as well be applied to 'ability' as to age, serving as a justification for the stability of streamed groups.

Hargreaves (1972) argued that believing in the child's potential for improvement, often in the face of contradictory evidence, and the communication of this belief to the child, was the key to releasing this potential. In 1967 he had studied the effects of streaming on pupils in a secondary modern school, pointing to the development of subcultures within the lower streams. Sporting norms and values at variance with those of the school, these groups became alienated from the mainstream aims. Disenfranchised from status positions within school, which were bound up in high achievement, pupils in the lower streams gained status instead from deviant behaviour. This perpetuated the lack of movement between streams.

Mixed ability teaching

When comprehensive schooling was introduced in the late 1960s it was hoped that the problems created by using streaming as a form of differentiation would abate. Initially however, a certain resistance to change and a lack of experience in teaching pupils of all abilities together simply led to a replication of the secondary modern/grammar groupings of pupils on a smaller scale within the comprehensives. The DES (1978a) stressed the social arguments for mixed ability groupings: for the individual there would be increased equality of opportunity, less rejection and classification; for the teacher there would be greater control since mixed grouping avoids the emergence of a sink mentality and promotes group cooperation, better relationships and a reduction in competitive/aggressive behaviour; and, for society, class differences would be counteracted helping to create a non-competitive, non-elitist society.

Keddie, in 1971, observing the introduction of a new humanities curriculum within a comprehensive school, found a relationship between perceived ability and social class. She argued that teachers classified children in terms of an ideal type of pupil even though the classes were of mixed ability. Pupils meeting the teachers' stereotype of an 'A'-stream type pupil were given access to higher-grade knowledge, even though all pupils were supposed to be taught the material in the same way. The result was the differentiation of an undifferentiated curriculum.

By the late 1970s mixed ability grouping had become widespread but neither research nor HMI reports could find evidence to support the strategy because the grouping, whether banded, setted, streamed or mixed, did not in itself appear to improve teaching and learning (Bourne and Moon, 1994; Newbold, 1977; Slavin, 1990). The HMI findings (DES, 1978a) indicated that in the main teachers were teaching to the middle via whole-class teaching with the needs of the less and more able pupils being ignored. Both HMI and a study by Kerry (1984) found little evidence of task differentiation. Where attempts had been made to cater for the range of abilities in one class, these had of necessity to be so teacher directed that they limited the extent to which the pupil could be intellectually challenged. 'Death by a thousand worksheets' is a phrase with which many teachers of the 1970s can identify. It describes the overuse of differentiated worksheets within mixed ability classrooms (Toogood, 1984).

Ball (1981) reported on the change from banding (where pupils are placed in broad ability bands on the basis of results in English and mathematics and then setted further into ability groups for each subject) to mixed ability grouping in one comprehensive school in the 1970s. Later, in 1987, he commented that:

> At Beachside the implementation of mixed-ability as a teaching problem was left almost entirely to the teaching departments to cope with. Each department was asked by the head teacher to produce a report outlining their intended responses, but there was no follow-up to the reports, and in several cases the teaching strategies actually employed bore no resemblance to original stated intentions. (Ball, 1987: 40)

The political heat generated by the introduction of mixed ability methods was such that much energy was employed engineering and safeguarding them (Toogood, 1984). Clearly thought-out school policies for the teaching of these groups were rare; Toogood's text provides a retrospective explanation of the approach taken at one 'progressive' school and Kelly's (1975) collection of case studies describes the methods employed in five schools. Despite some innovative developments by individual teachers (Hart, 1996), there were few systematized approaches within either schools or local education authorities (LEAs) to galvanize these strengths and disseminate good practice. Along with political pressure, this helped seal the fate of mixed ability teaching which declined in the 1980s, to be replaced by setting within each subject.

Grouping for the 1990s

There is evidence (Bourne and Moon, 1994) that the introduction of the National Curriculum with its differentiated attainment levels has led to changes in grouping policy. The publishing of examination results forced the hand of many stalwart supporters of mixed ability teaching because of the risk of a perceived association between mixed ability teaching and poor examination results (Boaler, 1997). The very public arena in which schools increasingly function encouraged further abandonment of mixed ability teaching rather than efforts to develop more appropriate teaching strategies to support it (Weston, 1996).

Boaler (1997) has reviewed more recent research, finding that while there was a small, but not statistically significant, advantage for the most able pupils if they were setted, the losses for the less able were large if they were setted. Their attainment was significantly lower than the attainment of the less able who were in mixed ability groups. Boaler (1996) has conducted her own three-year study comparing the GCSE mathematics results of 310 pupils in two schools, one of which set the pupils while the other taught pupils in mixed ability groups. She found that results were significantly better among the latter group even though test results from Year 7 indicated the pupils were performing at the same levels (Boaler, 1996). When Boaler asked Year 11 pupils in the setted school about mathematics lessons the responses revealed a dissatisfaction with the fixed pace of progress. Some pupils, especially girls, found the pace too fast which occasioned them to become anxious; more of the boys reported that the pace was too slow. This was the case across the eight sets which is a striking finding, given that one would assume a limited range of ability within each set. The pupils preferred the arrangements lower down the school when they had been able to work at their own pace in mixed ability groups because they gained a better understanding. Many of the pupils who were negatively affected by setting were the most able. Boaler concluded that 'a student's success in their set had relatively little to do with their ability, but a great deal to do with their personal preferences for learning pace and style' (1996: 585).

Biott and Easen (1994) have called for a systematic enquiry into the best way to group pupils. Citing Johnson and Johnson (1992) and Terwel (1992), Dowrick explained that:

> The standard co-operative learning method has been to employ heterogeneous grouping. The argument in its favour has been that high-ability pupils benefit from mentally organizing their thoughts in order to explain them to their less able partners, and from reformulating them to make their explanations clearer when necessary, as well as from initially having studied new material more carefully in order to explain it later. Low-ability pupils are said to learn from their partners' explanations, especially as the explanations are likely to be more accessible than those given by a teacher, and from monitoring their own understanding before asking for help. (1996: 16–17).

These arguments are significantly different from the social ones of the 1970s since the rationale Dowrick describes for mixed, or heterogeneous, groups takes a clear academic focus. Indeed social problems have been found to exist within mixed groups; Dowrick (1996) has found evidence in Mulryan's (1992) study that low-ability pupils are looked down on by their partners. Work which makes clear the academic arguments against homogeneous grouping is now also available. Dowrick refers to Bennett and Dunne (1992) and Jones and Carter (1994) who have shown that, among older pupils, lower ability groups are unable to collaborate or stimulate each other sufficiently to make progress. In Japan, studies have indicated that ability is a much less central concern than effort (Purdie and Hattie, 1996). The western notion of ability is turned on its head, hence 'intelligence is viewed as an expression of achievement; it results from experience and education' (848).

Townsend and Hicks (1997) examined the relationship between academic task values (for mathematics and language) and perceptions of social satisfaction for 162 12- and 13-year-old pupils in New Zealand classrooms using a cooperative, interactive learning structure and in ordinary classrooms. Task values for engagement in learning activities were found to be higher in classrooms using a cooperative goal structure and to be associated with higher social satisfaction among pupils. The authors suggested that these findings imply a need to examine the coordination of multiple goals which extend beyond the academic domain. Brown, describing the learning communities she espouses, aims at: 'non-conformity in the distribution of expertise and interests so everyone can benefit from the subsequent richness of available knowledge . . . Teams composed of members with homogeneous ideas and skills are denied access to such richness' (1994: 10).

There seems, then, to be a complex relationship between grouping structures, pedagogical strategy, academic achievement and social satisfaction. It is possible to conclude that the classroom strategies employed are of greater significance to the quality of learning than is the organization of the teaching groups. Slavin has suggested that what is needed is a better understanding of how to choose teaching methods which work at appropriate times with particular pupils in different group structures, since 'it does not move the discussion forward at all to note that students differ and then to assume that all achievement differences must be dealt with through some sort of grouping' (1993: 13). A very common approach nowadays is to differentiate learning experiences, tasks and materials for learners.

Defining differentiation

Two principles that inform the concept of a differentiated approach to learning can be identified. The first lies in changing notions of the rather nebulous term 'ability' which we see has become 'abilities' in the following definition of differentiation: 'the matching of work to the abilities of individual children, so that they are stretched, but still achieve success' (NCC, 1993: 78). This suggests a shifting, wide-ranging set of skills, interests and talents rather than a singular ability which is stable across a range of contexts and has been recognized increasingly by authors (see for example Daw, 1995). The idea of responding to, or matching work to, this range of abilities is the natural corollary of adopting this definition of ability. Thus Visser defines differentiation as: 'the process whereby teachers meet the need for progress through the curriculum by selecting appropriate teaching methods to match the individual child's learning strategies, within a group situation' (1993: 15).

The common-sense notion of an all-embracing ability derived from IQ theory has been replaced by a more finely tuned, diagnostic assessment of what each child is capable of at a particular time, with a particular teacher, in a particular subject, using a particular learning strategy. Howard Gardner's explanations of the proclivities learners have for different aspects of their learning can help inform teachers' responses to learners' needs. Chyriwsky (1996) has emphasized the need for subject-specific identification of ability, eschewing the global IQ testing approach. Leo and Galloway (1996) highlighted the impact of children's own conceptions of ability on their goal orientations, citing the work of Dweck (1991) and Nicholls (1989). These studies have indicated a tendency for adolescents to conceive of ability as stable and fixed, which leads to performance-oriented goals. Their commitment to make an effort in class can thus be undermined by the expectancy of it having little effect on their achievement. Younger children are more likely to conceive of ability as changeable, something which is affected by effort; this can orient them towards learning goals. Leo and Galloway also suggested that teachers' conceptualizations of ability affect the way they teach pupils. Those holding a view of ability as a fixed, stable entity 'might behave in ways which impede effective development of mastery learners' (1996: 43).

The second principle of the new differentiation lies in the emphasis on process; thus: 'Differentiation is a planned process of intervention in the classroom to maximise potential based on individual needs' (Dickinson and Wright, 1993: 1). Tubbs placed the teacher at the centre of this intervention, defining differentiation as: 'the means by which a teacher intervenes in every pupil's education in order to provide effective and relevant access for them to the curriculum' (1996: 49). Stradling et al. identified teacher–pupil dialogue as one manifestation of this intervention process: 'The commonest characteristics of differentiation between individual learners tend to be an emphasis on dialogue in the form of regular review between teachers and individual pupils about their progress and their learning needs' (1991: 11).

Groups of pupils, whether setted *or* mixed ability, will display differences in their interest in the topic, presentation skills, ability to work cooperatively or independently, listening skills, parental support, learning styles, gender, ethnic group, cultural background and so on. These differences have an impact on scholastic achievement (Maqsud, 1997). In responding to these differences by differentiating the learning the teacher's aim is itself to make a difference, the difference between where a pupil is now and where he/she has the potential to be. This resonates clearly with Vygotsky's (1978) work on zones of proximal development when he explained that what a child does in cooperation with others, he/she will learn to do alone. The clear implication of this social constructivist approach then is that the teacher's intervention will vary from child to child; as Warnock explained: 'The purpose of education for all children is the same; the goals are the same. But the help that individual children need in progressing towards them will be different' (DES, 1978b: 5).

Two essential principles which characterize a differentiated approach to facilitating learning have been established:

1 Pupil performance is not a function of a simply defined ability, but of a range of interrelated internal and external factors; it is more helpful to use the notion of contextually dependent sets of skills and aptitudes as the underpinning to achievement.
2 The teacher's focus will be on the learning process rather than on the learning product.

These principles are manifestly more complex than those identified by the National Curriculum Council (NCC) in 1990 which explained that the National Curriculum would help teachers to:

- assess what each pupil knows, understands and can do
- use their assessment and the programmes of study to identify the learning needs of individuals
- plan programmes of work which take account of their pupils' attainments and allow them to work at different levels
- ensure that all children achieve their maximum potential (Hart, 1996: 21).

While committed to the potential of individuals, the NCC, in linking differentiation to an assessment of attainment, placed the same ceiling on expectations as that occasioned by the streaming of the 1960s. In contrast, the two principles outlined above recognize the complex nature of attainment, and in pursuing process rather than product, encourage a liberation of learner potential.

The publication of examination results has led to schools adopting tactics such as cramming sessions for pupils on the C/D grade boundary of GCSE to boost results (Pyke, 1996). More recently this has even extended to Year 6 primary school children in order to boost a school's percentage of level 4s in the core subjects. The culture of national benchmarks based on assessment and other performance indicators along with parental and employer pressure are recurring features of school life. The current Labour government has endorsed these ideas by publishing, annually through OFSTED since 1998, benchmarking data for schools to determine their examination targets in relation to the achievements of schools in similar situations. Significant by its absence, however, is any mention of how classroom learning is to be enhanced (Reynolds, 1997). The externality of all these ideas to the learner is very evident. Thus, the ramifications of individual differences in attainment are more far-reaching than a single child's performance in examinations. This now goes hand in hand with the implications which that single child's performance has for the aggregated results of a school.

Conclusion

Research into the ecology of development, suggestions about different types of intelligence, new understandings about the effect of underlying cognitive style on learning approaches and strategies, and an acknowledgement of the impact of social and emotional factors on motivation and achievement all contribute to a richer understanding of individual development through education. The varying influence of different psychological theories can be seen when examining policy changes and in shifts within pedagogical 'trends' such as in the differentiation of pupils, the curriculum offered to them and the learning media employed.

The influence of social-constructivist ideas currently felt within institutions of education is very strong. These have built upon, rather than usurped, many of the ideas previously in favour. Even discredited notions of a single, measurable intelligence persist in our common-sense discourse of ability. The implications of more fluid ideas about intelligence, about the construction and site of knowledge and about the impact of greater learner autonomy through technologized forms of learning have yet to impact in a major way on conventional wisdom about individual learning and achievement. As psychological research continues to refine theoretical ideas about learning, students of education will enjoy a fascinating perspective on them.

Student activities

1 Find out what views your tutors and colleagues have about intelligence. Do they know anything about newer ideas of intelligence? Is there a tendency to think of intelligence as innate and fixed or do people conceptualize intelligence more fluidly? Try to explore this with any schoolteachers you know. How fundamental is their view of intelligence to the way they help pupils learn?

2 Think about your own learning style: do you write essays incrementally, piecing together the components one upon another or do you like to have a generalized idea of the whole essay before you start writing? Do you see pictures and images when you are thinking or reading, or do you find yourself thinking in words? Relate this to a review of some of the learning styles literature (see Riding and Rayner, 1998, for references).

Recommended reading

In addition to Bee (2000) and Child (1997) recommended in the last chapter:

Kozulin, A. (1998) *Psychological Tools: A Sociocultural Approach to Education*, Cambridge, MA: Harvard University Press. This is an advanced text for those who are particularly interested in Vygotsky's work. It is a fascinating reader but requires application by the reader.

Riding, R.J. and Rayner, S. (1998) *Cognitive Styles and Learning Strategies*, London: Fulton. A comprehensive text which cites up-to-date research studies and explains clearly the many theoretical positions within style research. Well written and structured effectively, this book will be useful to those who want a deeper understanding of style constructs and their implications for education.

Sigston, A., Curran, P., Labram, A. and Wolfendale, S. (eds) (1996) *Psychology in Practice with Young People, Families and Schools*, London: Fulton. An edited collection which offers a psychological perspective on a diverse range of topics including adolescent health, refugee children, media influences on young people, family therapy, abuse and neglect, adoption and inclusion of students with special needs.

6

Social Perspectives on Education

This chapter describes the major ideological perspectives on the structure and functions of society and their implications for education. How we understand the relations between education and society is of great importance for practitioners, researchers and students of education alike. To this end, social factors in education are examined briefly from a historical perspective and the prevailing 'liberal ideal' is analysed. Critical studies which challenged these liberal assumptions are outlined. In essence, the chapter grapples with the issue of whether education is designed to broaden minds and develop all pupils in the creation of a better society or is really about reproducing economic and social inequalities by supporting existing power structures.

Introduction

Research into the influence of social factors on achievement in education has frequently challenged the dominant, functionalist paradigm that represents education simply as working in the interests of all its participants. The focus on social influences on achievement has been able, implicitly, at least, to open up debates about the form and function of the curriculum. A number of significant questions arise. What are its ideological foundations and effects? To what extent does the curriculum really serve the interests of powerful minorities and to what extent does it cater for the aspirations of different groups? What about the institutions of education and their culture and values? What is the characteristic form of the school as an institution and from what different perspectives can we see it? Is it possible, still, to think of state education as a mechanism for social reform with the aim of distributing social benefits more evenly?

Perspectives on education and achievement

Social theories and education

There are various perspectives on society and education which, though substantially different, may overlap in parts. There is a tension in these perspectives between the idea of social *action*, what people do in their social existences, and social *structures*, the institutions, practices and ideas that have a determining influence on behaviour, identity and belief. At the centre of this difference is the question posed by Marxism and neo-Marxism of the relations between the material *base* of society and the ideological *superstructure* in society. In some accounts of social structures, the material base, the economic forces that drive social conduct, will be seen to be what determines the general social structure. In others, cultural practices, ideas and institutions will be seen to have a life more or less of their own with relative independence from the economic forces at work in society. One view is to see schools, colleges and universities as *superstructural* institutions, concerned to promote and reproduce ideas but concerned also to produce identities and positions for individuals that are useful for the economic base. As we have seen though, educational institutions might be described from a liberal perspective as being unrelated to economics, being fundamentally concerned with learning, knowledge and the personal development of individuals independently of their economic life.

Functionalist views

Functionalism views society as a system where interconnected parts function in relation to an integrated whole. Functionalism depends on the idea that social systems are significantly determined by fundamental human need. In this way it tends to be seen as a 'conservative' ideology. Functionalism also works with the idea of functional prerequisites: some social phenomena are simply there as they are necessary for the society to work for the benefit of all its different members. All societies have some form of social stratification, for example, so this is interpreted as a necessary condition of social order. Some needs are common to all societies implying the idea of a general human condition independent of cultural differences. Socialization, for example, a concept closely allied to education, is seen as a functional prerequisite of all societies (Durkheim, 1947). Durkheim emphasized social facts as a kind of network of constraints. Society shapes members and their actions and also 'manages' the beliefs and actions of individuals. Durkheim outlined a social reality as existing over and above the perceptions of individuals. Beliefs and values are transmitted to individuals rather than created by them and are related to positive social functions. They provide reasons and explanations, and enable individuals and groups to make sense of their own experience of the world and to function within the given social structure. Society is seen as a system with necessary laws, in the sense of constraints on behaviour that are both legal and tacit components of a kind of unwritten social contract.

Parsons (1937; 1951) describes society in terms of a general value consensus. Modern societies, though complex and fractured, according to this view, are capable of expressing common goals. They operate according to established norms that positively express the shared common goals of society. Social equilibrium is an ideal state of balance. It will be more or less realized in social structures. The family and the school are the positive and necessary institutions through which social values and cohesion are maintained. Parsons takes a thoroughly systemic view of social structure which he accounts for in terms of four principles: adaptation, goal attainment, integration and pattern maintenance. His theory encompasses the possibility of social change through gradual evolution.

One main criticism of functionalist perspectives is the way that they see social structures according to a hidden logic of cause and effect. They fail to detect alternative ways of engaging with different social phenomena. Vital questions about conflict and difference in societies are explained away by functionalist perspectives. Institutions are seen as expressing necessary social functions, and dysfunctional social phenomena are regarded as outside the true functional pale of the social, blips in the system rather than problems with the system itself. There are vital questions that tend to be suppressed by functionalist perspectives about institutions, for example, whether they have to be seen as necessary or whether they might be seen as contingent, as in post-structuralism and postmodernism. These theories of 'contingency' emphasize the idea that social institutions may have arbitrary roots, that they may be thrown up more or less accidentally by history and do not necessarily perform the functions they appear to be designed for. Functionalist theories tend to be 'monologic'. Social phenomena are seen as having single and simple, surface causes. Social conflicts are minimized and the normative elements of social life are emphasized. Functionalist theories can be valuable in describing how societies and their various elements work together in coherent patterns but are less successful in accounting for change and conflict. One of the big questions that haunts education is whether or not schools are functional in a positive or negative sense. In other words, do they provide a necessary and important function for all their 'members' or do they work only in favour of certain groups?

Conflict perspectives

From early years we are encouraged to see education positively, as offering benefits to all. But what if, as some social theorists and education researchers have claimed, education is more about promoting dominant ideology and dividing populations into different class and occupational segments? Conflict perspectives propose that schools perform certain social functions but not necessarily to the benefit of all. Some have suggested that they serve the system well but that the system they serve is based on inequalities that schooling or education in general should be challenging.

Marxism

Conflict perspectives have been dominated by Marxism, a historical perspective that places conflict as the driving force of human development. Marxism borrows its theory of history and society from Hegel's dialectics. Put simply, this suggests that social change is caused by the relationship and interaction between opposed forces. Marxism sees history as necessarily progressive. Conflicts in society are working towards resolution. Human societies are characterized by necessary development through history towards the final end point of communism. Marxism tends to emphasize the material basis of social life as giving rise to contradictions and to conflict. Capitalism gives rise to alienation as workers are divorced from the products they are required to produce in an alienated social condition. Class is a relatively clear-cut affair in Marxism. Capitalist societies are divided into the bourgeoisie and the working class, who are in constant conflict with one another. Class-consciousness arises from conditions of existence and becomes the motive force of history.

Marxism has represented the most serious sustained body of ideas to challenge dominant thinking about education in western nation states. At the centre of Marxism is a deep suspicion of the 'bourgeois state' which is predisposed in all its operations to favour the interests of 'capital', of the wealthy and privileged and more recently of the large multinational corporations that dominate the world economic scene. Marx's original description of capitalist society was founded on the idea of struggle and conflict. It emphasized the brute relations of oppression that characterized the social landscape of the nineteenth-century post-industrial revolution that he inhabited. For Marx conflict and contradiction were the engines of history. Conflict in capitalist states inevitably grew out of the unequal distribution of wealth that both symbolized and realized the differences in power between groups of people. Marx's conclusion was the inevitable collapse of the capitalist state.

Post-Marxism

Marx's predictions, however, about the future of capitalism and its inevitable demise, the coming of communism and the gradual withering away of the state, now seem very remote from reality. Nevertheless, the Marxist inheritance continues to provide powerful critiques of inequality and injustice, and has been transformed by successive generations of Marxists and others to address contemporary issues. The failure of major predictive elements of Marxism and some of the gaps in its analyses have, it could be said, been compensated for by the developing body of thought that has grown out of classic Marxism.

But what does the Marxist analysis of capitalism and the 'bourgeois state' have to do with the practices of education systems and the daily workings of schools? In contemporary terms it could be said that there is still a case to be answered in relation to Marxist-inspired critiques of systematic inequalities in education. Some of the key critical positions, theories and researches developed in modern times have been influenced, directly or indirectly, by Marxist thought: Bernstein (1971; 1973), Labov (1972), Bowles and Gintis (1976), Bourdieu (1991), Willis (1979), all in different ways and to different degrees, have been influenced by Marxism. Althusser in the 1960s and 1970s was concerned to return to Marx's ideas about the relations between base and superstructure. Althusser formed the concept of ideological state apparatuses (ISAs), a development of the concept of government and class relations (Althusser, 1984). Ideological state apparatuses are significant in terms of maintaining ruling-class ideology and are an important part of the means through which the capitalist state maintains control. The particular role of education is apparent here.

Gramsci (1985; 1991) claims that ownership of the means of production cannot be enough to guarantee class rule. The ruling class must also work for 'hegemony', a key concept signifying the cultural rule of dominant ideas. Gramsci's view of society emphasizes the importance of ideas. It includes a sense of class accommodation. It points out that the ruling class needs to actively win the support of other members of society and indicates how ruling-class concessions have to be made. Gramsci makes a distinction between political society and civil society. In constructing this divide, Gramsci puts great emphasis on civil institutions and cultural practices as fields for political action and intervention. This implies a broad idea of the state, political power and authority as being located in everyday practices and ideas. Hegemony is achieved by continual negotiation and has to be constantly worked at. Thus we see the importance of the education system. Gramsci's social theory is complex. It proposes a kind of dual consciousness rather than monologic ideology. The dominant class can never, therefore, totally monopolize power as beliefs and ideas are constantly being contested in everyday practices (in education, for example). As a consequence, social change (revolutionary action) can be located in existing institutions and everyday social practices.

Habermas, a later member of the so-called 'Frankfurt School' of Marxist social theorists, has more recently been responsible for a different reinterpretation of Marxism. This is a modified Marxism, interested in culture above all and in the idea of civil society. Habermas refers to the current global condition as 'late capitalism'. The predicted economic crisis of Marx has turned out not to be so inevitable. The modern capitalist state intervenes to manage, to delay impending crises, to sustain ruling-class authority. In fact, according to Habermas, the modern state has become part of the economic base of society. But Habermas, like Gramsci, is more superstructural. As opposed to a theory of direct conflict, he identifies class compromise, notes concessions by the ruling order and views the real crisis of capitalism not as leading to an impending bloody revolution but as being in the realm of ideas – a 'legitimation crisis'. According to Habermas, ideas of equality, justice and freedom are actually at the centre of the capitalist state but the state must also represent the interests of the ruling economic class. There is a serious threat to social stability in this contradiction. As non-material factors are critical in Habermas's social theory which emphasizes language as a vital component of human social being (Habermas, 1984a; 1984b), education represents an important arena for political struggle. The field of education is one significant section of the social landscape where *cultural politics* is in play. Marxist and post-Marxist social theories continue to express interest in education as an important arena for social action and social reform.

Social interactionism

Social interactionists emphasize the *actions* of members of society as the source for understanding social phenomena and institutions rather than overarching *structures*. Weber (1958; 1963) was interested in uncovering the meaning behind social actions. The perspective of 'symbolic interactionism' comes out of the development of Weber's thinking and American sociological traditions. George Herbert Mead is often cited as the 'founder' of symbolic interactionism. According to Mead (1934), human beings interact through symbols which define the world and the roles of social actors. This position emphasizes the importance of culture in social formations, institutions and practices such as education. Culture specifies roles, symbols and interpretations of symbols. Symbolic interactionism is a 'superstructural' theory par excellence. Symbols enable the social actors to make sense of their world. While symbols in social interactions must be shared, individuals interpret the actions, meanings and intentions of others. Social life involves an ever active role. Mead emphasizes the critical importance of role-taking and interpretation in the development of the 'self'. The idea of the coherent self is learned and cultivated. Social institutions such as schools are composed of many roles. These roles can be chosen to some extent and are interpreted and adapted by the actor, for example, parenting can be carried out in many ways. Thus culture is not monolithic and constraining. Subcultures exist and are constantly changing. Cultural meanings often indicate possibilities rather than requirements. Social roles are dynamic and, to some extent, fluid.

While Marxism emphasizes *structures* as the dominant forces determining the shape and form of institutions and behaviours, interactionists emphasize *agency* or the freedom and ability of the individual to decide. In recent times, the sociologist Antony Giddens (1985) has argued for a theory of social action that sees structure and agency as interdependent: 'structuration' relates structures to action. Giddens writes of the 'duality of structure'; structures do exist but have no existence outside of the consciousness of the agents who act upon them and define them in everyday activity. Language provides Giddens with a model for 'duality of structure'. Language must be rule governed and therefore structural. It depends for its existence on the utterances of individuals who make it happen. Languages though are different and constantly change. Human agents can change as well as reproduce structures. Rules as procedures to follow in social life can be shifted. The social system is a pattern of social relations that exists over time: agency and reproduction – a duality of structure. Giddens warms to Willis's work on schooling, for example, indicating how structures are reproduced by activities of agents and as unintended consequences of actions (Giddens, 1985; Willis, 1979).

Post-structuralist and postmodern perspectives

Some powerful and influential ideas about culture and society come in the form of theories referred to as 'post-structuralist' and 'postmodernist', though neither of those terms can be used in any very straightforward sense. The importance of these ideas within education is that they challenge dominant discourses and practices by suggesting that, while these things may be fixed in behaviour and institutions, they are at another level provisional. They also indicate the importance of culture, language and identity – key features of the inequalities that operate through education.

Post-structuralism provides opportunities for rethinking the school as an institution. It considers the nature of knowledge, about how this changes through history and according to culture. It also is aware of how knowledge works in relation to different forms of subjectivity. Discourses of knowledge position subjects, exert power and are force-fields of power at the same time (see Derrida, 1987; Foucault, 1977b; 1988a). Post-structuralism is critical of the deep-seated ideas that infuse education systems and traditions. On the whole it is anti-essentialist and anti-traditionalist. It is suspicious of ideas like truth and aware of the historical 'contingency' of ideas and 'systems of thought'. With its emphasis on the importance of language and culture, post-structuralism provides the means for examining all the mundane practices of institutional life and posing questions of them, from what texts get read in English lessons, to how discourses of science and knowledge represent gender. Similarly, Lyotard's (1986) postmodern account considers the fragmentation of knowledge and how the knowledge of powerful groups dominates (see Chapter 3).

Differing social perspectives, such as those described in this section, are important in the study of education. It is vital to work towards some idea of the relations between the social structure and the institutions of education and the education system itself. Tracking these relations is complex and problematic but important. An examination from a historical perspective can help.

A brief historical perspective on social structures and education

We saw in Chapter 3 how the development of the school as a key component of civic life, particularly in urban centres, transformed the nature of society and the 'citizen' (Hunter, 1994). In its early phases (from 1870) the school was primarily designed to produce this new form of 'citizen' who was basically literate, trained in certain disciplines of conduct and who had learned some basic facts about the world (Donald, 1992). It was during this period that the many still relatively new urban centres in Britain became governed and ordered locally. Amenities and systems for cleanliness and health were provided, for example public baths, drainage systems, new technologies of hygiene and waste disposal. It is possible to see the school as one very important manifestation of this civic concern and it is certainly important to recognize the extent to which the early elementary school represents a vast extension of government in the name of both social control and social improvement (Wardle, 1970). The early education system was thus concerned with the moral, physical and spiritual condition of the population. Domestic economy and the civic virtues of cleanliness and personal self-management could be taught and some of the negative effects of urban poverty could be dealt with by health care and large-scale feeding programmes managed through schools (Horn, 1989).

The elementary school emerged in the nineteenth century as a new form of institution with a newly formulated social mission. The school as we know it is closely related to this recent ancestor. These 'new' elementary schools that appeared like 'beacons of the future' over the urban landscapes of the industrialized nation were quite different from the 'monitorial' schools that had successfully drilled working-class children in the basics of literacy and numeracy. The new elementary schools were often constructed using a grand architectural design which strongly resembled the nineteenth-century factory buildings dominating the post-industrial revolution skylines of urban industrial centres. Indeed, these were conceived of and developed as responses to urbanization and industrialization, as responses to the problems of population management. They became complex institutions for the governance *and* for the transformation of populations (Hurt, 1979). They represented a new form of aspiration for mass urban populations and, architecturally, presented a socio-cultural symbolism in their (early) grand designs and were structured and embellished accordingly (Donald, 1992; Lowe and Seaborne, 1977).

They also operated a more subtle pastoral and disciplinary regime than the monitorial system with its huge drill rooms. In the elementary school the teacher was brought closer to the pupils in smaller classrooms and the culture of the children met with the supervisory gaze of the teacher in the playground. The collective space of the hall could be utilized for the promotion of collective identity and moral guidance. The elements of the elementary school combined into a new structure that would be the basis for the development of an entirely new kind of 'human technology' capable of producing responsible and self-governing citizens. This self-governing aspect of the school's characteristic way of working remains very powerful. It is deeply embedded in the work ethic that prevails in schools and in the contemporary drive to develop a self-managing, self-governing citizenry through state-funded education.

After the First World War, state-funded education in Britain was regarded as important in improving the quality of life of the oppressed classes. Social reformers and revolutionaries saw it as a mechanism for enabling class inequalities to be challenged and swept aside. The more radical versions of this view were expressed by left-wing demands for the eradication of public schools in England and Wales and for the institution of a new 'comprehensive' school system (CCCS, 1991). After the Second World War, there was a socialist government in England and Wales and the welfare state was instituted. In a radical agenda of social transformation, nationalization accompanied a fresh vision for social welfare and social mobility. People of all political persuasions welcomed the 1944 Education Act, which gave secondary education to all for the first time. The number of young people attending universities was also expanded and there was the expectation that working-class children would have access to education of the most 'complete' kind as well as of the highest quality. This advance was seen as essential as much on the grounds of realizing the nation's economic and industrial potential as on grounds of social justice. A new vision of the nation as cohesive and purposeful with common goals seemed to be on the verge of realization.

The new education system was fraught with problems. While it certainly did have the effect of enabling more working-class young people to gain access to an expanded higher education system, it remained shot through with inequalities. Statistics produced by large-scale studies of social differences in educational attainment grimly revealed that significant numbers of working-class children were failing to succeed, either by not passing the 11-plus examination which determined whether they went to secondary modern or grammar school, or by being unable to capitalize on opportunities that were on offer if they were given a place in a grammar school through a lack of financial and cultural resources (Halsey et al., 1980).

The capacity for working-class children to take advantage of the opportunities that were apparently being placed freely before them became the crux of big debates about the state of education. Questions centred on where failure was to be located: the children themselves, the parents and their lack of educational *nous*, the school system or the whole of working-class culture which became increasingly significant in the discussion (see Douglas, 1964). There were at the same time large-scale popular, 'parental' concerns over inequalities in the tripartite system that the comprehensive school was at least partly designed to confront (see Jackson and Marsden, 1962).

By 1965 the idea of the comprehensive school was well established in public consciousness. It was conceived of as a major political break-through in the development of the principle of equality of opportunity. 'Comprehensivization', though, was not to make a dramatic break with the thinking and practice of the time. Schools were still to be streamed according to 'ability' (*Circular 10/65*, 1965) though the divisions between differently labelled pupils would be more fluid and open to movement. It would appear that, while the goal of social mobility dominated, the desire to relinquish ability-based organizational structures was more muted. The comprehensive school was, however, intended to enable greater flexibility and opportunity to those whose fate had hitherto been determined at the moment of the 11-plus examination.

We can conclude that, since the Second World War, industrial societies have seen the development of education systems in terms of the social democratic ideals of social equality. Schools and the processes of schooling are viewed as instruments of social advancement. Expansions of the higher education system during the late 1940s, the 1960s and the early 1990s represent significant phases in the development of this ideal. During these periods the school was increasingly seen as a route towards the social advancement that higher education appeared to offer. This represents a very significant difference from the situation before the Second World War under the elementary school system. The transition to the tripartite system and later to comprehensive schooling was designed to enable greater numbers of working-class children to make progress through the school to higher education and thereby to social advancement. The education system, at least in the state sector, was being redefined in this process as meritocratic.

Questioning the liberal ideal

Comprehensive reorganization represented a moment of optimism about education and its power to realize both the full development of individuals and to accentuate the social and economic development of the nation. This was optimism about a new social future in which all sectors of the populace would have access to education. Equality, or at least equality of opportunity, became a key term. This powerful liberal ideal can still be seen embodied in governmental policy statements and in school mission statements. It hovers behind the conception of education as a vehicle for self and general social improvement (see Marples, 1999, for discussion of the liberal tradition in education). According to this ideal the real function of education is to realize the full potential of individuals, especially perhaps their intellectual potential, but also recognizing their physical, artistic, spiritual and emotional development. An important product of this theory is that the education system is always a flawed version of the ideal. Why do so many fail to achieve this potential? More positively, though, it follows that this ideal view of education can be used as a lever for social reform. To sustain ideas about equality and democracy in relation to education is important in terms of keeping education alert to matters of opportunity and access.

The work of Gardner (1993) on multiple intelligences, for instance, bears the stamp of this liberal ideal that probably finds its most complete early expression in the writings of John Dewey. In Gardner's contemporary version the theory of multiple intelligences enhances the idea that each individual is unique and of intrinsic worth. The liberal view of education, however, leaves a number of important issues untouched and fails to address some of the fundamental features of education. It assumes that there is an unproblematic relationship between the knower and the known, that the development of knowledge and understanding is an end in itself and that it will lead to personal growth, fulfilment and, by a kind of necessary osmosis, will improve the quality of social life for individuals and for society as a whole. It assumes that the field of knowledge is also relatively knowable and stable. Advances occur and positions may shift from time to time but, on the whole, the substantive content of knowledge is given and the forms of knowing are more or less constant, though subject to the law of progressive development. The liberal view also holds that the primary unit of education is the individual. Personal freedom will naturally give rise to a desire for learning as part of the 'natural' development of the individual (Bentley, 1998).

The liberal ideal has been powerful throughout the twentieth century. It has influenced educators like A.S. Neill, the founder of the radical progressive school, Summerhill, and the tradition of progressive state education that found expression and embodiment in some state schools in the 1970s, Countesthorpe College in Leicestershire perhaps being the most famous instance (Watts, 1977). It is very evident in the

Plowden Report (CACE, 1967) with its emphasis on the innate nature of the child and in traditions of teaching, particularly English teaching, that developed during the 1960s and that espoused an ideology of personal growth (Dixon, 1967). One of its most radical expressions is in the work of Ivan Illich who advocated the deschooling of society. Illich was convinced from his experiences of New York schools that the ideal solution for the realization of true, liberal education would be 'deschooling', the dismantling of schools as institutions intrinsically inimical to the true spirit of liberal education. Illich was particularly concerned with the fact that significant numbers of immigrant children in New York seemed to be getting nothing out of the school system. In fact, they were dropping out in large numbers. The school as an institution seemed incapable of meeting their needs. In identifying and centralizing the problem of exclusion Illich's work highlighted a critically important focus of modern educators. This is to explain and to find solutions to the problems of class inequalities in a system that is ostensibly designed to meet the needs of the whole population, not to cater more or less exclusively for the social aspirations of the middle classes. For the majority, according to Illich, schooling is designed to produce a mindless conformity. The school is more an instrument of social pacification than a centre of creativity and learning. Schooling confuses teaching with learning, qualification with education and certification with competence. In other words the school does not provide individuals with real knowledge, competence or learning skills and experiences. Schools have a kind of life and logic of their own. As institutions, their primary function is not educative (Illich, 1971).

Liberal education has the positive virtue of being directed towards personal fulfilment. It might be contrasted with a more instrumentalist version of education that tends to promote the idea of economic efficiency through education. In this sense liberal education has failed to address concerns about inequalities. In subscribing to what David Hargreaves has called 'the cult of the individual', liberal education and liberal perspectives on education fail to address the social politics of the school system. A major consideration of the liberal position is that it is deeply embedded in our familiar, 'common-sense' thinking about education. The idea, for example, that education is about personal growth, that education offers opportunities for self (and therefore social improvement) seems somehow obvious and inevitable. These ideas are often alluded to in government policy-making. The 1999 National Curriculum review by the Qualifications and Curriculum Authority (DfEE/QCA, 1999) refers, for example, to a powerful version of the liberal model of education. Critical social studies have often sought to challenge the ruling liberal assumptions about education by identifying hidden practices, deep-seated inequalities and cultural biases. Exploring the effects of education in terms other than the dominant liberal paradigm has on occasions produced powerful alternative theories that enable the social and cultural politics of education to be seen more clearly.

Education and inequality: critical studies

Mostly deriving from Marxist and post-Marxist social theories, critical traditions of the analysis of society have led sociologists to conduct researches into the social inequalities in education. The famous study conducted by A.H. Halsey and others into social class inequalities in education provided some of the impetus for a reconsideration of the education system that led to comprehensive schooling (Brown et al., 1997). This major study, conducted across several generations in England and Wales, concluded that the changes in the education system had hardly made an impact on social inequality. Although working-class children were staying in the education system for longer their relative chances of gaining access to higher education, and to significantly enhancing their economic and social status, were not much changed by post-war reforms. The study indicated that the levels of qualification required for going into work had been raised during the period in question (1913–52) and insufficient numbers of working-class children were staying on at school. Halsey et al.'s work had provided detailed evidence of the results of changes that had been designed to produce a more meritocratic society but which had not had that effect. The Halsey study divided the populations it was looking at into three categories – the service class, the intermediate class and the working class – and found considerable differences in levels of educational achievement across the period. More recent studies indicate similar class differences in university attendance leading to significant variation in educational qualifications. The problem of explaining why schooling had failed to realize its aim of providing equality of opportunity increasingly became of interest to sociologists and theorists of education.

In England and Wales, the tripartite system had been founded on commitment to secondary education for all, but made assumptions about children's innate, inherited intelligence. This was reflected in the tests used to determine whether children would progress at 11-plus to secondary modern schools or grammar schools. Grammar schools provided a more academic education essentially designed for progression to university and secondary modern schools were more skills and work oriented, more like an extension of the elementary schools they had partly been designed to replace. At least the tripartite system seemed to offer the chance for all to gain access to a grammar school education. All children would be sifted through the testing net. As noted in Chapter 4, educational psychologists of the period, notably Sir Cyril Burt, had promoted the idea that intelligence was an inherited characteristic. But studies indicating that class was a decisive factor in success or failure in 11-plus tests would seem to contradict the idea of innate intelligence, unless we accept the idea that working-class intelligence is somehow 'lower' than middle-class intelligence levels (Silver, 1973).

A number of powerful critiques of the education system emerged to challenge the very idea of innate intelligence and to indicate the fact of working-class underachievement in schooling. Popular dissatisfaction with the tripartite system gave rise to the Labour government circular (*Circular 10/65*) that initiated the comprehensive school system that seemed to be founded much more on a notion of equality of opportunity. However, at the same time, during the early 1960s, a number of studies and theories emerged which challenged the very notion that state education systems were, or could be, instruments for social transformation and for democratic inclusion of the whole population.

Labelling theory and research

Symbolic interactionists see individual existence as always being bounded and impinged on by external forces. We are what we are by process rather than by fixed characteristics or identity. Identity is produced by the relation between your view of yourself and the way others view and react to you. Identity is always being worked on. It is in a state of flux and it may well vary considerably according to context. In addition, the institutions we inhabit impose social roles upon us like that of pupil or teacher. Within these roles there are a range of 'options' for difference. There is a repertoire of behaviours and positions. Sociologists who work from this perspective attempt to understand the interactions that give rise to various positions in schools. They see social actors rather than statically positioned classes or groups and try to understand the process whereby patterns of behaviour develop. Subcultures are a strong element of this theory and can explain how it is that different value systems come into contact and conflict within one institution. David Hargreaves's study, *Social Relations in a Secondary*

School (1967), indicates how the school effectively (and not always at a conscious level) defines pupils as conformist or non-conformist, successful or not successful. This sets up a dynamic of social relations that produces broadly differentiated subcultural groups in the pupil population. So pupils who find themselves being negatively defined in relation to the dominant values of the school in terms of behaviours, attitudes and academic work may themselves accept this definition. They may also transform it into a positive form of identity so that an alternative form of high status can be achieved by rule-breaking and general non-conformism.

In *Deviance in Classrooms* (Hargreaves et al., 1975), factors such as appearance, attitudes to discipline, ability to work, 'likeability', relations with other pupils, personality and deviance rating were found to contribute to the way that teachers distinguish and define pupils. Teachers then elaborate and test out their original hypotheses and finally stabilize their sense of a pupil's identity. Teachers thus make sense of the pupils in their charge and define them in relation to their potential to meet the criteria for success established by the school which may be radically different from the pupil's or the pupil subculture's sense of success and value. For pupils who are negatively valued it is extremely difficult to achieve a positive identity. Other researchers have confirmed important aspects of this perspective in different contexts. Rist's work in American kindergartens indicated that teachers quickly labelled and defined pupils as soon as they entered school and that the crucial factor in determining positive and negative identities was social class (Rist, 1970). Becker (1971) conducted research in Chicago to discover how teachers defined the 'ideal pupil' and found that teachers saw pupils from non-manual backgrounds as most nearly conforming to this ideal and saw 'lower-class' students as furthest from it.

Labelling, then, influences the way teachers see pupils, the roles and identities pupils develop and, crucially, the academic progress and success of pupils. Another American study found that pupils might be defined negatively as representing a conduct problem in relation to a number of factors of personal style, such as posture, gait, speech patterns and so on, all of which can be markers of class difference (Cicourel and Kitsuse, 1971). Labelling theory suggests that as types get imposed upon pupils this affects their sense of themselves and their identity and in the long run influences their performance and potential to achieve. Related to this the *self-fulfilling prophecy* indicates how the definitions that teachers make of pupils will powerfully influence how well they do and is a factor in determining their level of academic school success (Rosenthal and Jacobson, 1968). Various studies have confirmed this theory, indicating how teachers react differently to pupils when given different types of information (whether that information is true or false). Other studies have challenged the apparently deterministic nature of the labeling idea, examining counter-cases where pupils have actively resisted the negative stereotypes imposed on them by schools (Fuller, 1984).

Perhaps the most insistent and remorseless form of labelling that goes on in schools is banding and streaming, the organization of pupils into populations according to supposed 'ability'. Both banding and streaming can have the rather drastic effect of producing quite different forms of education within the same school. Again, studies of the practices of particular schools have given rise to theories of labelling that are class oriented. Some studies have indicated how both streaming and banding follow patterns according to social class. Pupils who found themselves in the higher streams and bands were much more likely to have fathers who were not manual workers, for instance. In addition, once pupils were labelled and streamed or banded they received different treatment, effectively a different curriculum and education from the pupils in the higher bands. While this pattern does not hold true for all cases of banding or streaming, and some pupils escape the negative labelling, it remains broadly very significant. In addition, it was found that certain types of knowledge were regarded as more significant than others. Knowledge made available to pupils depended on teachers' judgements about the ability of pupils to use it and about their readiness. Once again a social-class factor was found to be important and was strongly influential in how teachers made judgements about pupils' relative 'abilities'. From these studies it is clear that pupils are classified and evaluated in schools. There is a strong component of social construction at work in this process. Similar evaluations and classifications of knowledge occur in schools in interaction situations. So it is that 'appropriate' knowledge is directed towards 'appropriate' pupils (Ball, 1981; Keddie, 1973).

Language, class and culture: Bernstein, Labov and ebonics

A major issue in relation to the school, social differences and equality that came to the fore during the late 1960s was language and culture. Basil Bernstein had been commissioned to examine inequalities in education. His main focus was language but he was also interested in the school as a social environment that operated through 'culture'. Bernstein (1971; 1973) saw language differences as expressive of deep-seated differences in culture, particularly between middle-class and working-class children. The 'elaborated' and 'restricted' code distinction that Bernstein deployed in his study, corresponding to middle-class and working-class speech patterns, engendered controversy among educators, raising the heat on questions about education, language, culture and class in the early 1970s.

Bernstein proposed that language differences lead to different levels of achievement between class groups. In Bernstein's work language is an essential component for a description of the way that social structure and stratification works through education. Experience is organized through language but language differences are related explicitly to social systems. According to this position, language does not simply reflect the world but actively organizes the world into categories of experience. Linguistic systems or dialects reflect different types of social experience, expressing the forms of life and dispositions particular to their social environments. Children therefore come to school from different linguistic environments that are not matched by forms of language used in schools. The acquisition of language and processes of socialization could be said to be one and the same process producing cultural orientations. In effect, language differences represent different 'symbolic orders' for different groups (Bernstein, 1971; 1973). In schooling, dominant forms of language may relate negatively or positively to the linguistic, symbolic legacies of sections of school populations. Bernstein writes: 'The different focusing of experience . . . creates a major problem of educability only where the school produces discontinuity between its symbolic orders and those of the child' (Bernstein, 1971: 122). Language and culture became very important themes in the powerful sociological critiques that emerged through the 1970s from Bernstein (1971), Bowles and Gintis (1976), Bourdieu and Passeron (1977) and Willis (1979), among others.

Halliday (1979) defines the effect on the child of Bernstein's account of the differences in verbal practices that inhere in different class speech environments: 'The child who is not predisposed to this type of verbal exploration in this type of experiential and interpersonal context "is not at home in the educational world" as Bernstein puts it' (Halliday, 1979: 26). In other words, children may experience alienation in school through language. Certain ways of organizing experience in socially differentiated language forms and habitual practices, those that approximate most nearly to 'standard' English, are more in tune with the linguistic environment of schooling. Dialects and registers vary and diverge according to a number of factors including, crucially, social class.

In describing Bernstein's account of the character of the socially differentiated nature of languages, Halliday refers to the idea of subculture: 'what determines the actual cultural linguistic configuration is, essentially, the social structure, the system of social relations, in the family and other key social groups, which is characteristic of the particular subculture' (Halliday, 1979: 24). Bernstein defines the relations between language differences and social relations as linguistic forms or 'fashions of speaking'. Allied to these socially structured differences in speech are (and herein lies the source of the controversy in Bernstein's work on education) different forms of behaviour:

> A number of fashions of speaking, frames of consistency, are possible in any given language and . . . these fashions of speaking, linguistic forms or codes, are themselves a function of the form social relations take. According to this view, the form of the social relation or, more generally, the social structure generates distinct linguistic forms or codes and these codes essentially transmit the culture and so constrain behaviour. (Bernstein, 1971: 122)

The danger in the position expressed by Bernstein in relation to class, language and education was the attribution of *essential* qualities to the differences between working-class language and middle-class language, and the potential correlation of working-class culture with less expressive linguistic forms. The use of the distinction between working-class speech as 'restricted code' and middle-class speech as 'elaborated code' became infamous as it seemed to imply a hierarchy of expressive power. This position was tackled positively in the work of Labov and in the development of socio-linguistics by Halliday who refined Bernstein's thought with a more acute sense of the arbitrary nature of symbolic linguistic power (Halliday, 1979). Both Labov and Halliday were keen to shift the argument away from the taint of deficit models of working-class language implied by Bernstein. While Halliday reminds us of the *social* dimension of educational failure, he also reminds us of the *linguistic* aspect of educational failure: 'Educational failure is really a social problem, not a linguistic one; but it has a linguistic aspect' (Halliday, 1979: 24). This focus on language indicates how cultural difference may be a crucial factor in achievement in education.

Labov's work had offered a challenging theory to call into question the 'juridicial' issue of the cultural linguistic authority of the school:

> In this area, the deficit theory appears as the notion of 'verbal deprivation': black children from the ghetto area are said to receive little verbal stimulation, to hear very little well-formed language, and as a result are impoverished in their means of verbal expression. It is said that they cannot speak complete

sentences, do not know the names of common objects, cannot form concepts or convey logical thoughts. (Labov, 1997a: 4)

The argument rendered problematic liberal assumptions about the positive function of education, including the egalitarian pretensions of the new comprehensive school system, and indicated clearly a lack of awareness in matters of class and culture. Labov's work was significant as a radical departure in debates about language and education, insisting as it did consistently that 'the logic of non-standard English', the grammar and the expressive power of non-standard forms were in all ways comparable with the standard, dominant and educationally privileged forms (Labov, 1973). The effect was to deflate the myth of linguistic deprivation, while also insisting that the domination of standard English was essential to inequalities of access. This question about the relations between standard language and varieties of language relating to ethnicity, class and culture remains powerful and unresolved.

If the debate or issue of language and language differences has largely withered away from the UK context, it remains very powerfully alive and urgent in other national contexts, particularly in the USA and in South Africa. This is partly to do with the intense political pressures that have been brought to bear on some key questions of equity and inequality in these two different but related national contexts. In the USA, the question of language has been at the cutting edge of great controversy, especially in relation to the underachievement of large sectors of the population, particularly African-Americans who have consistently fared less well through state-funded education than any other sizeable ethnic group. The educational underachievement of black Americans through processes of schooling is powerfully illustrative of the role of language in education and of its critical relations with culture and cultural difference. In the USA black communities and educators have chosen in some cases to adopt what appears to be a radical approach. Schools, it is well known, are regulatory environments and promote certain values and norms. This works through language as much as through anything else. Schools are also constantly promoting ideas about language and promoting linguistic norms. These norms are not shared equally by all pupils. Certain groups may actually have quite different linguistic norms as part of their upbringing or lived cultural heritage. This means that many children, black American children particularly, may experience the school as a linguistically and culturally alienating environment. Rather than have their children and pupils suffer the kind of cultural negation that can come from being unrecognized by the official and unofficial language of the school, some activists decided to adopt an alternative approach. They decided that as the best way to ensure that the culture of the school was not alienating for the children from African-American background they would use the language of black Americans, called 'ebonics', as a medium of instruction. They decided to take positive measures to celebrate the linguistic heritage of their charges and to teach the characteristics of ebonics and draw comparisons with the characteristics of so-called standard English.

The ebonics issue has many implications for questions about language in education, particularly concerning the school as a linguistic environment. It indicates the extent to which language is a decisive factor in educational success and failure. It raises questions about the nature and social role of standard English in education and particularly in relation to practices of assessment. It highlights the tension between the cultures of pupils in schools and the culture expressed in the dominant practices of the school, the curriculum and the language environment. Delpit (1995) and Smitherman (2000) have written about the need to make schools user-friendly cultural and linguistic environments for African-American pupils and have demonstrated how ebonics may be used to effect changes in the rates of success for African-American children in state schools. The ebonics movement has been politically contentious, partly because it challenges the given order of things and partly because it has been misread as an attempt to offer a non-academic curriculum to African-American children (Labov, 1997b). But it remains an important movement that has made significant inroads into educational practices in schools in the USA. Some of the issues it raises have considerable general importance in other contexts.

Social reproduction and correspondence theory

Bourdieu (1991) has argued consistently that class culture is a major factor in determining educational success and failure. The failure of working-class children in education relates to the systematic bias of the system, rooted in culture. In schools working class culture is either not recognized and simply negated or is denigrated as an inferior form of culture, a kind of anti-knowledge.

Cultural reproduction, the process of handing down beliefs, values, ideas, practices and knowledge, may seem to be a vital if not absolutely essential function of the education system. But reproduction through schooling is primarily concerned with the reproduction of dominant class culture, a position it holds arbitrarily. In fact, the dominant form of culture as embodied in schooling gets represented as, in some way, culture itself. Other forms of culture are unrecognized (they are not really culture) or are defined negatively (they are a debased form of culture). This is quite clearly illustrated in the case of narrative fictions in the subject English which privileges certain kinds of narrative fictions, (Shakespeare, for instance,) that are more likely to fall within the cultural experiences of middle class-children than others. Media narrative fictions, for example, that are likely to enjoy a more central position in the cultural experiences of working-class children, are given lower academic status. Bourdieu argues that middle-class children arrive at school with a ready established bank of cultural attributes including the style of speech referred to as standard English. Bourdieu develops a Marxist influenced concept of 'cultural capital' to explain how the cultural dice are loaded in favour of the culturally dominant group or groups. Dominant culture is a set of properties, characteristics, behaviours, orientations that dominant class groups already have and that subordinate class groups must strive to acquire if they want to compete for educational success. This means there is much more cultural 'work' for working-class children in schools to do. The ingrained cultural characteristics of 'social-class dispositions' are usually acquired early in life. Schooling builds on the given cultural attributes of children. Middle-class children are already attuned to the codes and meanings of schooling, whereas for working-class children these are likely to be opaque.

For Bourdieu success in schooling is a matter of adopting a certain 'style' of being. The school reward system recognizes certain 'styles' positively and others negatively. The whole process of schooling, as well as the institutional habits and demands, are likely to be much less amenable to working-class children's culture than to middle-class children's culture. Social inequalities are not simply based on wealth. Bourdieu introduces the idea of cultural capital, the accumulation of cultural attributes that can be reinvested into education with a positive return for their holder. This form of 'capital' is visible in social habits, styles of speech, and modes of conduct that belong to the general way of being known as 'habitus'. 'Habitus' corresponds to the class/cultural environment of your upbringing. Middle-class children come to school well endowed with cultural capital which they can translate and transform through education into both social and economic capital. Middle-class children know more readily the styles of behaviour demanded of them in school. Middle-class children better understand how to speak, how to behave with books, how to sit at storytelling time and how to conduct themselves as good pupils in general. They know this not because they are more clever and adaptable but because the required modes of behaviour of the school are the modes of behaviour they are generally inducted into from the earliest age, and belong to their way of life. Middle-class children, therefore, have a built-in advantage as they are brought up with dominant culture and trained in its behaviour patterns. Through the various gradations of the education system they accumulate more cultural capital which later translates into wealth and power. Their academic success can be cashed in for a well-paid and high-status job (Bourdieu and Passeron, 1977). In later work, Bourdieu addressed questions and issues of culture, not necessarily in the context of schooling, and found that cultural practices, habits and preferences were expressions of ways of life of socially stratified groups of people. Cultural practices followed patterns of economic division of labour. Similarly, linguistic differences can be seen as expressions of different class orientations. Habits of speech, attitudes towards, and practices of, writing are differentiated in line with social class, economic and ethnic differences (Bourdieu, 1991).

Bowles and Gintis (1976) coined the infamous phrase 'hidden curriculum', expressing the idea that going to school is less about learning mathematics or literacy and more about learning how to behave, to conform and to accept your position in the order of things whatever it may turn out to be. The major study they produced, *Schooling in Capitalist America*, was initially an account of the failure of the school reform movement and of wave after wave of school reform legislation to alter the deep-seated, class-based patterns of achievement in American state schools. Bowles and Gintis give priority to the regulatory practices of the school: uniform, timekeeping, rowed seating in classrooms, rules for corridor movement, the countless injunctions to maintain order and so on. They point out the training in boredom represented by the majority of school time, spent on passively being instructed or in actively performing tasks that have no obvious meaning or visible use. They highlight the training in accepting relations of subordination. In all this the school forms a sound preparation for working life and prepares the majority of its pupils particularly well for a waged life working for a corporation or institution that will deploy similar tactics and practices for economic gain.

If these accounts of the school as a training in subordination and as culturally restricted and excluding environments make the sociology of education seem rather a serious pursuit, Paul Willis's (1979) amplification of the position expressed by Bowles and Gintis offers an often entertaining though not always comfortable account of school failure as a deliberately chosen option. Certain groups of pupils who have a strong sense of class cultural affiliation realistically weigh up the possibilities and make a more or less conscious decision in adolescence to eschew the value system of the school and to dedicate their energies to the varied practices of 'having a laff' and 'mucking about'. Willis's study of the mythical school of 'Hammertown' (based on a real case) provides a graphic illustration of how a segment of the school population can be seen making active decisions and constructing resistant practices in the face of Bowles and Gintis's grimly deterministic controlling school. The social consequences of the two positions are the same – 'working class kids get working-class jobs' as Willis memorably puts it. But Willis's account is at least enlivened by a sense of working class 'lads' exerting *agency* and being anything but passive dupes of an all controlling system. Nevertheless the lads fail at school and fail to achieve the possibilities for social advancement that liberal educators would say is at the heart of the comprehensive ideal of state schooling (Willis, 1979).

Conclusion

Education remains a contested field in which tensions exist between different ideologies and differently positioned groups. In the USA in recent times these tensions have come to the fore particularly in relation to the systemic disadvantage suffered by African-American pupils in schooling, a disadvantage that has a deep and abiding history (Delpit, 1995). Attempts to challenge this inequality by activists inside and outside education have focused, at least partly, but very significantly, on the culture and language of schooling. Questions of cultural authority, identity and representation, and knowledge and understanding have been powerfully addressed by post-structuralism, postmodernism, linguistics and cultural studies. Addressing these matters cannot change the social structures that schools operate within, but they can very importantly change the culture and practices of schooling, and make schools and education professionals more properly aware of the cultural power of the institution and its relations with changing forms of knowledge and being.

Others, however, have argued that schools remain an important vehicle for social transformation. Schools are important sites, according to this position, for the legitimation of inequality. They justify social stratification and legitimate success and failure, making them seem natural consequences of individual differences. While schools cannot cure social inequalities on their own, they must be seen as an important component of any strategy for social change (Karabel and Halsey, 1977). Stewart Ranson's recent work on 'voice' and community is one serious attempt among many to recover the 'true spirit' of the comprehensive ideal and to continue to work towards the unrealized, unfinished project of comprehensive community education (Ranson, 2000). In all of these positions, the question of 'achievement', failure, inclusion, exclusion, equality and inequality remains very much alive.

Student activities

1 Analyse your experiences of education using the different social perspectives of functionalism, Marxism, interactionism and postmodernism in turn. Share your accounts with those of other students.
2 Consider education as a vehicle for social reform. What different kinds of evidence can be gathered to support this view? What conclusions do your researches lead you to?

Recommended reading

Lowe, R. (1997) *Schooling and Social Change, 1964–1990*, London: Routledge. This book explores the history of education and the social effects of education at the level of policy and at the level of the curriculum. Examining the shifting trends in educational provision, rhetoric and practice, the book asks questions about equality of opportunity and keeps a sharp and critical focus on social factors that determine or influence differences. The book provides a critical account of the modern history of education and asks some serious questions about the future of state funded schooling.

Willis, P. (1979) *Learning to Labour*, Aldershot: Gator. This book is an ethnographic study of the culture of the school that explores the different value systems held by a group of 'lads' and the school authorities. It seeks to get inside the thinking of the lads and to understand their world picture and why it leads them to reject the official values of the school and to adopt a position of 'resistance'. Much of the book includes a good deal of lively and entertaining dialogue from interviews conducted with the lads and some transcripts of their exchanges with teachers. The book also includes some very dense theoretical material. It can be read in a number of ways.

7

The Influence of Social Factors on Achievement

Chapter 7 explores the relationship between social factors and achievement in education. While accepting that factors such as intelligence and motivation are important in the success of individuals, wider social influences have also been seen for many years as significant. Research findings relating to class, race and gender are examined using explanations from the perspectives discussed in the previous chapter. The issue of equality of opportunity, which is so often taken for granted, is challenged. The assumption that schooling is one of the main determinants of a pupil's success is questioned in relation to the influence of wider social factors. New research is discussed which points to the perpetuation of inequality. The impact on education of discourses of gender and race is evaluated and current topical issues such as concerns about boys' underachievement and school exclusion rates among African-Caribbean boys are discussed.

Introduction

The growth of concern with social factors and their relationship to educational achievement can be seen to correspond to the rise of policies of access and equality in western nation states. Perhaps the most significant and enduring achievement of recent studies in relation to social factors in education has been to put questions of class, culture, gender and ethnicity at the centre of descriptions of educational processes and institutions.

A number of questions arise. How might the specific practices of education be exclusive and excluding? In what ways do the everyday activities of the classroom, for instance, alienate children from various different types of background? What is the general culture of the school? How can it be described? How does it affect children from different backgrounds? At the centre of these lines of inquiry is the big question about whether education is doomed to replicate the inequalities in society or whether it can be an engine for challenging inequality and for promoting social justice.

The state of educational achievement

According to official statistics from the DfEE educational achievement has increased steadily during the last two decades. End of Key Stage assessment has shown an increase in pupil attainment in the core subjects of English, mathematics and science (DfEE, 2000a). At every level of academic attainment more people hold qualifications and fewer people hold no qualifications. Most young people (16–18) stay on in full-time education, 71 per cent in 1995 as opposed to 47 per cent in 1985 at age 16, 40 per cent as opposed to 17 per cent at 18 (DfEE, 1997a).

Educational achievement in higher education has also increased in the past decade. This has been accompanied by an increase in the number of students in higher education – since 1980 it has more than doubled. It might seem that the benefits of educational qualifications and access to higher education have been made available to the population as a whole. There is some truth in this, although what the figures mean in terms of patterns of inequality in society in general needs to be closely examined. More education for all does not necessarily mean more equal education. There are issues to confront about the distribution of education resources and benefits throughout the population. Inequalities in provision and achievement exist between individuals for a host of complex reasons but also, more significantly perhaps, between social groups and 'population categories'.

Pupils at different types of school achieve different levels of success in public examinations. Selective schools, whether in the private sector or the maintained sector, have much higher percentages of their pupils achieving top grades than comprehensive (non-selective) schools. Grant maintained (now foundation) schools also achieve greater success in public examinations than their LEA maintained equivalents (MacKinnon et al., 1999). In addition, there are large, and fairly abiding, patterns of inequality associated with specific social groups. Social class, gender and ethnic group have been and remain key factors of inequality in education. The interaction between these three factors produces an even more powerful set of inequalities for many children. 'All pupils have a gender, class and ethnic identity – the factors do not operate in isolation' (Gillborn and Mirza, 2000: 23).

Social class

Although social class is felt to be an important factor in educational achievement and has been on the 'agenda' of education studies for some time, it is not a category that is widely used in official statistics of education. Nevertheless, surveys which included class as a significant category have indicated that, by just about every criterion of achievement, middle-class pupils in maintained schools do better than working-class children. This imbalance was documented through a series of reports in the 1950s and 1960s when the question of class became a significant issue in education policy (Crowther Report, 1959; Gurney-Dixon Report, 1954; Newsom Report, 1963). These raised the issue of what kind of schooling was appropriate for a post-war democracy founded on ideals of social hope in which 'all our children' are cultivated to their fullest capacities (Jones, 2000).

It has been explained in Chapter 3 how the maintained education system developed from 'elementary' education through significant shifts occurring in 1902, 1944 and 1965. In 1907 legislation granted scholarships for elementary school children to attend grammar schools. The idea was to offer state intervention to allow bright working-class children access to grammar school education since the majority of children attending grammar schools were middle class and fee-paying. This situation remained in place until 1944 when working-class children had the opportunity to enter grammar schools via the 11-plus examination. Between 1920 and 1940 methods were developed for testing the 'inherent ability' of pupils in the belief that the population could be rationally divided into the able and the not so able. The tripartite system established from the 1944 (Butler) Education Act was founded on this belief in innate ability. Then, as now, fee-paying private schools and the more prestigious 'public' schools remained outside the system.

Although we may be tempted to assume that social change in the direction of equality has been significant, figures for Great Britain published in 1997 indicate that the link between social class, defined by parental occupation, remains strong. Seventy-nine per cent of 18-year-olds from 'social class I', the 'professional' class, were reported as participating in higher education as opposed to 12 per cent of 18-year-olds from 'social class VI', the unskilled manual class (GSS, 1997). While these figures represent a slight reduction of class differences in recent years, there remains a question about the 'currency' of higher education qualifications in the labour market. The sector expanded significantly in the early 1990s so more places became available. Statistics do not distinguish between institutions of different status but Oxford and Cambridge remain socially powerful and there exists an important social distinction between so-called new universities that were previously polytechnics and the established universities. These figures about social-class origins and higher education seem to confirm the view that occupational levels of parents affect educational attainment of their children.

While pupils in independent schools represent a small percentage of all school pupils, just 7 per cent in 1991–92, independent schools achieve higher levels of success in public examination than those in maintained comprehensive schools but lower than those at maintained selective schools. For example, 87 per cent of pupils in independent schools attain five or more passes at GCSE grades A–C compared with 44 per cent at maintained comprehensive schools and 95 per cent at maintained selective schools (DfEE, 1997a). Despite a general increase in GCSEs obtained at state schools, the gap between GCSE achievement of children from managerial/professional backgrounds and children from unskilled manual groups has widened in the past decade (Gillborn and Mirza, 2000). In 1988 52 per cent of the former group and 12 per cent of the latter group gained five or more GCSE grades A–C. In 1997 the proportions were 69 per cent and 20 per cent.

On the whole it can be seen that British society cannot be regarded as meritocratic in relation to educational opportunities across classes. Education may influence the class position of individuals but class background itself is very important in determining levels of success in education.

Gender

Levels of GCSE achievement have been improving in recent years. The proportion of pupils gaining five or more higher grade passes (A–C) has risen dramatically during the 1990s to 47.9 per cent in 1999 (Gillborn and Mirza, 2000). The overall improvements are almost entirely due to changing success rates in state maintained schools. The same research indicates that girls have improved at a faster rate than boys (Gillborn and Gipps, 1996; Gillborn and Mirza, 2000).

Currently, it is the case that girls do better than boys overall in school examinations at all levels. Girls are outperforming boys at both GCSE and at A level (Gillborn and Mirza, 2000; GSS, 1997). However, differences in achievement do not favour girls in all cases uniformly across subjects (Arnot, 1998). Girls do achieve higher numbers of passes in some subjects and boys achieve higher numbers in others. At GCSE girls do better in English, history and French but do worse in mathematics and physics, for example (DfEE, 1997a). At A level, girls do significantly better in English and French and obtain significantly fewer passes in mathematics and physics (DfEE, 1997a). In all three end of Key Stage assessments girls are currently outperforming boys in English (DfEE, 2000a).

Broad evidence confirms the now widely held view that girls achieve at higher levels than boys in schools and it is interesting to note the extent to which this has captured the media's imagination. It is also worth noting, however, that in some schools boys' achievement has been higher than girls' and these exceptions perhaps provide a challenge to the norm. The data from these schools have come to light through the collecting of evidence by QUASE (Quantitative Assessment in Secondary Education) and YELLIS (Year 11 Information Service). Studies of such schools are attempting to define what it is about them that challenges the general pattern. Such aberrations provide a useful reminder that quantitative data often need to be made sense of by reference to 'qualitative' analysis. Only by examining the practices and the cultures of such schools can the nature of differences be illuminated and practices be challenged and changed.

Since 1996 there are virtually equal numbers of men and women in full-time higher education in the UK, though women outnumber men among part-time students (GSS, 1997). Women obtain marginally more first degrees than men, and men achieve marginally more higher degrees than women. In spite of the strong tendency for overall levels of achievement for girls to be improving, it remains the case that gender imbalances in 'influential occupations' remain weighted in favour of men. This may have a number of causes and indicates a remaining deep gender bias in society as a whole that cannot be accessed simply by reference to statistics but that needs to be addressed through matters of social practices and culture. The 'common-sense' correlation between educational success and levels of occupational success needs to be reviewed in the light of this fact.

Ethnic groups

Performance at GCSE examinations at 16 shows widespread overall improvements but not all pupils have shared equally in this trend. In many LEAs the gap between the highest and the lowest achieving groups has increased, in fact. It is more difficult to get hold of information about educational differences between ethnic groups as ethnic differences are not categories used in national collections and publications of official statistics on educational achievement. Achievement according to ethnic difference varies also according to class.

Concern for the educational performance of ethnic minority groups was expressed in the government-sponsored Swann Committee report, *Education for All* (DES, 1985b), which indicated that, overall, ethnic minority groups did less well in education in the maintained sector. The report also found important differences between ethnic minority groups. From a survey of five LEAs, it was found that pupils of Asian background did almost as well as whites or 'others', as they were identified in the report, at GCE O level or CSE in terms of achieving five or more graded results. The average performance of pupils from African-Caribbean backgrounds was considerably lower than white pupils. Only 5 per cent of the pupils of African-Caribbean background passed an A level and only 1 per cent went to university.

More recent research (Jones, 1993) indicates that members of ethnic minority groups are more likely to stay on in full-time education between the ages of 16 and 19 than are whites. Quoting the statistics from the *Labour Force Survey* for 1988–90, 37 per cent of whites, 43 per cent of those of African-Caribbean background, 66 per cent of those of African-Asian background and 58 per cent of those of Indian background were in full-time education (Jones, 1993). While this may seem a positive statistic, Jones suggests that the greater tendency for ethnic minority young people to stay in education is partly due to difficulties in gaining employment in the labour market where racism and discrimination are still common.

Some common patterns of GCSE higher-grade passes emerge in UK state schools (Youth Cohort Study conducted for DfEE, 1999c). Percentage improvements in the GCSE achievements of pupils in African-Caribbean, Indian, Pakistani and Bangladeshi groups has been greater than that of white pupils in recent years, but it is important to note that the gap between attainment of white pupils and African-Caribbean pupils has grown overall in the last decade (Gillborn and Mirza, 2000). Pupils of Indian background achieve more highly on average than their white counterparts and by comparison with pupils from other South Asian backgrounds. Pupils of Pakistani background tend to achieve less well than white and Indian pupils. Pupils of Bangladeshi background have achieved less well than those of other ethnic groups on the whole although in the past two years their attainment of higher-grade GCSE passes has risen by more percentage points than any other ethnic group. Pupils of African-Caribbean background have not shared equally in generally rising rates of educational achievement. In many LEAs their average achievements are significantly lower than other groups. Recent research in Birmingham, however, has indicated that African-Caribbean pupils attain higher levels of achievement in Key Stage 1 tests and yet achieve considerably less well in GCSE (Gillborn and Gipps, 1996). Reported again in 1998, this trend still persisted (Gillborn and Mirza, 2000).

Patterns of inequality persist, but can be difficult to interpret. Statistical information does not speak for itself. An interesting case study, conducted by Ghaill (1992) in Birmingham in the late 1980s, questioned the nature and extent of racism and racial difference in the education system specifically from the point of view of the ethnic minorities concerned. The students interviewed referred to the pervasive racism of British society in relation to immigration laws, housing and labour markets but varied in their accounts and assessment of racism in education. Some who felt that education was structurally racist and had experienced negative attitudes in school nevertheless persevered with their studies and were 'successful' in conventional academic terms.

Some important conclusions can be drawn from this brief overview (see Gillborn and Mirza, 2000):

1 Despite the great interest in girls generally achieving better than boys, the gender gap is considerably smaller than the inequalities associated with ethnic origin and social-class background.
2 There are persistent underlying ethnic inequalities which indicate that African-Caribbean, Bangladeshi and Pakistani pupils do not enjoy equal opportunities. This places these pupils at a disadvantage in future education and work and increases the likelihood of social and economic exclusion in later life.
3 Inequality in GCSE achievement has increased in recent years for African-Caribbean and Pakistani pupils.

Research into differential achievement

Race and gender were very much on the political programme of education in the 1980s, in the form of equal opportunities policies, multiculturalism and anti-racism, following the Sex Discrimination Act (1975) and the Swann Report (DES, 1985b). These policies engaged with important questions about education, in relation to identity, the formal structures of knowledge and institutions, and about equal opportunities and achievement. Inequalities in education are still rife, however, and have been scrutinized within a number of studies in recent years (see Gaine and George, 1998, for a summary of this research).

Studies of race and ethnicity

The influence of ethnic difference on levels of achievement in state schooling systems remains one of the great scandals of contemporary western-style state education systems.

One of the problems of beginning in this area is the problem of the term 'race'. As post-structuralist perspectives will indicate, the word 'race' is not, and cannot be, innocent. It is imbued with the history of colonialism and carries connotations of difference that can be dangerously essentialist. Differences of race are often conceived of, and deployed, as though they are biological differences. This position has been radically challenged, not just by philosophers and sociologists, but also by geneticists in recent times and with human genome discoveries particularly. Steve Jones, eminent geneticist, declares that ideas about 'race' differences have no scientific basis. Human beings according to Jones are much more biologically homogeneous than other species. 'If you were a snail it would make good biological sense to be a racist' (see 'We are all cousins under the skin', Jones, *Independent*, 12 December 1991). Race is associated with some of the worst atrocities of the twentieth century. It is well known that Nazi views on race were frequently backed up by 'scientists' who strove to demonstrate the biological inferiority of the Jewish race and the superiority of the so-called 'Aryan' race (Sereny, 2000).

The term 'race', then, has to be used with caution, provisionally and always under qualification. It has been closely associated at times with the term 'ethnicity' which signifies more the cultural differences between groups of people. Both terms, 'race' and 'ethnicity', are significantly loaded in social terms and carry with them important considerations for education particularly in the area of inequality. Issues of race and ethnicity give rise to important questions about schools as cultural environments. Schools very obviously are places where power relations exist and define what counts as knowledge, learning and culture. How much do schools and the processes of schooling either replicate or challenge inequalities and prejudices in the wider social context?

The idea that education is, in some simple and obvious way, a route towards social advancement is what the sociology of education has been at pains to critically examine. The idea is seriously threatened by the statistics cited earlier in this chapter which clearly indicated that black children of African-Caribbean origin leave with the poorest examination results and thus have acquired less cultural capital and enter the labour market less well qualified than any other group. In spite of radical improvements in race relations in the USA since the 1960s, black Americans continue to 'lag in school performance' quite significantly (Ogbu, 1994). To get to the causes of these alarming statistics it is necessary to examine how matters of ethnic difference and 'race' interact with educational opportunity. This issue is complicated by other social considerations, such as the fact that there is an 'ethnic-penalty' factor incurred by ethnic minority groups in the job market. The degree of penalty varies across different ethnic groups (Brennan and McGreevor, 1990).

Clearly, this flies in the face of the idea that the key social processes of selection for social advancement or 'upward mobility' should be determined by meritocratic principles. Some commentators have consequently decried the idea of meritocracy and its relations with post-Second World War education as a myth (Goldthorpe, 1996; Hayek, 1976). According to some researches racial inequality persists because changes have occurred mainly in one aspect of racial stratification, that is, barriers in opportunity structure, but not in other domains. The implication here is that racial stratification is related to, but different from, class stratification. Definitions of social stratification refer to the arrangement of social groups or social categories in a hierarchical order of subordination and domination in which some groups so organized have unequal access to the fundamental resources of society (Tuden and Plotnikov, 1970). A conservative, functionalist point of view may take these differences and inequalities as inevitable, but it is hard to see how it is possible to justify or explain away the radical differences in levels of opportunity sustained by different racial and ethnic groups in different nation states. Much research into inequality in education has been concerned to reveal and address the root causes of inequalities, rather than simply to explain and accept them. Marxist and other structurally oriented perspectives on society will see them as the inevitable but unacceptable consequences of the division of labour and the unequal distribution of economic and cultural capital.

This means that some people, by virtue of belonging to a certain group, have almost unimpaired access to the strategic resources while some other people, by virtue of belonging to other social groups, have various impediments in their access to the same strategic or fundamental resources. In addition, different groups in the social hierarchy are separated by cultural and other distinctions that serve to maintain social distance between them. This differentiated opportunity system is usually supported by ideological explanations for the differences which seek to naturalize them or to make them seem almost normal or inevitable. These can be both popular and scientific. There are several types of stratification in societies. These can be organized according to class, gender, ethnicity, age and caste.

In the Marxist view, social class refers to a group's relation to the 'means of production' – to how goods are produced, who owns what and who has access to the profits of production. Classic Marxism tends to privilege the importance of the group's relations with the means of production seeing as it does the economic base as determining the social and cultural superstructure. Racial stratification, however, also depends on other factors, although economic factors are critically involved. Racial stratification operates by consciously and unconsciously, explicitly and inexplicitly, assigning different status values to people according to racial or ethnic identities. Racial categories, moreover, tend to be more fixed than social-class categories because of the traditions of non-mobility that exist. This can be illustrated by the fact that for over 100 years after the emancipation of slaves in the USA black Americans have endured a period of social 'summation'. In other words their occupational roles and educational opportunities were defined in terms of their membership of a racially subordinated group rather than in terms of individual attributes or capacities. While in the USA black Americans have to some extent entered higher social strata, this has tended to be through professions that primarily served the needs of the black community: the law, teaching, medicine, business and preaching. They remained largely excluded from other higher-paying, higher-status professions such as architecture, civil engineering, accounting, chemistry and management. In the USA the legacy of slavery and the ghettoization of black communities in urban centres were influential factors in creating systematic poverty and lack of advancement through education.

Correlational studies indicate that children achieve in school according to how their social class and cultural backgrounds meet with the value and social systems of schools. The problem with this position in the context of race, however, is the fact that they cannot explain how children from similar social-class backgrounds but from racially different backgrounds statistically achieve at very different levels from one another. In one study in the USA it was found that black children of higher social and economic status still fared less well than white children of lower social status (Ogbu, 1997). A great deal of research has confirmed this alarming pattern. White children whose parents have little educational success will still achieve more than black children at the same school whose parents have experienced some success. The same pattern, however, does not follow with other ethnic minority groups.

Ogbu (1997: 773) defines the 'school-performance gap' in terms of:

1 Societal educational politics and practices, including unequal resources, segregation ensuring blacks do not receive equal education in terms of both quantity and quality.
2 The perception of black students in schools, including cultural, linguistic and intellectual denigration.
3 Community forces: black people's own perceptions of, and responses to, schooling, and the context of their overall experience of social subordination.

According to Ogbu, black Americans are not merely passive victims helpless in the face of racial subordination and the study is at pains to point out the 'well-documented history of their collective struggle' (Ogbu, 1997: 773). When black Americans did not perceive that significant numbers of their communities were achieving social advancement through education, their reaction was varied but coherent. While popular black conceptions of social advancement (in television programmes such as *The Cosby Show*) may include reference to education, many black Americans do not accept this idea at face value. It is measured against their more common perceptions of education as denying real opportunities, of the dice being loaded against them. As a consequence in many communities there is no developed black 'effort optimism'. Ogbu defines this position in terms of its being a reasoned and perfectly rational response to a negative position. An important factor is how young black Americans perceive and make sense of cultural and language differences they encounter in and through the school. The cultural linguistic environment of the school often collides with collective identity that has community resonances and that is rooted also in survival strategies (Smitherman, 2000). For some black youths accepting school values was an affront to self-respect as academic effort and participation is equated with a denial of black cultural identity (Labov, 1972a).

Race as an issue in British education can be seen against a historical background of immigration and eugenic ideas. Ethnic minority groups were variously regarded as problematic, either in terms of their being in the country in the first place, or in terms of their 'integration' into British society. By the early 1970s 'multiculturalism' had become established as a kind of educational orthodoxy, strongly promoted by the DES (Gaine, 1995). The Bullock Report was multiculturalist in many of its recommendations about language and culture and 'the home' (Bullock Report, 1975). The 1977 DES Green Paper proclaimed a pluralist view of contemporary society as multiracial and multicultural. Key local authorities, including the Inner London Education Authority (ILEA), implemented multicultural policies at the same time. There was even an attempt to import teachers from the Indian subcontinent and an explicit attempt to enlist African-Caribbean teachers into the profession (Ghuman, 1995).

A crisis was precipitated by the disaffection of black youth symbolized in disturbances in 1981 in urban centres in England. The crisis raised some awkward issues in relation to race and education, and confronted liberal 'consensus' views with some difficult facts and positions. Multicultural programmes came to be seen as naive and inadequate, largely in terms of how they ignored institutional racism in education (Williams, 1981). Some even suggested multiculturalism was itself racist and a cause of disaffection (Mullard, 1981). It was argued that multiculturalism was nothing more than a form of social control, a misguided form of tokenism designed to integrate rather than to enable serious cultural differences to be properly expressed. In spite of these protests, multiculturalism remained (and remains) a position adopted by institutions at different levels of the education system. Crucial government-sponsored reports including Rampton (DES, 1981) and Swann (DES, 1985b) backed multicultural education as the proper means towards a multicultural society, although both favoured anti-racist initiatives in schools. The process of change that has occurred since 1988 involving competition between schools for places, OFSTED reports and the publication of 'league tables'of examination results, has ensured that the curriculum remains ethnocentric in orientation and that anti-racist initiatives cannot occupy a central position in public education agendas.

Meanwhile, the 1981 Nationality Act betrayed much central government education attitude and policy. Ministers ignored or rejected elements of Rampton and Swann which emphasized anti-racism because it was considered to be against 'our fundamental values and institutions' (Grosvenor, 1994). Popular fears were played on by the tabloid press and exacerbated by a further round of disturbances in 1985. New right think tanks and policy groups placed 'Englishness' high on their agendas. In 1988 further restrictive legislation on immigration was passed. A new 'debate' was constructed around nationalism and national identity that became reflected in some of the emphases of the 1988 Education Reform Act itself – a reversion to fairly traditional notions of language and literature in English, an emphasis on 'Christian' assemblies and the abolition of the ILEA (Gaine, 1995). A number of campaigns appeared in the popular press to deny the wisdom of anti-racist initiatives, culminating perhaps in Margaret Thatcher's famous question: 'What is anti-racist mathematics, anyway?'

Grosvenor claims that education policy has systematically followed the state's construction of black people as problematic since the early 1960s (Grosvenor, 1995). The effect of persistent failure of policy to address structural racism combined with economic and social marginalization has been 'to alienate and marginalize black youth within the education system' and also to 'generate significant contrasts in employment opportunities' (Lowe, 1997: 128). The relative success of some ethnic minority groups opened up prospects of social advancement through education but overall the pattern of underrepresentation in higher education has persisted, echoing the North American experience, with inevitable economic and social consequences. There is a double penalty here as those African-Caribbean youths who do not attain access to higher education are likewise subject to discriminatory practices when it comes to getting and keeping employment.

Lisa Delpit has described the more or less systematic, though often unconscious, denigration of black culture and identity in education and seeks to address this by an equally systematic restoration and positive reconstruction of the value of black identity. Delpit is also anxious to listen to the voices in black communities, even when they are not saying the kinds of things that politically aware black educators might want to hear. In recent times there has been a tendency among black educators working in the field of culture to draw on the rich resources of black popular culture to engage students' interests and to redefine the relations between teachers and learners, the school and the minority individual and group. This has meant addressing questions about the cultural authority of the curriculum. In the UK context, commentators have noted that the National Curriculum itself is guilty of cultural bias likely to disadvantage ethnic minority children (Troyna and Carrington, 1990). Others have noted the tendencies in the National Curriculum to represent an exclusive and excluding ethnocentric view of the world (McNeil, 1988). The most radical critique of education in the British context on race grounds has come from Bernard Coard who claims that the education system actually promotes the denigration of black children. This occurs through attitudes expressed in the processes of education about speech, the inbuilt racism of common forms of language which are not dealt with, the denial of black existence in the contents of the curriculum and the failure to tackle generally racist attitudes that are explicit outside of the institutions of education and implicitly accepted within them (Coard, 1971). A study conducted in British inner-city primary schools by Cecile Wright (1992) found that, while teachers were concerned about equality of opportunity, the practices of the institutions often worked against it. The study found that Asian girls received a good deal less of the teacher's time than other pupils and African-Caribbean boys received a disproportionate amount of negative attention from teachers. Wright et al. (1999) and Majors (2000) have reported on the worrying phenomenon of disproportionately high school exclusion rates among African-Caribbean boys in the UK and USA. These experiences could be crucial to further developments within the education system for the groups and individuals involved.

To understand the issues involved in questions of race it is important to explore the field within which education operates. This means understanding what the issues are for contemporary cultural politics. Recent theories represent some significant shifts in how we can think about the relations between culture, identity, institutions and practices. The idea of globalization, for instance, has impacted on how we understand the nature of contemporary societies, nations and peoples. The facts of post-colonial global migrations remain significant in the cultural and educational landscape where communities with different value systems, forms of identity and social practices may live side by side with one another, mingle and interact. Abdullah Sahin has explored the business of identity formation in relation to Moslem youth in Birmingham, asking questions about how this complex process engages with processes of education. The findings of this study are challenging and suggest that identity formation is actually much more fluid and dynamic than common-sense notions would suggest. The implications of Sahin's study also indicate that education could play a more active and positive role in providing opportunities, experiences and structures for a range of different cultural identities to find positive expression (Sahin, 2000). The post-colonial legacy has given rise to what has been referred to as the postmodern condition, the idea of a world without fixed bearings, where the old grand narratives and big explanations no longer apply and where cultural intermingling is the order of the day. It is in this shifting and uncertain world that education must operate to manage knowledge, conduct, culture and values. Failure to engage with and positively recognize different identities may result in the continuation of damaging inequalities.

Accounts of gender

We are all gendered subjects living within a world where gender is being represented in different ways all the time. Questions about gender enter into education in all contexts at all levels, whether in terms of how many girls get science qualifications at 16+, how many women physics teachers or secondary headteachers there are, how many men train to be primary teachers, how women get represented in set Shakespeare texts in the English National Curriculum or what reading practices are encouraged in relation to gender.

In the 1970s and 1980s there was much research into how the social processes of education led to discrimination on the basis of gender. Oakley (1975) looked at the socialization of young children and how they acquire their gender roles from home, school and peers. Children learn gender expectations from the society surrounding them and these lessons are reinforced through play. Whyte (1983) looked at gender stereotyping and bias in the primary school curriculum. This was displayed through reading schemes and lesson content that emphasized the different positions of men and women in society. Sharpe (1976) considered the influence of gender stereotypes in secondary schools and how this encouraged teenage girls to behave in 'feminine' ways and to develop gendered career aspirations. Spender (1982) investigated interaction in the classroom, language and the curriculum. She noted the marginal position of girls in the classroom and the message this gave about their future roles in society. Strategies were developed to make the curriculum more girl-friendly in response to such concerns. Murphy and Gipps (1996) have suggested that although these worked for many, mainly middle-class, girls, they have been singularly unsuccessful for a great many others and, in fact, have provoked a male backlash.

Feminism is the name roughly given to various movements that have sought to put questions about gender and equality on the agenda of public life. Feminism has been particularly powerful in challenging and rethinking education practices. It is not, in spite of how it is represented (or misrepresented, often), a singular and fixed position, set of beliefs or values. It does represent a general trend that offers a shift in perception and thinking, though. Liberal feminism came to promote the idea that individual women should be as free as men to determine their own social political roles. This position contends that laws should protect rights, freedoms and equal opportunities. Liberal feminists believe reforms can be achieved through democratic processes and gradual shifts rather than revolutionary changes in economic, social and cultural life.

What came to be known as 'second wave feminism' was influenced by Friedan's *The Feminine Mystique* (1963), civil rights and anti-Vietnam campaigns in the USA and ideas derived from Marxism. Firestone's (1970) the *Dialectic of Sex* sought to redefine society in terms of a sex/class system, proposing a feminist 'revolution'. Clearly this radical reinterpretation must have serious and far-reaching consequences for education. If there is systemic injustice then the whole system is likely to stand in need of critique. Out of radical feminism the concept of 'patriarchy', the structural inequality of gender, became a cornerstone of modern feminist thought used to account for women's oppression throughout society. In this sense, modern feminism had much in common with Marxism. The upshot of this position is that patriarchy is seen to operate at all levels of society and that it is vital to recognize the 'universal oppression of women' (Millett, 1971). We can see how this radical feminist position would see inequalities at work in the curriculum, the social order of the institution, in the culture and even in the very language of education.

From radical feminism came the idea of consciousness-raising. To become aware of the effects of patriarchy, and to liberate themselves, women need to undergo a process of education or re-education. This position gave rise to new forms of knowledge as well as new educational perspectives. In academic contexts, women's studies courses began to appear. Feminist perspectives became influential in literary studies, in media studies, cultural studies, history and in other established and emerging discourses of education and knowledge. Feminism drew on powerful new theories of subjectivity and contributed significantly to theoretical developments. Chris Weedon's *Feminist Practice and Poststructuralist Theory* (1987), for example, provided a neat exemplification of the uses of post-structuralist theory in the textual and subject politics of gender (Weedon, 1987). Through the carefully thought-out application of new theories of identity and meaning, conventional readings could be disrupted, established reading practices could be challenged, the language of patriarchy could be exposed and questions asked about the effects of certain kinds of knowledge and representation and of certain kinds of reading practices (those that were 'gender-blind', for instance).

Second-wave feminism generated both a general intellectual and political movement (Rowbotham, 1989). A cluster of issues arose from the determination of women's groups to create new forms of knowledge on areas of gendered experience: sexuality, pornography, media representations, pay and other workplace inequalities, childcare, violence and many others. These issues were often dealt with through interventionist strategies rather than through the formal channels of representation. The personal became the political. During this period it can be said that gender politics were seen to be at work in all walks of life, both formal and informal: in the school, in the factory and in the family. Radical feminism sought to challenge practices at all levels of society and also to challenge habitual ways of seeing, feeling and knowing in all spheres of social activity (Mitchell and Oakley, 1986).

Different perspectives gradually emerged to challenge both liberal and radical feminism. Socialist forms of feminist thought appeared, producing new relations between different discourses such as feminism and Marxism (Barrett, 1980). The complex interplay between gender, culture and society was explored through new models and methods, and with new research agendas. Marxism applied to gender inequality could expose the material and historical basis of capitalism's patriarchal division of labour. According to some Marxist feminists, gender and class are very closely related locations of inequality within capitalism (Macdonald, 1981). An important movement came in the form of black feminism. Their critique, based on triple oppression of black women through the triad of race, class and gender, included new emphasis on economic and social oppression and exclusions. Black feminists have been critical of any feminism not centrally aware of racism, critical, also, of the (allegedly) uncomplicated notion of patriarchy that does not account for the different position of black men within relations of oppression, for instance. Identity politics emerges from this mingling of discourses, organized around a specific form of oppression, but also asking questions about what is it that makes us what we are. Inevitably, some feminists begin to reinterpret education and to critique education from the specific point of view of 'a background of colonialism and imperialism' (Brah and Minhas, 1985). These perspectives afforded a new kind of cultural focus: institutions, knowledge, ideology and language, all vital components of education, could be viewed differently from the perspective of feminist thought.

Post-structuralist and postmodernist ideas have also been extensively deployed by feminists in descriptions and analyses of patriarchy and women's oppressions, especially in terms of how these positions challenge universalist, foundationalist and absolutist theories of knowledge. An anti-fundamentalist mentality emerged ready to take on the old rationalism and theoretical objectivity that was seen as complicit with patriarchy and all its problems and oppressions. A new emphasis is put on positionality as a conditioning factor of being and knowing. What you see, what you know, what you think and how you understand things depend significantly on where you are positioned in the order of things. This implies a very different kind of epistemology, or theory of knowledge, which is anti-essentialist. It challenges fixed positions, fights against the belief that things are as they are because they must be so, or because biology decrees it should be so. This tendency of thought is very congenial to the view of gender differences as being socially constructed and therefore open to both deconstruction and reconstruction.

Poststructuralist feminism is thus concerned with constructing new ways of seeing and knowing. In this sense post-structuralism's anti-essentialism, which is often represented as an ethically vacuous position, is a very positive way of examining and redefining a politics concerned with ideology, institutions and practices. In the emphasis given to differences it enables the possibility of formulating different ways of thinking about and engaging in critical practices. Identity politics is concerned with the shifting and contested nature of gender identity where subjectivity is being contested constantly (Weedon, 1987).

The implications of feminism for education are thus many and varied. Just as there are different positions within the feminist movement, so there will be different interpretations, practices and strategies within the field of education. Coffrey and Delamont (2000) contend that a feminist analysis of everyday classroom life is highly relevant in determining the extent to which women teachers have contributed to theoretical and practical aspects of teaching. The gender politics of education has thus become an established discourse. This can be seen in some legislation and in equal opportunities and feminist critiques that have infiltrated, or partially infiltrated, certain institutional practices (Lowe, 1997). All these developments indicate a partial shift in consciousness and in social practices. The feminist movement can be said to have opened up the issue of gender, not just indicating the obvious inequalities, but indicating, too, the cultural politics of gender in the institutions of education. The arbitrary exertion of patriarchal power in staffroom relations or in the very organization and ingrained habits of the curriculum remains a live issue. (See Arnot, 2000 for a feminist critique of educational policy over the past two decades.)

The underachievement of boys has recently given rise to growing concern in Britain. This issue of the relationship between education and masculinity has emerged as a significant discourse in public and academic arenas (see, for example, Francis, 2000, or Gilbert and Gilbert, 1998). Some have suggested a crisis of masculinity in relation to changing patterns of work, where certain forms of masculine identity could find expression. In addition, changing domestic arrangements where male roles are no longer as solidified as in the immediate post-Second World War period, are cited as being implicated (Mac an Ghaill, 1994). Paechter (1998), however, has suggested that despite improvements in girls' academic success, their education remains subordinated to that of boys. Murphy and Gipps (1996) suggest that the recent pattern of boys' lower examination achievement may be due to their learning approaches not being catered for in current pedagogical practice. This issue was touched upon in relation to teacher perceptions of boys' behaviour in Chapter 4. Some have suggested that it may be helpful to use a range of learning strategies to cater for the needs of different individuals regardless of gender, ethnic background and class.

The impact of discourses of gender on education has been far-reaching and profound, raising questions about all aspects of practice. Feminism has enjoyed a relatively high profile and has influenced education at many levels, from the curriculum to policy. But while recognizing the changes that discourses of gender have wrought in education practices, there remains a need to be cautious about the operating power that they have won which may often be 'disappointingly small' (Halsey et al., 1997). It is interesting and somehow predictable that the academic references that give some supposed guarantee of 'truth' in this chapter and this book as a whole will be dominated by the names of men. Questions about sexuality are interestingly absent from almost all policy discussions about citizenship in education, except in the form of sex education. There are serious questions to ask about how schools and the curriculum deal with gay and lesbian identities. There are few schools in England, for instance, that will offer explicit support to gay and lesbian pupils.

Conclusion

There is no doubt that the processes and effects of education can and do influence the life opportunities of individuals and particular social groups. In the past, alternative forms of education were openly provided for different social groups. It seemed reasonable to educate the children of the labouring classes to fulfil their future roles effectively. Likewise the sons of the middle classes needed to be equipped to take decisions fitting to their future station in life. Economic life and working conditions have changed greatly and today the emphasis is more on equality of opportunity and the adaptability of the workforce. But inequalities in education persist with the continued failure and effective exclusion of significant sections of the population.

Rising GCSE and A level results, increasing percentages of pupils staying in full-time education post-16, improved performance at all levels by females and ethnic minorities, and greater participation in further and higher education all seem to point to the opening up of opportunity. However, the continued development of specialist schools such as city technology colleges (CTCs) and grammar schools at the expense of comprehensive education, the problems of multiple deprivation faced by pupils from the poorest areas, the disproportionately high school exclusion rates and low GCSE results of African-Caribbean pupils, evidence of a deterioration in the motivation and achievement of boys in school, the abolition of student grants and the introduction of university fees, and the widening gap between the regional universities and the older elite research-based universities all seem to point to a perpetuation of inequalities.

These facts cannot be attributed solely to individual causes, to the failure of particular pupils, schools or teachers. They belong to the structures of schooling and are 'systemic'. These 'facts' about the school have been powerfully demonstrated and analysed in the past, often by Marxist influenced studies that have seen a 'correspondence' between inequalities in the social system at large and inequalities in the education system.

Student activities

1 Consider each of the following:
   (a) *Equal opportunities*. What are the principles that inform this idea? When did this idea become powerful in relation to education? Find evidence to support a new focus on equal opportunities in education.
   (b) *The various institutional locations of education*. What are their characteristic features? How might these enhance or inhibit the development of individuals and groups of learners?

Recommended reading

Delpit, L. (1995) *Other People's Children: Cultural Conflict in the Classroom*, New York: The New Press. This book explores the business of education from the point of view of the African-American experience. The underachievement of African-Americans in the education system is examined in terms of the cultural politics of teaching and learning. The book provides a powerful explanation for underachievement but also provides a set of ideas and proposals to redress the educational underachievement of African-Americans. From the outset, the business of teaching and learning is embedded in its social context.

Gaine, C. (1995) *Still No Problem Here*, Stoke-on-Trent: Trentham Books. This book explores the phenomenon of institutional racism in education and proposes methods for confronting the cultural biases that give rise to educational failure. It explores how racism and unproductive practices can be ingrained in the culture of institutions and makes proposals to address questions of race and ethnic difference in education. The book provides a useful introduction to some of the central and critical questions about education in an ethnically, culturally varied society.

8

Politics and Policy in Education

Having considered the way beliefs inform explanations of the nature and purpose of education and a range of theories for the differential achievement of pupils and students, we turn to the relationship between policy and political ideologies in education. Chapter 8 gives a historical overview showing the development of the state education system in England since the Second World War showing how policy in education is influenced by the constant interaction and struggle between differing sets of beliefs and wider political circumstances. The post-war political consensus during a period of reconstruction, the expansion in education and the growth of the comprehensive movement are outlined. The disillusionment which arose during the time of economic crisis in the 1970s is discussed. The development of a policy of market forces and, paradoxically, the increasing control of central government during the Conservative administrations of the 1980s and the first half of the 1990s is contrasted with the development of 'third way' politics by Labour in the second half of the 1990s. The influence of political ideologies on education is well illustrated through this analysis.

Introduction

Previous chapters have indicated that the development and organization of systems of education is not a straightforward matter. Education is not a neutral concept. We may wish for the development of 'the good society' but what this actually looks like and how we get there can be viewed very differently. A 'good society' may be based on the discipline and order shown by citizens or it may be a result of the freedom of all to develop themselves or a combination and balance of both of these things. Consider how often pupils are subjected to punishments and controls to make them comply, yet are also encouraged to question and explore. The purposes of education may be broadly agreed as developing minds, imparting significant knowledge, ensuring the continuation of social order and preparing young people for future employment. However, constructing the detail of an educational experience is a highly problematized, political activity.

Chapter 3 has shown how educators must grapple with issues of curriculum content and pedagogy. What must be taught and also, perhaps, what is best avoided? For instance, what do we tell young people about drugs and sex? Do we allow wide-ranging discussion on such topics in our schools? Which teaching styles and techniques are most effective? Should the emphasis be on disciplined learning or freedom to explore? Drawing back from the detail, it is also necessary to engage with issues about the universal nature of education. What aspects should be for all citizens? Will they be compulsory? If so, for how many years shall people be expected to study? Is the education provided different for different sections of the population? If so, in what ways and how is the populace to be divided? Is it to be paid for by the state or the individual? The answer to this final question may depend upon whether society or the individual is deemed to be the beneficiary. The circumstances an individual is born into can clearly be very important in determining subsequent educational experience.

Kelly (1999) suggests that education is a political activity whereby society prepares its young for adult life. Education and politics are 'inextricably interwoven' and it is not possible to discuss education without considering the political environment: 'The political context, then, is a major element in any scheme or system of education, and one without reference to which such a scheme cannot be properly understood, or, indeed, planned' (Kelly, 1999: 165). The history of the development of any education system illustrates competing views as to the purposes of education and how these are best met. These views are very much linked to how individuals would like to see their society develop (see Chapter 1 for a discussion of ideology in education). As education has to be paid for and may affect the quality of a future workforce, any system has to be seen in relation to the economy. Identifying who possesses the power to make decisions which bring about change is important and not always so clear cut.

The influence of different groups of people varies over time and, as education is clearly a central concern in our society, it is always an important national issue. Marsh (1997) suggests that the education received is a result of a complex relationship between decision-makers, stakeholders and other influences, in which no one group is in total control. We must not assume that because politicians pass a national curriculum that it will be interpreted in the same way by all of those operating at different levels of its delivery. He also suggsts that it is naive to assume that teachers have ever been in total control of the classroom. They are affected by forces outside the classroom as well as by the pupils within.

When examining the development of education systems some significant questions to be answered are: who decides what is to be taught, how it is to be taught and to whom? To illustrate we will look at the recent history of one part of the education system in England. In examining the compulsory sector (primary and secondary education) we will be able to see the effects of differing ideological beliefs and the pressure these bring to bear on the political process. Clearly any particular 'slant' placed on the telling of these developments may reflect the ideologies and backgrounds of the authors. Particular events may often be interpreted in various ways. We have made decisions, based on wider academic readings, about what to include as important in this brief historical analysis, and therefore what to leave out. Thus this history also reflects the beliefs of other authors concerning what education 'should' be about.

The 1944 Education Reform Act: towards reconstruction and consensus

The account will start as politicians in the depths of war consider the peace to come. The vision was to create a prosperous, thriving society. How to do this and what it would look like was seen differently by politicians of the left and the right. Whatever the political perspective, education was to play an important part in realizing the dream. In Chapter 3 we described the 1944 Education Act as a great political moment. As we saw, the Act enabled the introduction of the tripartite system of secondary education. In terms of the division of responsibility for the new national education system which the Act created there was a 'balance of control' (Coulby, 1989) between central government, local government and the schools. This system of checks and balances has been portrayed as a period of consensus or, alternatively, a triangle of tension between state, LEAs and teachers, which ensured that no one group obtained too much power in the running of the education system.

Apart from making religious education compulsory, the 1944 Education Act made no stipulations concerning the curriculum. This whole area was left to the discretion of the teachers and the individual schools. Barber (1996) gives two reasons why this may have been the case:

1 In the 1920s the government was concerned that teachers may have joined the growing labour movement and become affiliated to the trade union movement. This had occurred elsewhere in Europe and was seen as contributing to civil unrest in these countries. In order to keep teachers neutral they were incorporated to some extent as part-ners in the policy process and control over the curriculum was ceded to them (see Grace, 1987, for an account of how they were always vulnerable to having this privilege removed when the mood of suc-cessive governments changed).
2 At the time of the formulation of the 1944 Act Britain was still at war with the fascist powers. It was felt that controlling education, as part of a wider control of people's minds, was how enemy totalitarian regimes had operated and so democratic governments would not seek to interfere with the curriculum. Teachers, by being allowed to exercise their professional educational judgements over the curricu-lum, were seen to be helping to safeguard democracy. Tropp (1957) gave an account of the steady rise in the status of the teacher as a pro-fessional after the Second World War. Lawton (1989) refers to this period as the 'golden age' of teacher control of the curriculum.

The growth of the comprehensive movement

After the Second World War education was increasingly seen, in advanced industrial societies, as a key investment in both the promo-tion of economic wealth and social justice (Brown et al., 1997). This was a period of growth after the destruction of the war with full employ-ment and a steady rise in living standards. According to Chitty (1992) both major political parties were committed to the principles of the welfare state, along with full employment and a mixed economy. In education throughout the 1950s and into the 1960s the emphasis was on expansion. The economy was changing to processes of mass pro-duction and the growth in white-collar and professional employment meant that these new workers needed to have completed more educa-tion. Education became increasingly seen as an economic investment.

A link was perceived to exist between an educated workforce and an expanding economy. The future labour force was regarded as human capital and as such it needed to be developed.

The 1960s was a time of rising standards of living. It could be summed up by the election slogan of Conservative Prime Minister, Harold Macmillan, that 'You've never had it so good'. Many factory workers were now earning high wages, and could be seen to be living a 'new lifestyle' (see Goldthorpe et al.'s thesis of *The Affluent Worker*, 1968). The structure of society was altering and more people were seen as becoming middle class due to increasing affluence. Certainly the majority were materially much better off, and with these improved living and working conditions came raised expectations for the future. Thus the argument for increasing public expenditure on education became irresistible. The comprehensive school movement was born from an alliance of three groups. Leading sections of the Labour Party keen to promote social reform through education, the organized sectors of the teaching profession who favoured a more egalitarian system and some key intellectuals in the new education-related academic disciplines (see Silver, 1973) were able to exert some influence on government thinking. Comprehensive schooling was successfully sold to the electorate as an opportunity for making what was seen as valuable in grammar school education available to everyone. It was also presented as being essential for the needs of industrial modernization which would enhance the wealth of all. In this it was related to Harold Wilson's rhetoric of a 'technological revolution' (CCCS, 1981). This revolution would involve the reshaping of the social infrastructure of the country accompanying industrial expansion. Schools and the new universities would be egalitarian powerhouses to effect this dual transformation – a powerful vision. The detail of how investment in education would be transformed into specific economic benefits was never actually clarified (Chitty, 1992) and the concept of human capital always remained at a general level of application.

According to Chitty (1991), Labour was able to put what were seen as the sound economic arguments of developing human capital alongside desires for social reform as justification for the comprehensivization of state education. Crosland, the Labour Secretary of State for Education, issued *Circular 10/65* and then *Circular 10/66* which put pressure on LEAs to reorganize on comprehensive lines (see Brooks, 1991 for an outline of the arguments put forward by Crosland for this reorganization). Halsey et al. (1997) suggest that the focus on the link between education and social democracy at the time can be seen in the increasing movement for reorganization of secondary education. It was felt that in these compre-hensive schools pupils from varied social backgrounds would mix and tolerance and respect towards each other would be created. Comprehensives would provide greater opportunity as pupils would be allowed to develop rather than being separated out and discriminated against. This in turn would allow the development of social democracy: 'From the democratic-socialist perspective of the time it could be seen and still can be defended as a major advance in breaking down the bar-riers of class, gender, and ethnicity' (Halsey et al., 1997: 5). The trend with new schools was to make them community schools so that there would be joint use of facilities. This was a more efficient use of resources and also helped promote the social democratic ideals of the Labour Party.

In some LEAs the reorganization of the tripartite system into com-prehensive schools did cause problems with amalgamations between traditional grammar and non-academic secondary modern schools. There were issues of split sites and clashes of school cultures. For many, comprehensivization did not have the auspicious start hoped for (see Young, 1998).

Conflict and dissent

The post-war consensus has perhaps tended to be overstated (Coulby, 1989). Though there was a move towards comprehensive education, this was still not universally accepted. There was some opposition to these new forms of secondary school, particularly within the Conservative Party, where many saw a need to re-establish a Tory iden-tity. Many Conservatives felt that they had gone along with the con-sensus for long enough and that it was damaging both to the electoral prospects of the party and also the country. They pointed to an insid-ious move to the left, which had gone largely unnoticed, under the aus-pices of a national consensus. Britain was felt to be in decline, both morally and economically, by many Conservative politicians from the mid-1960s onwards (see Chitty, 1992; Lawton, 1994).

Economic crisis

There was little concern among the general public with problems in edu-cation so long as there remained full employment. This appeared to be the case in the 'swinging '60s' with the increasing affluence, a football World Cup win and hope for even more prosperity in the future. Rising standards of living for all sectors of society, while not reducing inequality, created at least a semblance of unity, according to Chitty. Economic crisis when it came in the 1970s had a significant effect and 'fundamentally altered the map of British politics' (Chitty, 1992: 6). Education had been linked with the rebuilding of society after the war, with secure employment, better living standards and the eradication of poverty. When there was recession, however, questions began to be asked about how effective education had been and the value gained from money previously invested. The whole of compulsory education came under scrutiny. Economic pressure to reduce spending focused attention back onto fundamental questions concerning the purposes of education.

Public outcry

Throughout the 1970s there was growing public concern regarding education, which was actively fuelled by the media, the press in particular. There was a public perception, whether based on fact or not, that education was in crisis (Dale, 1983). Standards were felt to be falling. There are ideological issues here about standards of 'what' and how they are being measured (see Kelly, 1999 for a discussion of the use and meaning of the term 'standards').

'Progressive' and 'child-centred' approaches adopted in primary schools, which had been promoted particularly in the light of the Plowden Report and much sociological and psychological research of the 1960s, were now questioned. It was felt that these approaches had led to indiscipline, lack of direction in pupils' learning and a resulting lack of knowledge acquisition. Pupils were no longer being taught the basic skills of reading, writing and arithmetic in any systematic way. Classrooms were portrayed as chaotic with little learning taking place.

These public concerns were highlighted by the William Tyndale case which made the headlines in 1976. Here, despite the worries expressed by parents, the headteacher of William Tyndale Primary School claimed the professional expertise to continue with progressive teaching methods. The Auld Report, which was set up to investigate the case, found many faults with how the school was being run. This instance, by the media attention it drew, strengthened the public mistrust of teachers, teaching methods and teachers' control over the curriculum (see Dale, 1979). In secondary schools, in particular, the curriculum was felt to be too academic for many young people. It was not practical and not relevant to their future and appeared to be out of touch with modern life. This was held to account for much pupil unrest which was perceived to be part of a growing discipline problem within schools and which was spilling over into the wider society. These new comprehensive schools now came under increasing criticism, and teachers and teaching methods were seen as the prime cause.

Mixed ability

Mixed ability teaching practices in secondary education had expanded throughout the late 1960s and early 1970s. Informed by child-centred ideologies which aimed to motivate pupils and encourage an individual approach to pupils' learning they were increasingly criticized by traditionalists. Having to cope with such a wide range of ability in each class put a great deal of strain on many teachers, whole-class teaching being inappropriate. Pupils still often felt labelled within their classes and disruption was made worse as the able were often not challenged while the less able could feel left behind. The perception was that comprehensives were producing mediocrity by teaching to the 'middle' with ability and potential being wasted as it had been in the tripartite system. Thus, as well as the secondary curriculum not being relevant, academic standards were also felt to be falling. By emphasizing individual development and equality, it was felt that comprehensives and also primary schools were discouraging the very competitive spirit that was needed to improve the economy. Comprehensives were at a further disadvantage in that they were often compared with, and in fact in some areas were in competition with, grammar schools that only taught able pupils (see Benn and Chitty, 1996).

The curriculum

The curriculum had changed in many comprehensive schools. Critics saw the traditional subjects and their content being diluted into themes or topics. History, geography and religious education were now often combined with aspects of sociology to form 'social studies' or 'integrated humanities'. Some felt this led to important traditional knowledge not being taught and being replaced by the transmission of what were portrayed as left-wing egalitarian beliefs. Teachers were not felt to be upholding traditional stable values and were stereotyped as 'lefty', indoctrinating, long-haired and lazy. Thus schools and teachers could be seen to be to blame for many of the country's problems. In an article in the *Times Educational Supplement* (Weinstock, 1976: 2.) entitled 'I blame the teachers', it was clear who industrialist Arnold Weinstock blamed for the economic and social problems of the time. These criticisms were cited and much of the growing unrest captured in a series of Black Papers written by a group of right-wing politicians and thinkers published in the late 1960s and early 1970s. They criticized falling standards and an associated moral decline and put both down to progressive teaching methods encouraged in the Plowden Report (CACE, 1967). The Black Papers claimed this ideology led to sloppiness, lack of rigour, decline in discipline and thus disruption in the education of all pupils.

The great debate

This can be seen as a humanist backlash upon the prevailing progressive and social democratic ideologies of the time which had also been linked to the reconstructionists. The solution suggested in the later of the Black Papers was to take control of the curriculum and the running of education away from the teachers and the educationalists and place them in the hands of the parents and employers. Thus a policy of market forces was proposed, where the power of the consumer, not the producer, determined the 'product'. These criticisms of the education system and those who had been running it reflected the growing importance of what became known as the 'New Right' within the Conservative party. They raised questions about the purpose of education in society including issues of what and how pupils should be taught. As value for money came to be seen as increasingly important in the growing recession, these questions were also asked by the Labour Prime Minister of the time, James Callaghan.

James Callaghan's 1976 Ruskin Speech

Under increasing economic pressure and with growing public concern being expressed over education, a speech made by Callaghan at Ruskin College in 1976 marked a significant point in the recent history of education policy. Callaghan's intentions for the speech are still debated (see Batteson, 1998; Chitty, 1999). It could be taken as a critique of a system in crisis or it could be interpreted as a desire to move to a more radical agenda. He did not openly condemn education, in fact he noted achievements, though this was done with faint praise.

Callaghan spoke of issues which caused him concern and where attention needed to turn. He felt that the curriculum was not appropriate for the needs of a modern economy, that many of the brightest pupils were not being encouraged, and were even being discouraged from taking up courses relevant to careers in industry. He noted the great strides in social aspects of education but was also worried that a number of pupils were not acquiring the basic academic skills needed in later life. Though teachers were professionally involved in the curriculum, he felt it should not just be left to them – others in society needed to be involved. To this end Callaghan proposed a 'great debate' concerning the curriculum. Certainly this can be seen as the first significant occasion since the 1944 Act on which teacher autonomy in curriculum matters was questioned by the government in power. What this speech signified was the growing public feeling, stoked by politicians and the media, that the education system needed to be more accountable. It was felt that teachers and LEAs needed to be responsive to the wider society which was, after all, paying for education. In ideological terms the focus was shifting away from the individual and more towards society and the importance of traditional knowledge.

When Labour lost the general election of 1979 there followed a substantial period of Conservative government up until 1997. The early Thatcher years were a time of economic and social upheaval. There was a change in emphasis from the social democratic policies of the consensus politicians to the rigours of monetarism and the free market. This was reflected throughout government policy and so, too, in education. Education had come to be seen as part of the national problem and it provided a convenient scapegoat for intractable economic and social issues. Education could also, while undergoing a process of reform, be seen as a future solution to many of the economic difficulties of the time. It could prepare suitable workers and instil social responsibility and respect for authority among the young. What had previously been an education programme for a new affluent society had come to be seen as politically biased and damaging to the nation's development. It was claimed there was a need to get back to basics, to eliminate political meddling in education, to return to traditional values and at the same time modernize education for the needs of a changing economy. There was an ideological shift taking place in public life from progressivism to classical humanism alongside instrumentalism and economic revisionism.

Conservative policy: ideological predicates

After the defeat of the Conservatives in 1974 there had arisen a movement for reform within the party. It was felt that for many years the two main parties, Labour and Conservative, had been similar in their 'centralist' approaches to government. The rhetoric of consensus which resulted had hidden a steady drift to the left which was illustrated by policies such as the comprehensivization of education (Chitty, 1992). Certain right-wing thinkers, such as the Black Paper authors, felt that it was this drift which had led to the decline in fortunes not only of the Conservative Party but also of the country. They argued that socialist policies had ignored traditional values and stifled the important characteristics of individual achievement and entrepreneurship. The stress on equality of opportunity had been at the expense of competitiveness and the developing welfare state had created a culture of dependency and conformity. These policies were considered inevitably to lead to a steady economic and moral decline.

The rise of the New Right

The Conservative policy became influenced by groups within the party identified by the term the 'New Right'. This was not a coherent force but what Walford called 'a disparate range of groups of individuals with often substantially different visions of the future' (1994: 7). Their point of unity was a common enemy in socialism. The potential internal conflicts of the New Right were overcome and factions within the party were held together by the strong leadership of Margaret Thatcher. The origins of the New Right can be seen in traditional strands of Tory thought stemming from the nineteenth century. These are a combination of a desire for order and stability in society along with the importance of individual freedom and enterprise. Both of these are needed in the creation of a thriving economy (see Lawton, 1992; 1994). These two positions can be described as neo-conservative and neo-liberal.

Neo-liberalism

Neo-liberals attest to the importance of a free market economy which involves freedom of choice for consumers and producers with minimum state interference. These ideas stem from the economic model of perfect competition. This assumes that in the running of an economy there are certain factors of production, these being labour, land and capital, which are pulled together by entrepreneurs. These factors will be used most effectively when supplying the goods which consumers demand. Producers will endeavour to provide what consumers want, to sell their products and make their profit. This profit enables them to expand and to be even more successful in the future. Those producers who do not make what the public want, or who cannot produce it as efficiently (cheaply) as competitors, will go out of business. Thus those who meet demand and are the most efficient will survive. The factors of production used by those who go out of business are released to be used by more efficient producers in this or other industries. Thus competition leads to the most effective use of resources which will ultimately benefit the whole society.

The neo-liberals advocate minimum interference by government in the market. They suggest that this only benefits the less efficient producers and allows the production of goods which the market has not demanded. Protected industries, like those which are nationalized, will never become truly efficient and will always need to be supported by taxpayers' money. Thus protectionism means we all pay more for our goods and leads to a weak economy that will ultimately fail in world markets. Free competition benefits us all by creating efficiency of production and a strong economy. It was suggested that education could be seen as another product. Competition would, as in other industries, lead to more efficient use of resources whilst satisfying consumer demand. This would put a stop to the educational establishment forcing its own view of what should be supplied as education on everyone. This competition would in turn make the system more cost-effective and be part of economic regeneration (see Tooley, 1993, for a view of how this could happen).

Neo-conservatism

Neo-conservatives believe in the importance of upholding standards and traditional values. Ball (1994) referred to this group as 'Cultural Restorationists'. This ideology stressed the importance of authority, a national identity and high traditional standards. Economic decline could be traced to moral decline of which the education system was a major cause. The neo-conservatives felt that this was largely due to progressive teaching which lacked an important stress on traditional values and discipline. There needed to be greater supervision over the work of teachers and LEAs alongside reform of the curriculum. Lawton noted that: 'whereas the neo-liberals tend to talk about choice, competition and the market in education, the neo-conservatives are more likely to advocate traditional values, traditional subjects, and less educational theory in the training of teachers, but greater immersion into the traditional values of good schools' (1992: 7).

New Right education policy

Certainly these different ideological strands revealed dissatisfaction with the developments of education in the 1960s and 1970s. One ideology emphasized freedom of choice and markets, the other the need for control and a return to tried and tested methods. There is potential conflict between these groups but certainly a view that things needed to change. In spite of their differences neo-conservatives and neo-liberals both had a mistrust of state professionals who prevented the development of a free market and efficiency and were also seen as subversive (Carr and Hartnett, 1996). A policy developed which reflected both ideologies while stressing one and then the other at different times. Lawton (1992) cites Gamble's view that Thatcherism was a combination of 'the free economy and the strong state'. Whitty suggested that: 'New Right ideology was a blend of moral and economic, academic and philosophical doctrines, sometimes complementary, but sometimes in tension' (1990: 17). He further suggested that provided it held public support its inconsistencies did not matter. Thus:

> greater consumer power over choice and management of schools, a neo-liberal response to criticisms of LEA and bureaucracies, and a National Curriculum, a neo-conservative response to charges that trendy teachers are subverting traditional moral values and selling the nation short, may both resonate with popular experience and be electorally attractive, even if the whole package does not add up. (Whitty, 1990: 17)

The policy was not totally contradictory. Whitty also suggested that it was necessary for central government to take control of the curriculum to allow the market to develop, thus preventing the producers, teachers and LEAs from stifling the development of competition by their control.

Though slow to turn its full attention to education due to pressures elsewhere, the Conservative government did introduce some changes in the early 1980s. Perhaps most significant of these was the setting up of the assisted places scheme, whereby able pupils from state schools were offered places at public school, with the state assisting the parents with the payment of fees. This can be said to show a mistrust of the state system and a belief that the private sector was superior. It also diverted public funds from the state to the private sector. The government's mistrust of teachers and suspicions as to their subversive motives were brought to a head in 1986 and 1987 in a prolonged industrial dispute over pay and conditions. This resulted in severe disruption in schools. By their actions the teachers lost much public support and the government became even more determined to reform schooling and to alter the balance of power in education (see Ball, 1988, for an account of the strike and its effects). The policies of many LEAs on equal opportunities, anti-racism and so on began to be seen as 'loony' by the Conservative government (Coulby, 1989). Increasingly it was felt that the producer control of the education system needed to be broken. The Education Reform Act of 1988 which followed illustrated most clearly the Conservative ideologies on education. This was arguably the most significant piece of legislation since the 1944 Act:

> To understand the importance of the 1988 Education Reform Act, you have to understand, too, the situation and the opinions which gave rise to it . . . Education, it was felt, was not coming up to standard: it was not meeting the needs of society, especially industry, and it was not enabling young people to get the best out of life. What was needed, it was felt, was an agreed curriculum framework with a greater degree of prescription, and this could be achieved through more government direction. (Pring, 1989: 29)

Policy into practice: the Education Reform Act, 1988

Though the government had already made a number of changes, and continued to do so, this Act was designed to clearly implement the ideology of the New Right. The proposals of the Act reflected the main ideological strands of policy. Some were designed to create the market of the neo-liberals, others to reinforce a more traditional morality of the neo-conservatives. They were to tip the balance of power away from the teachers and LEAs, sometimes towards the centre, at other times towards parents, thus giving choice to the consumers. The main proposals of the Act relating to compulsory education are now outlined.

Open enrolment of pupils

Up to this time the number of pupils on each school roll had been decided by LEAs. This enabled them to plan for the education of all pupils within their authority. It also meant that they could control intake for each school and thus balance the size of schools in the authority. Parents had comparatively little say in the schools their children were sent to by the LEA and it was usual for pupils to be allocated places at their local primary or secondary school.

Under the Education Reform Act parents were now able to choose which school they wanted their children to attend. They could send them to schools which offered the kind of education they wanted rather than to a school chosen by the LEA. This meant that schools now had to start attracting parents and marketing themselves if they were to maintain a sufficiently high intake of pupils. This was particularly important in the secondary sector as parents were able to consider schools over a wider travelling distance for their children. The LEA was no longer able to protect undersubscribed schools by giving them extra funding to cushion the fall in pupil numbers due to the introduction of 'local management of schools'.

Local management of schools

Previously the LEA was in control of the budgets for all maintained schools in its area and it allocated funds according to its own policy. Thus some schools may have been given more funds by the authority than others for a variety of reasons. In this way the LEA could protect schools from falling rolls and they could be given extra support if they were having particular problems. In effect this meant that some schools were subsidizing others. From the point of view of the neo-liberals this meant that the efficient were paying for the inefficient and there was no financial incentive for schools to become more effective or to make an effort to be more attractive to parents and pupils.

The Education Reform Act gave headteachers more control over their own budgets and forced LEAs to pass on to schools a high percentage of the money allocated to them by central government. The money was to be allocated on the basis of the number of pupils on roll. Schools which were successful and growing, as more parents opted for them, would receive more money thereby enabling them to build upon their success. Those who were unable to attract pupils and were suffering from falling rolls would need to act quickly if they were to survive. Thus the consumer would reign supreme in the market and schools would need to offer the sort of education which attracted parents. The LEAs were no longer able to interfere as they had lost much of their financial power.

The creation of city technology colleges and grant maintained schools

For parents to be able to exercise choice there needed to be different types of school available. Greater diversity would stimulate competition and force existing state schools to change more quickly. A new type of school, a city technology college, was to be jointly funded by the government and industry. These schools were to be technology and industry oriented for pupils of secondary school age. This epitomized the link between education and economic development. They were designed to offer opportunities to pupils from inner-city areas who were oriented towards technology. It was expected that these schools would provide models of good practice that other schools in the area would have to follow.

Schools that wanted the freedom to develop in their own way and to sever links from the bureaucratic LEAs could become grant maintained. This meant that they were funded directly from cental government and they were in total control of the whole of their budget. The government expected that the majority of schools would welcome this option.

Introduction of the National Curriculum

This was a very significant development which has been considered in some detail in Chapter 3. Politicians had before this time not dared to prescribe the curriculum for fear of appearing undemocratic. This fear had passed into history with the World Wars now so far behind. With the increasing public concern over education, a national curriculum was now seen as a way of ensuring an appropriate schooling for all pupils. For the New Right it was a way of breaking the subversive control which teachers exerted over the curriculum. The National Curriculum was to be compulsory for all pupils aged 5 to 16. It was to be assessed and it was envisaged that test results at the end of the four Key Stages would be made public in the form of league tables. The results would show how pupils are progressing, how schools are achieving, and how standards are being raised.

The subjects and their content were traditional and thus reflected clearly the influence of the neo-conservatives. The neo-liberal element of the party perhaps did not favour this traditional approach since it had no element of choice for the consumer. However, they did go along with it in that future changes in content could be made and it would certainly encourage competition with the publication of National Curriculum test results. These would provide large amounts of information about the 'output' of each school for the consumer. For a discussion of the proposals of the 1988 Education Reform Act see Bash and Coulby (1989) or Pring (1989).

Development of Conservative policy into the 1990s

The policy of developing the market while also increasing central control continued throughout the Conservative period of office. In 1993 a rigorous inspection service was set up under the newly created Office for Standards in Education. As well as checking on the running of each school, inspection reports were made public giving the consumer information on which to make informed choices. Schools deemed to be 'failing' would have to improve rapidly or be severely dealt with. League tables of school performance were developed in the first instance to show GCSE results. These would provide consumer information and encourage competition among producers. The aim was to expand the tables to include end of Key Stage results. Increasing diversity of schools was encouraged to further stimulate the market. Secondary schools were given the right to specialize in one or more curriculum areas – science, music, technology, modern foreign language or sport. The city technology college (CTC) concept was modified and widened, enabling more schools to join the City Technology Trust scheme, providing they were able to attract matching funding from industry.

The concept of an education system driven by market forces was becoming more and more influential towards the end of the Conservative administration in all sectors of education, and it was proposed to extend this further had they won the 1997 general election. There was also, paradoxically, a move to allow schools greater powers to select pupils. This was part of the neo-conservative ideal of schools for an academic elite as had existed before comprehensivization. The high-status selective schools would perhaps naturally be formed from those which were already oversubscribed.

However, it was not all plain sailing for the Conservative government and its education policy. The National Curriculum encountered a number of problems during its introduction. Large amounts of prescribed content implemented over a very short timescale, coupled with the fear of untried assessment methods, placed great strain on teachers and schools. This was exacerbated by government reforms on school management being introduced simultaneously. The curriculum was: 'trying to offer too many subjects in too much depth and assessing them in ways which were absurdly complex' (Sweetman, 1993: 5). This caused confrontation between teachers and the government and resulted in the boycotting of the early end of Key Stage tests. In response to increasing public disquiet the government set up the Dearing Commission to look into the curriculum. While its brief was to make a complex system more 'workable' the ideological basis of the curriculum was not open to question. The Dearing Report (Dearing, 1993) did recognize the unwieldy nature of the curriculum. There was far too much content and the assessment was very complex and time-consuming. It proposed a streamlining of the curriculum which would give greater flexibility to the individual schools and teachers in their planning. This allowed more time to be spent on mathematics and English in the early years and the possibility of subject choice and vocational options in the later years. The subjects were to be reviewed for September 1995 with a promise of no further changes for five years. Only the core subjects of English, mathematics and science were to be nationally tested, though teachers were expected to monitor pupil progress in the other subjects in relation to the National Curriculum levels.

A list of the Conservative achievements in education by the end of their term might include:

- The balance of power had changed with LEAs having lost much of their power to central government and individual schools.
- Control of the curriculum was still an area of contention but certainly was no longer clearly the preserve of teachers. It was now quality controlled and monitored by government agencies.
- A market had developed with the introduction of greater parental choice and financial control delegated to schools. This had a great effect on how schools were run. There was an increasing emphasis on management training, cost-effectiveness and efficiency. Schools now operated much more on the lines of individual businesses. The producers, in this case the headteachers running the schools, were able to respond to the wishes of the consumers, that is, the parents.

A list of Conservative disappointments in education by the end of their term could include:

- Only a handful of CTCs were created. This was due partly to the difficulty in attracting funding from industry and partly to strong local opposition in some areas from parents and politicians (Brooks, 1991). Companies generally preferred to spread their sponsorship across many schools (Roberts, 1994), fearing anti-company feeling if they were seen to spend large amounts on one school benefiting only the few pupils able to gain a place.
- Nowhere near as many schools opted for grant maintained status as the government had hoped. The anticipated flood of applications to leave LEA control did not materialize. In fact, once schools had gained control of a large proportion of their budgets, they valued the assistance and support networks the LEA could provide. There was

perhaps still a deeply ingrained ethos of professional collaboration among teachers rather than competition between them.

- Allowing parental choice actually caused problems for many parents. In each LEA certain schools, usually with good examination results and in the more affluent areas, became oversubscribed. This led to problems whereby increasing numbers of parents living outside the immediate area could not get their children into the school of their choice because it was full. Lengthy appeals ensued which caused anxiety and ultimately dissatisfaction among many parents. Schools with poor reputations often had difficulty in improving their image as middle-class parents living in their area tried to send their children to schools further away. These undersubscribed schools, often serving poor neighbourhoods, had to accept a number of pupils who for whatever reason could not get into other schools. In this way they came to be seen as sink schools and remained low in the performance league tables. This is a form of market failure and illustrates how free markets may actually fail to satisfy supply and demand. As pupil places were limited in oversubscribed schools then the choice again became that of the school (the producer). This was often based on set catchment area criteria and neither the school nor consumer had a free choice in reality.

- The status of teaching had changed. Teachers had suffered criticism for many years, had come under scrutiny from OFSTED and retained little professional control over the curriculum. Many education theorists talked of the proletarianization and deprofessionalization of teachers (see Apple, 1988; Bartlett, 1998; Ozga, 1995; Ozga and Lawn, 1988). In the labour market teachers' salaries were not competitive with alternative employment and, subsequently, problems of teacher recruitment emerged. By the end of the Conservative period of office the teaching force was ageing with fewer young teachers coming forward to replace them.

When the Conservatives came to office in 1979 there were mounting problems with an economy that was undergoing a major restructuring in terms of employment and production. Under their stewardship education policy shifted towards stressing traditional forms of knowledge, the needs of the workplace, and the promotion of enterprise through competition. This was reflected in the policy of the New Right which was a combination of neo-conservatism and neo-liberalism. Towards the end of their term of office, public opinion began to swing against the tyrannies of tradition and a free market in favour of modernism and governmental restraint of market excesses. Thus there was a move back towards liberal humanism and social democracy.

New Labour

Labour perspectives on education

After the defeat of the Callaghan administration in 1979 and in their first years out of office, Labour moved to the left with the growing influence of the militant tendency within the party. It was presented in the media as a party of extremists and the Conservatives were able to portray Labour as unelectable. During the next 20 years the 'modernizers' set about altering the image and policies of the party. These efforts finally bore fruit with the victory in the 1997 general election. Lawton (1992) suggests that Labour has never really held a distinctive view on education. This reflects its mixed origins, having been formed from a combination of socialist groups and the declining Liberal party. The Labour Party's prime task was seen by many as representing the working classes in the areas of employment, housing and social conditions and, according to Lawton (1992), there was little discussion of a socialist view of education. Education was a part of the present order of things and radically alternative structuring of society was not attempted: 'The Labour Party has usually merely taken the existing education system and suggested minor adjustments to it in order to make it serve the interests of working class children more fairly' (Lawton, 1992: 23).

Labour had supported the development of the tripartite system, believing that the 11-plus would provide equal chances to all children of obtaining a grammar school education. Grammar schools were seen as a route whereby working-class children could improve their futures. The inequalities of the selection process and its effects on maintaining social disadvantage were not acknowledged by Labour politicians at this time (see Chapter 7 on how social factors can influence achievement in education). In the 1960s the Labour policy on comprehensive education was never made compulsory. Many LEAs ignored their instructions and maintained the tripartite systems. Though wishing to use education for the benefit of all sections of society, Labour had no real image of how comprehensive schools should operate and no view on the curriculum. These important areas were left to educationalists to decide. The Labour feeling, as expressed by Harold Wilson when Prime

Minister, was that comprehensive schools should aim to provide a grammar school education for all.

Labour ideology rests on the social democratic principles of ensuring equality of opportunity and individual freedom within a strong state framework. The state protects us and thus allows us to become free. This is freedom with responsibility involving fellowship and cooperation. Under 'New Labour' this is expressed as a partnership between individuals and the state. Both are seen as having duties and responsibilities to each other if, ultimately, we are all to benefit from economic and social development (Avis, 1999). According to Tony Blair, New Labour is not so much:

> a set of rigid economic ideological attitudes, but a set of values and principles. The simple case for democratic socialism rests on the belief that individuals prosper best within a strong, active society whose members acknowledge they owe duties to each other as well as to themselves, and in part at least depend upon each other to succeed. (Wintour, 1994: 8)

New Labour sees a need to modernize Britain even if this means questioning traditional Labour beliefs. The 'modernization project' is how Prime Minister Blair is able to embrace the wider electorate. It is by calling for a pragmatic approach to the solving of Britain's problems, rather than so called dogma, that New Labour appeals to the 'middle ground'. It is this 'common-sense' attitude, and not being tied by traditional allegiances of left and right, that Labour presents as the 'third way'. This is seen to be for the benefit of the whole country and thus it is the Tories who are now presented as the intolerant extremists. Labour policy, in general terms, seeks to curb the excesses of the market while still aiming to gain its benefits. At the same time, there is a policy of social inclusion, where the aim is to ensure that all citizens are involved in and feel a part of society. This is a direct result of the social exclusion experienced by many groups during the excesses of a free market in the Thatcher and Major eras.

The tension between traditional Labour values and modernization is illustrated by policies which promote individual incentives at the same time as collective responsibility. These highlight the uneasy mix which is New Labour. Ball (1999) suggests that the 'third way' provides a post-socialist resolution to this conflict. He states that 'Blairism' operates for New Labour in a similar way as 'Thatcherism' did for the 'New Right' by pulling together loose alliances of what are at times potentially conflicting ideologies. This mix is reflected in the Labour education policy which stresses improving opportunities, raising participation and increasing achievement. Education is seen as important not only for eliminating social exclusion and allowing fulfilment of individual potential, but also for economic reasons. It is regarded as playing a significant part in future economic development especially with the explosion of information technology and the increasing importance of global competition for British industry. Labour has returned to a belief in the need to invest in the future workforce. As David Blunkett, Secretary of State for Education, stated:

> we are talking about investing in human capital in the age of knowledge. To compete in the global economy, to live in a civilised society and to develop the talents of each and every one of us, we will have to unlock the potential in every young person. By doing so each can flourish, building on their own strengths and developing their own special talents. We must overcome the spiral of disadvantage, in which alienation from, or failure within, the education system is passed from one generation to the next. (DfEE, 1997b: 3)

Avis points to the assumed relationship between education, economic performance and competitiveness: 'Such a relation underpins moves towards mass higher education as well as an education system orientated towards social inclusion and cohesion. The result of such practices will carry not only social, but crucially, economic benefits' (Avis, 2000: 39). It is this supposed relationship from which the ideas of lifelong learning have developed. Avis does actually question the nature of this relationship in the same way as the notion of education developing human capital was questioned in the late 1970s.

Change in government, change in policy?

Labour was elected in May 1997 with education as a central issue in its policy agenda. Labour politicians spoke of the need for a 'can do' culture which was central to the modernization project. To succeed they needed: 'the commitment, imagination and drive of all those working in our schools and colleges, if we are to set aside the doubts of the cynics and the corrosion of the perpetual skeptics. We must replace the culture of complacency with commitment to success' (DfEE, 1997b: 3). They wished to heal the atmosphere of hostility created by the Conservative years of confrontation and the mistrust of government that had developed among those working in education. 'Education is the key to creating a society which is dynamic and productive, offering opportunity and fairness to all. It is the Government's top priority. We will work in partnership with all those who share our passion and sense of urgency for higher standards' (DfEE, 1997b: 9).

Excellence in Schools

The White Paper *Excellence in Schools* was published in July 1997 and outlined the Labour strategy for raising standards. It espoused six policy principles:

- Education will be at the heart of government.
- Policies will be designed to benefit the many, not just the few.
- Standards matter more than structures.
- Intervention will be in inverse proportion to success.
- There will be zero tolerance of underperformance.
- Government will work in partnership with all those committed to raising standards (DfEE, 1997b: 5).

The following challenges and agenda for action were set out:

- to ensure that every child learns the basics of literacy and numeracy early and well
- to increase levels of achievement and opportunities in schools for all pupils
- to challenge schools to improve and take responsibility for raising their own standards
- to tackle truancy and reduce exclusions from school
- to reduce social exclusion by equipping all children to be active citizens and by encouraging young people to stay in learning after 18
- to modernize comprehensive secondary education for the new century
- to improve the quality of teaching and leadership in schools
- to involve parents and local communities in the education of children, to reduce social exclusion and to develop effective partnerships at a local level to raise standards (DfEE, 1999a: 3).

This strategy had wide-ranging implications for many areas of education. Let us consider some of these as they relate to the compulsory sector. Currently these are at different stages in their introduction and development. Each really needs to be looked at in detail but can only be referred to briefly here.

Managing performance

Extensive use of target-setting is being developed at all levels to plan and monitor change. Each school is required to set challenging targets for improvement with LEAs monitoring the progress of schools and helping them to meet their targets. Local education authorities must prepare an educational development plan, also with targets, showing how they intend to promote school improvement. Thus the LEAs appear to have an important role but they will continue to be closely monitored by central government. Schools and LEAs are to be inspected by OFSTED and, as under the Conservatives, will be severely dealt with if performance is deemed unsatisfactory and they are unable to rapidly improve.

Each school is developing a system of performance management of staff with teachers' pay being more directly linked to targets through an appraisal system. A new grade of 'advanced skills' teacher (AST) has been created and 'fast-track promotion routes' to leadership roles are being developed. Simultaneously, dismissal procedures have been speeded up for failing teachers. The purpose of these changes is to reward teachers for their work, to share best practice and eliminate 'ineffective' teaching, while making the teaching profession more attractive to high-flying graduates. The wish to punish those perceived as 'poor teachers' and a desire to weed out the weak goes back to Sir Keith Joseph's time as Conservative Secretary of State for Education (see the White Papers, *Teaching Quality* – DES, 1983 – and *Better Schools* – DES, 1985c – for a view of teaching standards at this time). A General Teaching Council has also been created. This is again designed to raise the professional status of teaching by allowing it to be more self-regulating in line with other professional bodies. This council will, of course, not be independent of government.

Although the assisted places scheme was abolished as soon as Labour came into office there has been no straight endorsement of the ideals of comprehensive education by this government. In its 'can do' approach, the results are what matter as much as the means, which may involve allowing the existence of different types of schools. In the White Paper (DfEE, 1997b) the government states that able pupils must be stretched and those needing support must be given it. It suggests that this will mean more examples of target grouping by ability and fast-tracking. This appears to be a criticism of mixed ability teaching methods and is certainly an endorsement of the setting and streaming of pupils.

The government has placed increasing emphasis on the basics of reading, writing and arithmetic in primary schools and has introduced the literacy and the numeracy hours into the primary curriculum. Much guidance has gone into schools on how to structure these sessions along with the production of ready-prepared teaching materials. There has been an emphasis on reducing class sizes for

7-year-olds and below, and creating nursery places for all 4-year-olds. Baseline assessment has been introduced for pupils on entering school to enable teachers to plan work for, and monitor the development of, these pupils more effectively.

Twenty-five Education Action Zones have been set up, mainly in inner city areas, to raise pupil achievement (DfEE, 1999a). This policy links the raising of educational standards with the regeneration of inner cities and the promotion of inclusion for all sectors of society. Extra resources are provided by central government with matched funding provided for any sponsorship the zones can attract from local industry. This scheme has since been expanded as more action zones have been created. Labour is certainly investing in education through these initiatives but is also keeping control of how the money is spent via systems of bidding and accountability.

Initial impact of Labour policies and reforms

While recognizing what Fielding (1999a: 175) calls 'the most committed, unremittingly focused attempt at educational transformation since the post-war national consensus', there are certain criticisms and reservations about the early effects of Labour's policy. The *Times Educational Supplement* responded to Labour's first White Paper on entering office, *Excellence in Schools*, by noting the government's intention to take central control of the education service (Hackett, 1997: 4).

Ball (1999) suggests that while Labour has introduced many policies aimed at monitoring and raising standards, it has dispensed with very little of what the Conservatives initiated. He suggested that we need to look at the continuities with Conservatives as much as the differences (see Avis, 2000; Ball, 1999). As noted earlier in the chapter, rather than presenting a radical view of education, Labour continues to tinker with what exists. Thus Labour politicians wish to improve standards but there is no questioning of the nature of these standards. They are taken as accepted. The term 'modernization' is used to 'encourage' those working in education to alter their practices but it is modernization based on old images of what is important.

Provision that appears to be taken from the Conservatives includes:

- choice and competition – the commodification and consumerization of education
- autonomy and performativity – the managerialization and commercialization of education

- centralization and prescription – the imposition of centrally determined assessments, schemes of work and classroom methods (Ball,
  1999: 196).

These three main strands of Labour policy are not separate. They work
together and are interwoven throughout the developments in education introduced by the government. Ball (1999) suggests that these policies are not so much 'lifted' from the Conservatives but are part of a
globalization process where all educational policy is moving in this
direction. Labour has very little option but to follow the pressure of
globalization (also see Avis, 1999).

Fielding (1999b) points to the increasing importance of performance
management. This is a way of monitoring, evaluating and improving
how schools and their staff perform using a process of target-setting and
review (DfEE, 1998a; DfEE, 1999b; DfEE, 2000b). It is assumed, as under
the Conservatives, that such industrial practices which stress accountability of the workforce can be applied to schools and that these practices themselves are effective. There is no awareness of criticisms of
these approaches or acknowledgement of alternatives.

Fielding explains how the setting of targets may be helpful when used
by individuals to guide their development but may become tyrannical
when the target becomes the overriding reason for action. If these specific
targets are met at the expense of other important development needs this
may be detrimental to a teacher's performance. Measurement by targets
can encourage subversion of the results and teachers and headteachers
may become adept at hiding damaging information and boosting
favourable figures. This is a practice common in industries which rely on
checking up on the workforce through such targets (see Deming, 1986).

Quality management theorists such as Scholtes (1998) point out that
as the target becomes more important the focusing of attention on
specifics may detract from the larger purpose. For instance, by concentrating on small numbers of pupils to improve test results, such as raising those just below a GCSE C grade to just above it, other pupils or
different aspects of school life may be neglected. The effort and expenditure to achieve one specific target may not be the best use of
resources. Thus a great deal may be spent on bringing truants back into
school, simply to reduce the rate, when the actual cause of truancy and
what may be best for all involved may not have been considered.

Linking an individual teacher's pay to targets as part of performance
management may actually be counterproductive as it is likely to
discourage openness and teamwork if teachers are to be compared with

one another. It also makes the assumption that important achievements in a pupil's education can be credited to an individual teacher
and that they can be measured by simplistic scores. Targets thus help to
encourage an image of teaching as a technical activity which can be
controlled by a management process (Bartlett, 2000).

Targets set at every level of the education system mean that greater
control over priorities, and the monitoring of progress towards them,
can be exerted by the centre. The Standards and Effectiveness unit, set
up by the Labour government, issues detailed guidance which serves to
promote the standardization of teaching. The Office for Standards in
Education continues with the process of constant inspection of the
work of schools and individual teachers. As the National Curriculum
has been slimmed down, so league tables have been developed further
and given more credence under Labour. With the continuation of
parental choice these external measures remain of crucial importance to
both school and parent.

Curriculum debate appears to have diminished and to have been
replaced by a concern with standards (Davies and Edwards, 1999). This
brings us back to Kelly's (1999) point about who decides what standards
are important. There is little discussion about the nature of learning and
how it takes place. Didactic teaching of facts to be tested is to the fore,
as are the measures of technical competencies of both teachers and
pupils.

Though equality of opportunity may also be part of the Labour
rhetoric the policies which encourage differentiation and specialization
do not match this. As Ball says:

> In all of this social justice issues seem peripheral. As previously, concerns
> about equity are tagged on to the list of Labour's priorities and are not central
> to their content or planning decisions about education. Further, the 'what
> works' ideology of the Third Way, which is presented as 'beyond' politics,
> obscures the class politics of current education policies. (Ball, 1999: 198)

Schools are encouraged to apply for specialist school status (see DfEE,
2001). They can also become technology colleges, part of the CTC development introduced by the Conservatives. There is no proposal to abol-
ish those grammar schools which still exist. Instead parents are now able
to vote on their abolition but this has so far proved difficult to organize.

The Labour rhetoric is of partnership, cooperation and to end the
conflict which has occurred in education over the last 20 years.
Working together as partners may be a truly social democratic
approach. However, an emphasis on measurable targets and account-

ability means that increasing control from the centre is also a distinct possibility. The tension appears to be between *true* partnership and a continuing centralization of the locus of control.

Conclusion

The post-1944 period began with what has been portrayed as a general consensus in terms of the desirability of development and expansion in education. There was hope for the future and the development of a better society. By the early 1970s there had been rapid curriculum development, an increase in the 'pupil-centred approach' to learning and the implementation of the first wave of comprehensive schools. By the mid-1970s there was an economic downturn and education increasingly became a focus of national concern through 'The Great Debate' on education. In some quarters it was felt that there had been a fall in academic standards and that schools had played a major part in the nation's moral decline. Teachers and their progressive teaching methods were depicted as being largely responsible.

With the election of the Conservatives in 1979 education policy was strongly influenced by the 'New Right'. This was a mixture of neoliberalism, which proposed the creation of the free market involving consumer choice and competition to raise standards, and neoconservatism, which advocated a return to the traditional values which had allegedly made Britain successful in the past. Disillusionment with this combination of traditionalism and a free market, lacking in adequate constraints, led to a move back towards the centre in terms of ideologies with the development of Labour's 'third way'. With their 'modernized' form of social democracy Labour seems to be attempting to reap the benefits of a free market while ensuring the exercise of social constraint and state support. In education Labour says its aim is to open access and raise standards for all sections of society by emphasizing partnership and the involvement of all concerned. This is said to involve recognizing the professionalism of teachers and increasing public spending on education. Conversely it also means the setting of targets and the increasing accountability of those working in education. At the same time the competition between schools, the traditionalist curriculum and the diversity of provision to maintain consumer choice will remain. Third-way politics can be characterized as a mixture of ideologies and an attempt at compromise which has been able to flourish, some would argue, because of the desire for conciliation following the confrontational approach of the Conservative years in government. However, many would claim that this eclectic approach to education policy is not very significantly modified Thatcherism and likely to fracture when put under pressure. There is clearly a dichotomy, for instance, between the rhetoric of professional recognition for teachers and greater accountability and control through performance management systems. Thus education is riven with ideological splits even if government and policy-makers have political motives for presenting educational practices as derivative of a consensus position.

This brief analysis has considered important developments in the compulsory age phases of education since the Second World War. Brevity can breed oversimplification and the emphasis of some points at the expense of others. Nevertheless we have at least highlighted how beliefs about the nature of education, the possession of political power, and economic and social circumstances all help to shape policy and lead to change in the education system. It is important to realize that there is no single, objective, unchanging vision of how education should be that is superior to all others. What should be taught, how it should be taught and issues of measurement and standards remain, as ever, dependent upon ideological belief. Successive governments develop their views of education in relation to their vision of society. To those in power, therefore, their proposals are generally not seen as contentious since they are for the good of society. Governments do find it difficult, at times, to do all they would wish because of opposition from those with alternative ideologies. This continuous political process leads to the evolution of the education system. Public opinion about the type of education which is desirable also changes with time and circumstances, so the resulting development of education is a product of the struggle between competing ideologies.

Student activity

1 Visit the DfEE website (www.dfee.gov.uk). Look up current publications on educational developments. Read through several of these and try to identify the key parts of Labour education policy. How do these key parts relate to the ideologies discussed in Chapter 1?

Recommended reading

There are many interesting texts which examine contemporary developments in education. They do tend to be for the more advanced student as they are based on at least some awareness of the ideological nature of education and how this inter-relates with politics.

Marsh, C.J. (1997) *Perspectives: Key Concepts for Understanding Curriculum 1*, London: Falmer Press. As the title suggests this is a basic text on curriculum. As such it introduces the student to the important part political philosophy plays in curriculum development.

Halsey, A.H., Lauder, H., Brown, P. and Wells, A. (1997) *Education: Culture Economy Society*, Oxford: Oxford University Press. This is a reader examining significant developments in education in the 80s and 90s.

Carr, W. and Hartnett, A. (1996) *Education and the Struggle for Democracy: The Politics of Educational Ideas*, Buckingham: Open University Press. This was recommended in the opening chapter. It is a sophisticated analysis of the development of education in England alongside ideas of democracy. Designed for the advanced student it is well worth spending time to read and consider.

Kelly, A.V. (1999) *The Curriculum: Theory and Practice*, 4th edn, London: Paul Chapman Publishing. This was also recommended in the first chapter as suitable for the more advanced student, being a detailed and challenging volume. It links curriculum theory and ideology to the developing education system.

Lawton, D. (1992) *Education and Politics in the 1990s: Conflict or Consensus?*, London: Falmer Press. This is now becoming rather dated but it does cover developments in compulsory education in the Thatcher era. It shows the link between ideology and policy in education. It is well written and very perceptive.

9

Education – a Contested Enterprise

It is argued in this chapter that to study education in any meaningful way requires an awareness of the interrelationship between the different disciplines involved, that is, to take a multidisciplinary approach. Education is presented as the result of continual conflict and interaction between competing ideologies at many levels. The chapter suggests that, inevitably, the ideologically charged area of education will always be at the heart of the development of any society and will remain a focus of political debate and struggle. Some reference is made to broader areas of education study which are beyond the remit of this book.

Introduction

The aim of this book has been to introduce the study of education. The approach has highlighted the value-laden nature of education and how both its policies and practices are informed by different sets of beliefs. These ideologies can be seen to permeate every part of the education process. Their various proponents bring them to bear on the principles and practices of education through the often politicized processes of developing theory to determine practice and extrapolating theory out of practice. In applying some of the research questions and analytical tools of the four disciplines – philosophy, sociology, psychology and history – to the study of education, we can both reveal and explore these theories from a number of perspectives.

Theory and practice in education

Common-sense perceptions often represent theory as being quite distinct from practice. This is sometimes the case in education where the classroom or 'chalk-face' is perhaps set against what are felt to be the vague irrelevancies of the world of theory. In fact, this common-sense view is itself a theory of how things are and – as with all theories – represents a particular way of looking at the world. As Eagleton (1990) argues, the sharp polarity between theory and life is not really tenable. All social life is theoretical and involves theoretical propositions about the world. It can be claimed that there is a live tradition of critical theory that seeks to rethink fundamental aspects of contemporary education. This theoretical tradition may be said to include, for example, the:

- reflective practice movement historically associated with Dewey and Schon
- tradition of enlightenment thought that runs from Kant in the eighteenth century to Habermas in the present day, contending that social justice can be achieved through the actions of rational autonomous individuals participating in open public debate
- emancipatory concerns of feminism and the liberationist education philosophy of Freire
- action research movement that seeks to develop educational practice by concentrating on the micro-environment of the classroom and that is sensitive to the uniqueness of classroom practice (Parker, 1997).

In addition, new forms of research and practice have emerged from theory that has challenged the enlightenment tradition in the work of Foucault (1977a) and Lyotard (1984) and that sees the field of social action as being fraught with conflict and difference. It is clear that the theory you espouse will determine both what and how you see the field of education and how you propose to make interventions – whether in practice or into thought and knowledge about education. It may be the case that the production of theory is remote from the locations and exponents of practice, though the action research movement has been a significant attempt to narrow this gap and to put theory at the centre of practice as well as to make practice the source of theory.

The traditional disciplines and education studies

Fundamental to any society, education and the processes it involves are of great interest to fields of study concerned with the human condition.

In particular we have referred in this book to philosophy, sociology, psychology and history.

We have seen how the philosophy of education illuminates the ideas which underpin action and thought in education. The questions philosophers ask concern the nature and purposes of education, such as what makes an educated person, how is knowledge organized and what should be learned? They are primarily interested in the beliefs, morals and values which permeate education. These are very important questions which are at the heart of the whole process and therefore appear in every aspect of the study of education. They are key to discussions of the nature of curriculum which derive from different ideological positions on education and the structure of knowledge. Such questions are also apparent when analysing how beliefs are translated into policy or when looking at issues of individual development and progression.

The psychology of education is mainly concerned with how people learn and develop. As such it asks questions about our maturation, intelligence, personality and motivation, as well as about the learning process itself. It is interested in the relationship between nature and nurture and the way they interact to influence individual development and achievement. We have seen how a psychological analysis involves philosophical issues of the nature of knowledge and understanding and shares an interest in sociological issues since the individual is seen to be part of wider social groups. An examination of pedagogy from a psychological perspective revealed the link between psychological and sociological theory as well as the different ideologies within which they existed and from which came the resulting education policy.

The sociology of education examines the wider social influences upon the individual in education. Sociologists ask questions about the influences of social class, race and gender upon achievement, and these are seen in relation to various ideologies which shape education. Sociological analysis is concerned with power operating at different levels in society and how this influences outcomes. This explains the sociologist's interest in the creation of education policy and its implementation. The sociologist accepts that social factors are not totally deterministic of success or failure in education and that the psychological explanations of individual achievement are also very important.

The history of education may reveal causal explanations for changes which punctuate the political and social timelines of educational development. These explanations owe much to philosophical, sociological and psychological theories as well as to political analysis. It has been argued, for instance, that to understand modern education systems it is vital to learn that institutions of education had very significant governmental functions and worked to shape populations and define the identities of subjects. While the purposes and scope of education have changed radically since the late nineteenth century, the pastoral and disciplinary functions of schools and other education establishments remain significant within education in modern western societies. A historical approach to researching education can thus reveal data on many of its key aspects and is central to an examination of the contested nature of the education process. This has been apparent when looking, for example, at the development of education research or theories of achievement in education and the temporal manner of their definition, as well as when charting the history and development of compulsory education since the Second World War.

Each of these four separate disciplines brings its own specific perspective to the study of education and each is interested in particular aspects as they relate to their own concerns. It is also clear that their areas of interest overlap. When education itself is the focus for the student, as in education studies, it is important to draw from these disciplines as appropriate. This eclectic view can provide a richer picture of the whole process and may produce new forms of knowledge and new ways of understanding.

Education as the focus of study

We have seen the impact of disparate ideological perspectives on education as an area of study; from the functionalist view of education existing to prepare citizens for society, to the Marxist view of education acting as an agency of the state in the reinforcement of class differentials; from the utilitarian position of education ensuring social order, to Rousseau's view that humans can, through the development of society, rise above their natural state. While in daily classroom life the complexity of competing ideologies which seek to influence education may not be very apparent, there are tensions and conflicts inherent in even the simplest curriculum and educational policy decisions. These are a consequence of the different belief systems which pervade the education system at every level. We have referred to the compulsory sector when analysing the relevance of these ideologies to education but the analysis is of course applicable to other sectors of education. Lifelong learning, early childhood education, post-compulsory education, for example, can all be interpreted in terms of these ideological influences.

There remains a deep conflict in ideas about knowledge, the curriculum and the school. Acknowledging the power of the curriculum to be a purveyor of beliefs and values raises important issues about the purpose and nature of education. Although a number of western nation states have adopted national curricula that are similar in content and structure, there remain big questions about the utilitarian value of curriculum knowledge and its cultural authority. Also significant is the way the curriculum acts as a vehicle for socialization and the different motives ascribed to this by competing ideologies of education. Pertinent to these issues is a consideration of the structural features of the curriculum. In the case of the English National Curriculum this would include an examination of, for example, the value of testing, of standard attainment targets, prescribed forms of teaching and learning such as the literacy and numeracy hours, and the means of communication and control. The 'story' surrounding the implementation of the National Curriculum is a fascinating example of ideological power struggles. We have only been able, in Chapter 3, to briefly introduce its development but an in-depth study would facilitate an analysis from philosophical, psychological, sociological and historical perspectives. The kind of learning promoted and cultivated by any curriculum reveals much about a society's fundamental premises and culture.

The attention paid to the planners', researchers' and teachers' views of the curriculum might suggest that the pupils/students are passive recipients in the education process. However, that is certainly not the case. Learners of all ages may be subject to various forms of teacher control. Frightened by the ogre, mesmerized or motivated by the raconteur or enthusiast, they generally accept the power differential between themselves and the teacher, and agree to conform at least to a certain extent. However, it should not be assumed that they have no say. Their power varies and depends upon a number of factors in the relationship between themselves and their teachers. Learners of any age can use different strategies to cause disruption during the teaching session. They may even leave the lesson and not come back. At least one of the authors has found it particularly disconcerting to find a student doing an essay for another subject during a lecture. When challenged the student simply replied that the essay was more important. Learners are thus able to exercise at least some degree of autonomy in many ways. In some situations the learner is granted 'legitimate' autonomy. For example, in higher education it is usual for students to design their own projects and independent programmes of learning with supervised help as part of their degree course. In pursuing 'off-task' behaviour in school or university learners are, of course, exercising 'unlegitimated' forms of autonomy which often involve resisting the official goals of the curriculum, school or college.

When considering the individual in education and influences upon their achievement we face a number of complex issues which are only resolvable from different perspectives. When we measure success in education what factors are we looking at? Achievement could be seen in academic terms measured in examination scores, it could be physical ability assessed by coordination and strength or social skills in terms of being able to cooperate with others or demonstrate leadership. Ultimately different institutions and agencies including government, schools, colleges and universities determine what should be measured and this is based upon what attributes are valued most highly.

Thus, as researchers of education, we are still interested in whether education develops individuals and gives them the opportunity to progress or whether it perpetuates inequalities. In Britain the question remains about the extent to which the education system is a meritocracy or whether such a concept is a myth designed to legitimate and help maintain inequality. Paradoxically, the education system can be shown to reproduce existing inequalities while simultaneously extending opportunities and access for all.

Education is a central force within society and is likely to play a significant part in the shaping of future generations. Being such a contested enterprise it is at the heart of the public political process. This process is played out at national level in law-making and parliamentary debate down to the local level of the school and individual teacher in terms of the day-to-day classroom-based decisions. An understanding of how different sets of beliefs and values compete in this process is central to the analysis. At any one time a number of ideological influences can be identified as seeking to influence policy.

Education, then, draws on particular disciplines to provide explanations and to inform research. In this book we have emphasized philosophy, sociology, psychology and history, but sometimes it is difficult to determine which of these discourses of knowledge is most relevant to the question in hand. In recent times the strict divisions of the curriculum and of different areas of knowledge, study and research have been challenged. A tradition running from Nietzsche in the nineteenth century to Richard Rorty at the end of the twentieth century has challenged the claims of official forms of knowledge to truth. These discourses and others – such as feminism, deconstruction and postmodernism – have deliberately sought to problematize the nature of truth and of knowledge, too. They have begun to influence the way that theorists of education think about and define systems, institutions, practices and effects (Parker, 1997). Education as a focus of study offers opportunities for the interaction between discourses and this can give rise to 'hybrid' forms of knowledge – as with gender studies, literacy studies, visual sociology, school culture research and social geography, for example (Prosser, 1999). This often means that the boundaries of education study are not fixed, which can have highly beneficial effects in terms of the construction of interdisciplinary forms and examples of knowledge.

Thus, a number of traditional and emerging disciplines contribute to our understanding of education. We contend that the disciplines individually would be unable to deal with the issues in such a cohesive manner. While drawing on the theories and research of the traditional disciplines, education studies is an increasingly significant area of study in its own right which can benefit too from analyses drawn from newer discourses. What remains to the fore of any study is the contested nature of education itself and how beliefs and values permeate every aspect of it.

The breadth of education studies

In this volume we have been unable to examine the full range of topics covered within education studies courses. Instead we have concentrated on outlining some of the major questions and issues with which education studies is concerned, using schools and the compulsory education sector to illustrate where appropriate. The reader will be aware that this is just one sector of formal education and that even this has not been examined in any great depth. We can only mention some of the other important areas which warrant further study as significant topics within the field of education studies. The fundamental questions raised in this volume concerning beliefs, values and purpose remain appropriate in respect of these topics.

The post-16 sectors of further and higher education have expanded rapidly over the last 20 years. While the great majority of the readers of this book have attended school, an increasing proportion will also have attended some form of further education institution. Most will currently be attending, or intending to enter, higher education. These post-compulsory sectors have become increasingly significant arenas for education as greater numbers of students remain in some form of education after the age of 16. It has now become unusual, as opposed to the norm of a few years ago, to leave school at 16 rather than continue with some form of post-compulsory education or training (see Hodkinson et al., 1996, for an analysis of the UK context of post-compulsory education and training).

Traditionally, higher education was regarded as an elitist sector for public school and grammar school pupils. Universities were for a minority of academically successful pupils. The 1960s saw the development of polytechnics run by LEAs which were designed to give an alternative to the traditional subject approach. They were to develop more applied courses at degree level which would be appropriate to meeting the needs of industry. However, over time, they also began to offer degree courses similar to those run by the traditional universities. In the Education Reform Act (1988) polytechnics were given their independence from LEAs. The binary line, which separated them from the traditional universities, was later abolished altogether and they became full universities.

A study of higher education might focus attention on the expansion of student numbers, funding the increased provision and the quality of degree study. There was a desire to expand access to higher education but a perennial problem is that of paying for this expansion. Higher education has suffered from a funding crisis as the number of students has rapidly expanded while central funding per student has decreased. Total spending on higher education can thus be said to have increased but it has to be spread across far more students. These 'efficiency savings' or 'cuts', depending upon one's point of view, have had a significant impact upon the sector.

The nature of teaching and learning has been under scrutiny by the central funding agency (the Higher Education Funding Council – HEFC) and within the higher education institutions themselves. Students are encouraged to be more self-directing with a growing emphasis on independent study and distance learning. The government has launched a major development in e-learning which aims to create a virtual university. These initiatives are presented as a process of increasing student autonomy. Others see them reducing the quality of provision as students have decreasing contact time with tutors. At the same time lecturers have been given greater teaching loads and larger groups. The quality of higher education has become an issue with the government promising to maintain standards while increasing student numbers and reducing costs. Universities are now inspected by the Quality Assurance Agency, subject by subject, and this is a significant factor in maintaining government funding. Department scores in these inspections now form part of the league tables developing in the media for higher education as universities are forced to compete in the marketplace for students.

The Robbins Report (1963) suggested that as society benefits from the quality of university graduates then society should pay the cost of their education. This was affordable when only a small proportion of the population partook of higher education. As the numbers entering higher education have rapidly expanded the new view is that it is the graduates that benefit most from higher education and therefore they should bear at least some of the cost. Current debates revolve around what proportion this should be. Thus, recent developments include the phasing out of student maintenance grants which have been replaced by loans and the introduction of a flat-rate enrolment fee. The effects of these changes on student enrolment remain to be seen. There is also the threat of a widening gulf between the traditional Russell group of universities (the established 'old' prestige universities including, for example, Oxford and Cambridge), which may demand greater fees from students, and the newer less-established institutions. The divide dispensed with by the abolition of the binary line is perhaps re-emerging between the elite universities and mass higher education institutions. Thus, issues of student access, individual achievement, teaching and learning methods, and the nature of the curriculum apply just as much to higher education as to the compulsory sector. Ideological conflict is, as it always has been, an important part of developments in higher education.

The experience of further education in many ways mirrors that of higher education. Further education institutions have faced similar changes since they were given their 'independence' from LEAs and became responsible for their own finances. This development was an important part of creating the market within further education provision. The introduction of this demand-led approach, coupled with a decline in central funding, has meant these colleges have had to become more flexible with increasing proportions of staff employed on part-time and temporary contracts. Both further and higher education have witnessed the development of management cultures in a similar form to that of business and industry. Education is considered a product which the consumer pays for 'up front'. The emphasis is on outcomes which may be linked to organizational inputs. The market has perhaps been quicker to develop in post-compulsory education where its customers, the students, choose to 'buy' the product. The analysis of the compulsory sector in Chapter 8 helps us to understand these developments as both further and higher education have become subject to similar policies of market forces and competition. The exercise of central control through inspection and monitoring has also become tighter as LEA involvement has been eroded in the former polytechnics and further education institutions. The new Learning Skills Councils will fund further education institutions and will inspect them in conjunction with OFSTED (DfEE, 1999c). As the post-16 sector expands, issues of accountability come into sharper focus, especially at a time when the government is promoting entitlement through the allocation of vouchers for learning which will enable students to shop around for their educational experiences.

The whole issue of lifelong learning and the development of a learning society has become increasingly high profile in political debate, and links to our earlier discussions concerning appropriate educational experiences. It is suggested that changes in the economy with the development of modern communications technology and the obsolescence of traditional skills mean that, rather than having one job for life, employees may follow several different careers during their working lives. They will need to be adaptable, continually learning and updating their skills (DfEE, 1998b). This concept of lifelong learning does not only apply to the workforce. Prolonged life expectancy means that citizens will remain active for longer and will want to develop a wide range of interests and skills throughout their lives. Thus, lifelong learning is promoted as a continuous process.

There are interesting issues to consider when thinking about how this lifelong learning will take place. While it may involve traditional forms of teaching and learning in the classroom, this approach is unlikely to be appropriate for all, or even the majority, of the adult population. The emphasis is likely to be on information and communications technology with the development of flexible and distance learning modes. The University for Industry was established in the mid-1990s to be a major influence in these developments. There is debate, however, as to whether we are actually moving towards a learning society or if the whole concept is political rhetoric linked to images of creating opportunity. While some would see lifelong learning as a liberating process, increasing learner autonomy and helping to create a more socially democratic society, others portray it as just another, though perhaps more sophisticated, form of control being developed through modern technology (Coffield, 1999; Tight, 1999). The relationship between lifelong learning and modern modes of employment is certainly open to question.

At the other end of the educational spectrum early childhood studies is rapidly becoming a subject in its own right. Early childhood studies considers physiological, psychological, sociological and legal aspects of child development. Interest in this area has increased with the expansion of educational provision for younger children in schools, nurseries and playgroups. Hotly debated issues of the appropriateness of particular educational early years experiences, coupled with differing theories of child development, create a rich source of study. A central policy plank of the current Labour government is the growth of early years provision and the baseline assessment of 4- and 5-year-olds on entry to school. We can only gesture to the ideological tensions inherent in these policies but they are worthy of thorough exploration. Recent research and its significance to developments within this field have been well documented by Aubrey et al. (2000).

Special needs has also become an important area of study in its own right and is of particular interest in education studies. Issues of access, equality and inclusion are significant in the current political agenda (Clough and Barton, 1998; Dyson and Millward, 2000). They relate to individual and social factors which influence success in education. A study of special needs considers the different forms in which learning difficulties are manifested and the way they impact upon individuals and society. There is also an imperative to consider how far social inclusion is actually developing or, whether conversely, much of the rhetoric is merely masking a lack of change.

Issues of social justice have also been harnessed to debates about education for sustainability. The environmentally unfriendly practices of the past are now a source of real concern in most societies, particularly as their consequences are visited differentially on individuals depending on where in the world they live and how rich they are. Since the United Nations made education one of four priorities in the quest for sustainable development, there has been increasing pressure in the academic literature for issues of sustainability to secure a central place in the curricula of schools, colleges and higher education (Fien, 1993; Shallcross and Robinson, 1999). Consideration of the global economy and its implications for environmental and social justice might be said to be proper elements of a citizenship curriculum for the twenty-first century.

All sectors of education are made up of organizations of various sizes: schools, colleges, universities, local education authorities. Organization theory and the study of behaviour in organizations constitute important elements in education studies courses. As many postgraduate students of education work in the field there is a particular interest in theories of management and their application as part of professional and academic study (see Bush and Coleman, 2000; Middlewood and Lumby, 1999). By considering organizations which are primarily people-centred an emphasis is placed on theories related to performance management or management by objectives, human relations management and also quality management. The whole area of institutional effectiveness, touched upon in Chapter 2, also falls within this remit.

Other aspects of organizational theory treat the nature and purposes of educational organizations as much more problematic when examining them. They are concerned with life in these organizations from different perspectives (Ball, 1981). Thus some studies consider the nature of being a pupil (Willis, 1979). Others examine the labour process of teaching and how this may be seen in relation to concepts such as deskilling, proletarianization, resistance and renegotiation (Apple, 1996; Bartlett, 1998b; Ozga, 1995). These approaches often characterize educational organizations as being less predictable, more unstable and micropolitical than more traditional management approaches tend to.

This book has limited itself to a consideration of the English education system. This, of course, can make us blind to alternatives and may lead us to assume that other parts of the world have had similar experiences to ourselves. It also encourages a distorted view of our own significance. If we had space in the book to take in a wider range of education systems, similar issues of purpose and ideology shaping curriculum design and models of learning would arise. The importance of comparing different systems and the significance of particular cultural influences to each system should be acknowledged. In addition the impact and pressures of globalization on education systems and their pedagogy has generated a great deal of interest among educators (Edwards and Usher, 2000). Globalization is a significant factor in shaping both policy and practice across the world as systems 'interfere' with one another and ideas, research, ideologies and institutions take on different shape and form.

This volume has argued for a critical multidisciplinary approach to the study of education. It also demonstrates the importance of treating education as a field of study in its own right. This enables us to look at the major issues, structural features and sources of controversy in education and to ask critical questions. The last question we would put to you is the same as the first,

What exactly is education?

To answer this question we need to go back to the beginning.

Bibliography

Adey, P. (1992) 'The CASE results: implications for science teaching', *International Journal of Science Education*, 14: 137–46.

Ahmad, A. (1992) *In Theory*, London: Verso.

Albert, R.S. and Runco, M.A. (1999) '*A history of research on creativity*', in R. Sternberg (ed.), *Handbook of Creativity*, Cambridge: Cambridge University Press.

Althusser, L. (1984) *Essays on Ideology*, London: Verso.

Altrichter, H., Posch, P. and Somkeh, B. (1993) *Teachers Investigate their Work: An Introduction to the Methods of Action Research*, London: Routledge.

Anderson, G. with Arsenault, N. (1998) *Fundamentals of Educational Research*, London: Falmer Press.

Anderson, J. and Bower, G. (1973) *Human Associative Memory*, Washington, DC: Winston.

Anderson, J.R., Reder, L.M. and Simon, H.A. (1996) 'Situated learning and education', *Educational Researcher*, 25: 5–11.

Anderson, J.R., Reder, L.M. and Simon, H.A. (1997) 'Situative versus cognitive perspectives: form versus substance', *Educational Researcher*, 26: 18–21.

Andrews, R. (ed.) (1996) *Interpreting the New National Curriculum*, London: Middlesex University Press.

Apple, M. (1996) *Cultural Politics and Education*, Buckingham: Open University Press.

Apple, M. (1998) 'Work, Class and Teaching', in J. Ozga (ed.), *Schoolwork: Approaches to the Labour Process of Teaching*, Milton Keynes: Open University Press.

Aries, P. (1962) *Centuries of Childhood: A Social History of Family Life*, London: Cape.

Arnot, M. (1968) *Recent Research on Gender and Education*, London: The Stationery Office.

Arnot, M. (2000) *Reproducing Gender: A Feminist Perspective on Two Decades of Reform*, London: Routledge.

Aronowitz, S. and Giroux, H.A. (1986) *The Conservative, Liberal and Radical Debate over Schooling*, London: Routledge and Kegan Paul.

Assessment of Performance Unit (1986) *Speaking and Listening, Assessment at Age 11*, Windsor: NFER-Nelson.

Atkinson, J. and Shiffrin, R. (1968) 'Human memory: a proposed system and its control processes', in K. Spence and J. Spence (eds), *The Psychology of Learning and Motivation*, vol. 2, London: Academic Press.

Atkinson, J.W. (1964) *An Introduction to Motivation*, Princeton, NJ: Van Nostrand.

Atweh, B., Kemmis, S. and Weeks, P. (eds) (1998) *Action Research in Practice*, London: Routledge.

Aubrey, C., David, T., Godfrey, R. and Thompson, L (2000) *Early Childhood Educational Research*, London: Routledge.

Ausubel, D.P. (1968) *Educational Psychology: A Cognitive View*, New York: Holt, Rinehart and Winston.

Ausubel, D.P. (1985) 'Learning as constructing meaning', in: N. Entwistle (ed.), *New Directions in Educational Psychology: 1. Learning and Teaching*, Lewes: Falmer Press.

Avis, J. (1994) 'Teacher professionalism: one more time', *Educational Review*, 46: 63–72.

Avis, J. (1999) 'Shifting identity: new conditions and the transformation of practice – teaching within post-compulsory education', *Journal of Vocational Education and Training*, 51 (2): 245–64.

Avis, J. (2000) 'Policing the subject: learning outcomes, managerialism and research in PCET', *British Journal of Educational Studies*, 48: 38–57.

Baddeley, A.D. (1997) *Human Memory: Theory and Practice*, 2 edn, Hove: Psychology Press.

Ball, S.J. (1981) *Beachside Comprehensive: A Case Study of Secondary Schooling*, Cambridge: Cambridge University Press.

Ball, S.J. (1987) *The Micro-Politics of the School: Towards a Theory of School Organisation*, London: Methuen.

Ball, S.J. (1988) 'Staff relations during the teachers' industrial action: context, conflict and proletarianisation', *British Journal of Sociology of Education*, 9 (3): 289–306.

Ball, S.J. (1990) *Politics and Policy Making in Education*, London: Routledge.

Ball, S.J. (1993) *The Micro-Politics of the School*, London: Routledge.

Ball, S.J. (1994) *Education Reform: A Critical and Post-Structural Approach*, Buckingham: Open University Press.

Ball, S.J. (1999) 'Labour, learning and the economy: a "policy sociology" perspective', *Cambridge Journal of Education*, 29 (2): 195–206.

Baltes, (1996) *Interactive Minds: Life-Span Perspectives on the Social Foundations of Cognition*, Cambridge: Cambridge University Press.

Bancroft, D. and Carr, R. (eds) (1995) *Influencing Children's Development*, Oxford: Blackwell in association with the Open University.

Bandura, A. (1977) *Social Learning Theory*, Englewood Cliffs, NJ: Prentice-Hall.

Banks, O. (1968) *The Sociology of Education*, London: Batsford.

Barber, M. (1996) *The National Curriculum: A Study in Policy*, Keele: Keele University Press.

Barnard, N. (2000) 'Could you do any better miss?', *Times Educational Supplement*, 23 June: 22.

Barrett, M. (1980) *Women's Oppression Today: Problems in Marxist Feminist Analysis*, London: Verso.

Barrow, R., and Woods, R. (1988) *An Introduction to Philosophy of Education*, London: Routledge.

Bartlett, F.C. (1932) *Remembering*, Cambridge: Cambridge University Press.

Bartlett, S. (1988a) 'Teacher perceptions of the purposes of staff appraisal: a response to Kyriacou, *Teacher Development*, 2 (3): 479–90.

Bartlett, S. (1998b) 'The development of effective appraisal by teachers', *Journal of In-Service Education*, 24 (2): 227–38.

Bartlett, S. (2000) 'The development of teacher appraisal: a recent history', *British Journal of Educational Studies*, 48 (1): 24–37.

Barton, L., Barrett, E., Whitty, G., Miles, S. and Furlong, J. (1994) 'Teacher education and teacher professionalism in England: some emerging issues', *British Journal of Sociology of Education*, 15 (1): 529–43.

Bash, L. and Coulby, D. (1989) *The Education Reform Act: Competition and Control*, London: Cassell.

Bassey, M. (1990) 'On the nature of research in education (Part 2)', *Research Intelligence* (37) Summer: 39–44.

Batteson, C. (1998) 'A review of politics of education in the "Moment of 1976" ', *British Journal of Educational Studies*, 45 (4): 363–7.

Becker, H.S. (1971) 'Social class variations in the teacher pupil relationship', in B.R. Cosin, I.R. Dale, G.M. Esland and D.F Swift (eds), *School and Society*, London: Routledge and Kegan Paul.

Bee, H. (1985) *The Developing Child*, 4th edn, New York: Harper & Row.

Bee, H. (1992) *The Developing Child*, 6th edn, London: HarperCollins.

Bee, H. (2000) *The Developing Child*, 9th edn, London: Allyn and Bacon.

Bee, H.L., Barnard, K.E., Eyres, S.J., Gray, C.A., Hammond, M.A., Speitz, A.L., Snyder, C. and Clark, B. (1982) 'Predication of IQ and language skill from perinatal status, child performance, family characteristics, and mother-infant interaction', *Child Development*, 53: 1135–56.

Bell, J. (1999) *Doing Your Research Project: A Guide for First-Time Researchers in Education and Social Science*, Buckingham: Open University Press.

Benn, C. and Chitty, C. (1996) *Thirty Years On: Is Comprehensive Education Alive and Well or Struggling to Survive?* London: Fulton.

Bennett, N. and Dunne, E. (1992) *Managing Classroom Groups*, Hemel Hempstead: Simon and Schuster.

Bentley, T. (1998) *Learning Beyond the Classroom*, London: Routledge.

Bernstein, B. (1970) 'Education cannot compensate for society', *New Society*, 387: 44–7.

Bernstein B. (1971) *Class, Codes and Control*, London: Routledge and Kegan Paul.

Bernstein B. (ed.) (1973) *Class, Codes and Control: Vol. 2*, London: Routledge and Kegan Paul.

Bernstein, B. (1995) *Pedagogy, Symbolic Control and Identity*, London: Taylor and Francis.

Biggs, J.B. (1978) 'Individual and group differences in study processes', *British Journal of Educational Psychology*, 48: 266–79.

Biggs, J.B. (1987a) *The Study Process Questionnaire (SPQ) Manual*, Hawthorne, Victoria: Australian Council for Educational Research.

Biggs, J.B. (1987b) *Student Approaches to Learning and Studying*, Hawthorne, Victoria: Australian Council for Educational Research.

Biggs, J.B. (1993) 'What do inventories of students' learning processes really measure? A theoretical review and clarification, *British Journal of Educational Psychology*, 63: 3–19.

Biott, C. and Easen, P. (1994) *Collaborative Learning in Staffrooms and Classrooms*, London: Fulton.

Blaxter, L., Hughes, C. and Tight, M. (1996) *How to Research*, Buckingham: Open University Press.

Bloom, B.S. (1956) *Taxonomy of Educational Objectives*, vol. 1, London: Longmans.

Boaler, J. (1996) 'A case study of setted and mixed ability teaching', paper presented at the British Education Research Association Conference, Lancaster University, September.

Boaler, J. (1997) 'Setting, social class and survival of the quickest', *British Educational Research Journal*, 23: 575–95.

Bottery, M. and Wright, N. (1999) 'The directed profession: teachers and the state in the third millennium', a paper given at the Annual SCETT Conference, Dunchurch, November.

Bouchard, T.J. and McGue, M. (1981) 'Familial studies of intelligence: a review, *Science*, 212: 1055–9.

Bourdieu, P. (1991) *Language and Symbolic Power*, Cambridge: Polity Press.

Bourdieu, P. and Passeron, J. (1977) *Reproduction in Education, Society and Culture*, London: Sage.

Bourne, J. and Moon, B. (1994) 'A question of ability?', in B. Moon and A. Shelton-Mayes (eds), *Teaching and Learning in the Secondary School*, London: Routledge.

Bowles, S. and Gintis, H. (1976) *Schooling in Capitalist America: Educational Reform and the Contradictions of Economic Life*, London: Routledge and Kegan Paul.

Brah, A. and Minhas, R. (1985) 'Structural racism or cultural difference: schooling for Asian girls', in G. Weiner (ed.), *Just a Bunch of Girls: Feminist Approaches to Schooling*, Milton Keynes: Open University Press.

Brennan, J. and McGreevor, P. (1990) *Ethnic Minorities and the Graduate Labour Market*, London: Commission for Racial Equality.

Brewer, W.F. (1999) 'Bartlett, Frederic Charles', in R.A. Wilson and F.C. Keil (eds), *The MIT Encyclopedia of the Cognitive Sciences*, Cambridge, MA: MIT Press.

British Educational Research Association (BERA) (1992) *Dialogue Series: Policy Issues in National Assessment*, Clevedon: Multilingual Matters.

Broadbent, D. (1958) *Perception and Communication*, London: Pergamon Press.

Bronfenbrenner, U. (1979) *The Ecology of Human Development*, Cambridge, MA, Harvard University Press.

Brook, A. (1999) 'Kant Emmanuel', in R.A. Wilson, and F.C. Keil (eds), *The MIT Encyclopedia of the Cognitive Sciences*, Cambridge, MA: MIT Press.

Brooks, R. (1991) *Contemporary Debates in Education: A Historical Perspective*, London: Longman.

Brown, A.L. (1994) 'The advancement of learning', *Educational Researcher*, 23: 4–12.

Brown, S. (1990) 'Assessment a changing practice', in T. Horton (ed.), *Assessment Debates*, London: Hodder and Stoughton.

Brown, P., Halsey, A.H. and Stuart Wells, A. (1997) 'The transformation of education and society: an introduction', in A.H. Halsey, H. Lauder, P. Brown and A. Wells, *Education: Culture Economy Society*, Oxford: Oxford University Press.

Bruner, J. (1966) *Towards a Theory of Instruction*, New York: Norton.

Bruner, J. (1983) *Child's Talk: Learning to Use Language*, Oxford: Oxford University Press.

Bruner, J.S. (1972) *The Relevance of Education*, London: Allen and Unwin.

Bryant, I. (1996) 'Action research and reflective practice', D. Scott and R. Usher (eds), *Understanding Educational Research*, London: Routledge.

Bullock Report (1975) *A Language for Life*, London: HMSO.

Burden, R. and Williams, M. (1998) *Thinking Through the Curriculum*, London: Routledge.

Burgoyne, J. (1994) 'Stakeholder analysis', in C. Cassell and G. Symon (eds), *Qualitative Methods in Organisational Research: A Practical Guide*, London: Sage.

Burt, C. (1955) 'The evidence for the concept of intelligence', *British Journal of Educational Psychology*, 25, 158–77.

Burton, D. and Anthony, S. (1997) 'Differentiation of curriculum and instruction in primary and secondary schools', *Educating Able Children*, 1 (1): 26–34.

Burton, D.M. (1998) 'The changing role of the university tutor within school-based initial teacher education and training: issues of role contingency and complementarity within a secondary partnership scheme', *Journal of Education for Teaching*, 24 (2): 129–46.

Bush, T. and Coleman, M. (2000) *Leadership and Strategic Management in Education*, London: Paul Chapman Publishing.

Canter, L. and Canter, M. (1977) *Assertive Discipline*, Los Angeles: Lee Canter Associates.

Carr, D. (1997) 'The uses of literacy in teacher education', *British Journal of Educational Studies*, 45: 53–68.

Carr, W. (1995) *For Education: Towards Critical Educational Enquiry*, Buckingham: Open University Press.

Carr, W. and Hartnett A. (1996) *Education and the Struggle for Democracy: The Politics of Educational Ideas*, Buckingham: Open University Press.

Carr, W. and Kemmis, S. (1986) *Becoming Critical: Education, Knowledge and Action Research*, London: Falmer.

Cattell, R.B. (1963) 'Theory of fluid and cristallized intelligence: a critical experiment', *Journal of Educational Psychology*, 54: 1–22.

Cattell, R.B. (1970) *The Technical Handbook to the 16 PF*, Illinois: Institute for Personality and Achievement Tests.

Central Advisory Council for Education (CACE) (1967) *Children and their Primary Schools* (Plowden Report), London: HMSO.

Centre for Contemporary Cultural Studies (CCCS) (1981) *Unpopular Education*, London: Hutchinson.

Centre for Contemporary Cultural Studies (CCCS) (1991) *Education Limited*, London: Unwin Hyman.

Child, D. (1986) *Psychology and the Teacher*, 4th edn, London: Cassell.

Child, D. (1997) *Psychology and the Teacher*, 6th edn, London: Cassell.

Chitty, C. (1992) *The Education System Transformed*, Manchester: Baseline Books.

Chitty, C. (1999) 'The "Moment of 1976" revisited', *British Journal of Education Studies*, 46 (3): 318–23.

Chitty, C. and Dunford, J. (1999) *State Schools: New Labour and the Conservative Legacy*, London: Woburn Press.

Chomsky, N. (1965) *Aspects of the Theory of Syntax*, Cambridge, MA: MIT Press.

Chyriwsky, M. (1996) 'Able children: the need for a subject-specific approach', *Flying High*, 3: 32–6, Worcester: The National Association for Able Children in Education.

Cicourel, A.V. and Kitsuse, J.I. (1971) 'The social organization of the high school and deviant adolescent careers' in B.R. Cosin, I.R. Dale, G.M. Esland and D.F. Swift (eds), *School and Society*, London: Routledge and Kegan Paul.

Circular 10/65: The Organization of Secondary Education (1965), DES, London: HMSO.

Clough, P. and Barton, L. (eds) (1998) *Articulating with Difficulty. Research Voices in Inclusive Education*, London: Paul Chapman Publishing.

Coard, B. (1971) *How the West Indian Child is Made Educationally Subnormal in the British School System*, London: New Beacon Books.

Coffield, F. (1999) 'Breaking the consensus: lifelong learning as social control', *British Educational Research Journal*, 25 (4): 479–98.

Coffrey, A., and Delamont, S. (2000) *Feminism and the Classroom Teacher: Research, Praxis, Pedagogy*, London: Routledge.

Cohen, L. Manion, L. and Morrison, K. (2000) *Research Methods in Education*, 5th edn, London: Routledge.

Cole, M. and Scribner, S. (1974) *Culture and Thought*, New York: Wiley.

Collins, A.M. and Quillian, M.R. (1969) 'Retrieval time from semantic memory', *Journal of Verbal Learning and Verbal Behaviour*, 8: 240–8.

Cooley, C.H. (1902) *Human Nature and the Social Order*, New York: Scribner.

Cooper, C. (1999) *Intelligence and Abilities*, London: Routledge.

Copeland, I. (1999) *The Making of the Backward Pupil in Education in England 1870–1914*, London: Woburn Press.

Coulby, D. (1989) 'From Educational Partnership to Central Control', in L. Bash and D. Coulby, *The Education Reform Act. Competition and Control*, London: Cassell.

Covington, M. (1998) *The Will to Learn: A Guide for Motivating Young People*, Cambridge: Cambridge University Press.

Cox, B. (1991) *Cox on Cox*, London: Hodder and Stoughton.

Cox, B. (1995) *The Battle for the English Curriculum*, London: Hodder and Stoughton.

Cox, C.B. and Dyson, A.E. (eds) (1969a) *Fight for Education: A Black Paper*, Manchester: Critical Quarterly Society.

Cox, C.B. and Dyson, A.E. (eds) (1969b) *Black Paper Two: The Crisis in Education*, Manchester: Critical Quarterly Society.

Craik, F. and Lockhart, R. (1972) 'Levels of processing: a framework for memory research', *Journal of Verbal Learning and Verbal Behaviour*, 11: 671–84.

Craik, K. (1943) *The Nature of Explanation*, Cambridge: Cambridge University Press.

Creemers, B. (1994) 'The History, Value and Purpose of School Effectiveness Studies', in D. Reynolds, B. Creemers, P. Nesselrodt, E. Schaffer, S. Stringfeld, and C. Teddlie (eds), *Advances in School Effectiveness Research and Practice*, Oxford: Pergamon Press.

Crowther Report (1959) Ministry of Education *15 to 18*, London: HMSO.

Crozier, R. (1997) *Personality Differences in Education*, London: Routledge.

Cuff, E. and Payne, G. with Francis, D., Hustler, D. and Sharrock, W. (1984) *Perspectives in Sociology*, 2nd edn, London: Allen and Unwin.

Curry, L. (1983) 'An organisation of learning style theory and constructs', in L. Curry (ed.), *Learning Style in Continuing Education*, Halifax, Nova Scotia: Dalhousie University.

Dale, R. (1979) 'The Politicisation of School Deviance: Reactions to William Tyndale', in L. Barton and R. Meighan (eds), *Schools: Pupils and Deviance*, Driffield: Nafferton.

Dale, R. (1983) 'Thatcherism and Education', in J. Ahier and M. Flude (eds), *Contemporary Education Policy*, London: Croom Helm.

Darling-Hammond, L. (1994) 'Performance-based assessment and educational equity', *Harvard Educational Review*, 64: 5–30.

Darwin, C. (1859) *On the Origin of the Species by Means of Natural Selection*, London: Murray.

Davies, M. and Edwards, G. (1999) 'Will the curriculum caterpillar ever learn to fly?', *Cambridge Journal of Education*, 29 (2): 265–75.

Davis, B. and Sumara, D.J. (1997) 'Cognition, complexity and teacher education', *Harvard Educational Review*, 67: 105–21.

Davis, K. and Moore, W.E. (1967) 'Some principles of stratification', in R. Bendix and S.M. Lipset, (eds), *Class, Status, and Power*, London: Kegan Paul.

Daw, P. (1995) 'Differentiation and its meanings', *The English and Media Magazine*, (32): 11–15.

Dearing, R. (1993) *The National Curriculum and its Assessment: Final Report* (Dearing Report), London: School Curriculum and Assessment Authority.

Dearing, R. (1994) *A Review of the National Curriculum*, London: School Curriculum and Assessment Authority.

Deem, R. (1984) *Coeducation Reconsidered*, Milton Keynes: Open University Press.

DeFelipe, J. and Jones, E.G. (1991) *Cajal's Degeneration and Regeneration of the Nervous System*, New York: Oxford University Press.

Delpit, L. (1995) *Other People's Children: Cultural Conflict in the Classroom*, New York: New Press.

Deming, W. (1986) *Out of the Crisis: Quality, Productivity and Competitive Position*, Cambridge: Cambridge University Press.

Denzin, N. (1970) *The Research Act*, Chicago: Aldine.

Department of Education and Science (DES) (1978a) *Mixed Ability Work in Comprehensive Schools*, HMI Matters for Discussion 6, London, HMSO.

Department of Education and Science (DES) (1978b) *Report of the Committee of Enquiry into the Education of Handicapped Children and Young People* (Warnock Report), London, HMSO.

Department of Education and Science (DES) (1981) *West Indian Children in our Schools* (Rampton Report), London: HMSO.

Department of Education and Science (DES) (1983) *Teaching Quality. London:* HMSO.

Department of Education and Science (DES) (1985a) *The Curriculum from 5 to 16*, London: HMSO.

Department of Education and Science (DES) (1985b) *Education for all* (Swann Report), London: HMSO.

Department of Education and Science (DES) (1985c) *Better Schools*, London: HMSO.

Department of Education and Science (DES) (1987) *Statistical Bulletin 10/87: The Secondary Schooling Staffing Survey – Data on the Curriculum in Maintained Secondary Schools in England*, London: HMSO.

Department of Education and Science (DES) (1989) *National Curriculum: From Policy to Practice*, London: HMSO.

Department of Education and Science (DES) (1988) *The Education Reform Act*, London: HMSO.

Department of Education and Science (DES) (1989) *The Task Group on Assessment and Testing: A Report*, London: HMSO.

Department of Education and Science/Welsh Office (DES/WO) (1989) *Records of Achievement: Report of the Records of Achievement National Steering Committee*, London: DES/WO.

Department for Education and Employment (DfEE) (1997a) *Statistics of Education: Public Examinations: GCSE and GCE in England, 1996*, London: The Stationery Office.

Department for Education and Employment (DfEE) (1997b) *Excellence in Schools*, London: The Stationery Office.

Department for Education and Employment (DfEE) (1998a) *Teachers Meeting the Challenge of Change*, London: The Stationery Office.

Department for Education and Employment (DfEE) (1998b) *The Learning Age: A Renaissance for a New Britain*, London: The Stationery Office.

Department for Education and Employment (DfEE) (1999a) *Meet the Challenge. Education Action Zones*, Sudbury: DfEE Publications.

Department for Education and Employment (DfEE) (1999b) *Performance Management Framework for Teachers: Consultation Document*, London: DfEE.

Department for Education and Employment (DfEE) (1999c) *Youth Cohort Study: The Activities and Experiences of 16 Year Olds: England and Wales 1998*, London: The Stationery Office.

Department for Education and Employment (DfEE) (1999d) *Learning to Succeed: A New Framework for Post-16 Learning*, Nottingham: DfEE Publications

Department for Education and Employment (DfEE) (2000a) *National Curriculum Assessment of 7, 11 and 14 Year Olds by Local Education Authority*, London: DfEE.

Department for Education and Employment (DfEE) (2000b) *Performance Management in Schools: Performance Management Framework*, London: DfEE.

Department for Education and Employment (DfEE) (2001) *Schools Building on Success*, London: DfEE.

Department for Education and Employment/Quality and Curriculum Authority (DfEE/QCA) (1999) *The National Curriculum*, London: HMSO.

Derrida, J. (1987) *Positions*, London: Athlone.

Dickinson, C. and Wright, J. (1993) *Differentiation: a Practical Handbook of Classroom Strategies*, Coventry: NCET.

Dixon, J. (1967) *Growth through English*, Oxford: Oxford University Press.

Donald, J. (1992) *Sentimental Education*, London: Verso.

Donaldson, M. (1978) *Children's Minds*, London: Fontana.

Douglas, J.W.B. (1964) *The Home and the School*, St Albans: Panther.

Dowrick, N. (1996) ' "But many that are first shall be last": attainment differences in young collaborators', *Research in Education*, 55: 16–28.

Doyle, B. (1989) *English and Englishness*, London: Routledge.

Driver, R. and Bell, J. (1986) 'Students thinking and learning of science: a constructivist view', *School Science Review*, 67 (240): 443–56.

Dunn, R. (1991) 'How learning style changes over time', presentation at the 14th Annual Leadership Institute: Teaching Students Through Their Individual Learning Styles, 7–13 July, New York.

Dunn, R., Dunn, K. and Price, G.E. (1989) *The Learning Style Inventory*, Lawrence, KS: Price Systems.

Durkheim, E. (1947) *The Division of Labour in Society*, New York: Free Press.

Durkheim, E. (1970) *Suicide: A Study in Sociology*, London: Routledge and Kegan Paul.

Dweck, C.S. (1991) 'Self-theories and goals: their role in motivation, personality and development', Nebraska Symposium on Motivation, 38, University of Nebraska Press.

Dyson, A. and Millward, A. (2000) *Schools and Special Needs: Issues of Innovation and Inclusion*. London: Paul Chapman Publishing.

Eagleton, T. (1990), *The Significance of Theory*. Oxford: Blackwell.

Eagleton, T. (2000) *The Idea of Culture*, Oxford: Blackwell.

Ebbinghaus, H. (1885) *Memory: a Contribution to Experimental Psychology Refurbished*, 1964 edn, New York: Dover.

Edwards, R. and Usher, R. (1994) *Postmodernism and Education*, London: Routledge.
Edwards, R. and Usher, R. (2000) *Globalisation and Pedagogy: Space, Place and Identity*, London: Routledge.
Elliott, J. (1991) *Action Research for Educational Change*, Milton Keynes: Open University Press.
Elliott, E.S. and Dweck, C.S. (1988) 'Goals: an approach to motivation and achievement', *Journal of Personality and Social Psychology*, 54: 5–12.
Elliott, J. (1993) 'What have we learned from action research in school-based evaluation?', *Education Action Research*, 1 (1): 175–86.
Elliott, J. (1998) *The Curriculum Experiment. Meeting the Social Challenge*, Buckingham: Open University Press.
Engestrom, Y. (1993) 'Developmental studies of work as a testbench of activity theory', in S. Chaiklin and J. Lave (eds), *Understanding Practice: Perspectives on Activity and Context*, Cambridge: Cambridge University Press.
Entwistle, N.J. (1981) *Styles of Learning and Teaching*, Chichester: Wiley.
Erikson, E.H. (1980) *Identity and the Life Cycle*, New York: Norton.
Eysenck, H.J. (1947) *Dimensions of Personality*, London: Routledge.
Eysenck, H.J. (1967) *The Biological Basis of Personality*, Springfield IL: Thomas.
Festinger, L. (1957) *A Theory of Cognitive Dissonance*, Evanston, IL: Row, Peterson.
Feuerstein, R., Klein, P. and Tannenbaum, A. (eds) (1991) *Mediated Learning Experience*, London: Freund.
Fielding, M. (1994) 'Why and how learning styles matter: valuing difference in teachers and learners', in S. Hart (ed.), *Differentiation and the Secondary Curriculum: Debates and Dilemmas*, London: Routledge.
Fielding, M. (1999a) 'Editorial. Taking education really seriously: two years hard labour', *Cambridge Journal of Education*, 29 (2): 173–81.
Fielding, M. (1999b) 'Target setting, policy pathology and student perspectives: learning to labour in new times', *Cambridge Journal of Education*, 29 (2): 277–87.
Fien, J. (1993) *Education for the Environment: Critical Curriculum Theorising and Environmental Education*, Geelong: Deakin University Press.
Firestone, S. (1970) *Dialectics of Sex*, New York: Paladin.
Flavell, J.H. (1979) 'Metacognition and cognitive monitoring', *American Psychologist*, 34: 906–11.
Flavell, J.H. (1982) 'Structures, stages, and sequences in cognitive development', in W.A. Collins (ed.), *The Concept of Development: The Minnesota Symposia on Child Psychology*, 15: 1–28.
Fodor, J. (1975) *The Language of Thought*, Cambridge, MA: Harvard University Press.
Fodor, J. (1983) *The Modularity of Mind*, Cambridge, MA: MIT Press.
Fodor, J. (2000) *The Mind Doesn't Work That Way: The Scope and Limits of Computational Psychology*, Cambridge, MA: MIT Press.
Foucault, M. (1977a) *Discipline and Punish*, London: Allen Lane.
Foucault, M. (1977b) *The Archaeology of Knowledge*, London: Tavistock.
Foucault, M. (1980) 'Power/knowledge', in C. Gordon (ed.), *Selected Interviews and Other Writings 1972–77*, London: Harvester.
Foucault, M. (1988a) *Technologies of the Self*, London: Tavistock.
Foucault, M. (1988b) 'What is an author?', in D. Lodge (ed.), *Modern Criticism and Theory*, London: Longman.
Francis, B. (2000) *Boys, Girls and Achievement. Addressing the Classroom Issues*, London: Routledge.
Freud, S. (1901) 'The psychopathology of everyday life', republished in 1953, in J. Strachey (ed.), *The Standard Edition of the Complete Psychological Works of Sigmund Freud Vol 6*, London: Hogarth.
Friedan, B. (1963) *The Feminine Mystique*, London: Gollancz.
Fuller, M. (1984) 'Black girls in a London comprehensive school', in M. Hammersley and P. Woods (eds), *Life in School, the Sociology of Pupil Culture*, Milton Keynes: Open University Press.
Gagne, R.M. (1977) *The Conditions of Learning*, New York: Holt International.

Gaine, C. (1995) *Still No Problem Here*, Stoke-on-Trent: Trentham Books.
Gaine, C. and George, R. (1998) *Gender, 'Race' and Class in Schooling: A New Introduction*, London: Routledge.
Galton, F. (1869) *Hereditary Genius*, New York: Macmillan.
Gardner, H. (1983) *Frames of Mind: The Theory of Multiple Intelligences*, New York: Basic Books.
Gardner, H. (1993) *Multiple Intelligences: The Theory in Practice*, New York: Basic Books.
Gardner, H. (1995) 'Reflections on multiple intelligences: myths and messages', *Phi Delta Kappan*, 77: 200–3, 206–9.
Gavin, H. (1998) *The Essence of Cognitive Psychology*, London, Prentice Hall Europe.
Gessell, A. (1925) *The Mental Growth of the Preschool Child*, New York: Macmillan.
Ghaill, M.M. (1992) 'Coming of age in 1980s England: reconceptualizing black students' schooling experience' in D. Gill, B. Mayor and M. Blair (eds), *Racism and Education: Structures and Strategies*, London: Sage.
Ghuman, P. (1995) *Asian Teacher in British Schools*, Bristol: Clevedon Press.
Gibbs, G. (1992) *Improving the Quality of Student Learning*, Bristol: Technical and Educational Services.
Gibson, J. (1979) *The Ecological Approach to Visual Perception*, Boston, MA: Houghton Mifflin.
Giddens, A. (1985) *The Constitution of Society*, Cambridge: Polity Press.
Giddens, A. (1993) *Sociology*, Cambridge: Polity Press.
Gilbert, R. and Gilbert, P. (1998) *Masculinity Goes to School*, London: Routledge.
Gillborn, D. and Gipps, C. (1996) *Recent Research on the Achievement of Ethnic Minority Pupils*, London: HMSO.
Gillborn, D. and Mirza, H. (2000) *Educational Inequality: Mapping Race, Class and Gender: A Synthesis of Research Evidence*, London: Office for Standards in Education.
Gipps, C. (1993) 'The structure for assessment and recording, in P. O'Hear and J. White (eds), *Assessing the National Curriculum*, London: Paul Chapman Publishing.
Gipps, C. and Stobart, G. (1993) *Assessment*, London: Hodder and Stoughton.
Glaser, B. and Strauss, A. (1967) *The Discovery of Grounded Theory*, Chicago: Aldane.
Glass, D. (ed.) (1954) *Social Mobility in Britain*, London: Routledge and Kegan Paul.
Gleeson, D. (ed.) (1987) *T.V.E.I. and Secondary Education: A Critical Appraisal*, Milton Keynes: Open University Press.
Goldthorpe, J.H. (1996) 'Problems of meritocracy', in R. Erikson and J.O. Jonsson (eds), *Can Education be Equalized?* New York: Westview Press.
Goldthorpe, J.H., Lockwood, D., Bechhofer, F. and Platt, J. (1968) *The Affluent Worker: Industrial Attitudes and Behaviour*, Cambridge: Cambridge University Press.
Goleman, D. (1995) *Emotional Intelligence*, New York: Bantam.
Goodson, I.F. (1994) *Studying Curriculum: Cases and Methods*, Buckingham: Open University Press.
Government Statistical Service (GSS) (1997) *Educational Statistics for the United Kingdom*, London: The Stationery Office.
Grace, G. (1987) 'Teachers and the State in Britain: A Changing Relation', in M. Lawn and G. Grace, *Teachers: The Culture and Politics of Work*, London: Falmer Press.
Gramsci, A. (1985) *Selections from Cultural Writings*, London: Lawrence and Wishart.
Gramsci, A. (1991); *Prison Notebooks*, New York: Columbia University Press.
Green, A. (1990) *Education and State Formation*, London: Macmillan.
Greenfield, S. (2000) *Brain Story*, London: BBC Worldwide.
Greeno, J.G. (1997) 'On claims that answer the wrong questions', *Educational Researcher*, 26: 5–17.
Greeno, J.G., Smith, D.R. and Moore, J.L. (1993) 'Transfer of situated learning', in D.K. Detterman and R.J. Sternberg (eds), *Transfer on Trial: Intelligence, Cognition and Instruction*, Norwood, NJ: Ablex.

Grosvenor, I. (1994) 'Education, history and the making of racialized identities', PhD thesis, Birmingham University.

Grosvenor, I. (1995) ' "Race", racism and black exclusion', *Forum*, 37 (3), Autumn: 81–2.

Grosvenor, I., Lawn, M. and Rousmaniere, K. (eds) (1999) *Silences and Images*, New York: Lang.

Guilford, J.P. (1950) 'Creativity', *American Psychologist*, 5: 444–54.

Guilford, J.P. (1967) *The Nature of Human Intelligence*, New York: McGraw-Hill.

Gurney Dixon Report (1954) *Early Leaving*, London: HMSO.

Habermas, J. (1972) *Knowledge and Human Interests*, London: Heinemann.

Habermas, J. (1984a) *Legitimation Crisis*, London: Heinemann.

Habermas, J. (1984b) *The Theory of Communicative Action*, vol. 1, London: Heinemann.

Hackett, G. (1997) 'Labour tightens the reins of power', *Times Educational Supplement*, 11 July: 4.

Hadow Report (1926) Board of Education, *The Education of the Adolescent*, London: HMSO.

Halliday, M.A.K. (1979) *Language as Social Semiotic*, London: Arnold.

Halsey, A.H. and Anderson, C. (1961) *Education, Economy and Society*, New York: Free Press.

Halsey, A.H., Heath, A.F. and Ridge, J.M. (1980) *Origins and Destinations*, Oxford: Clarendon Press.

Halsey, A.H., Lauder, H., Brown, P. Wells, A. (1997) *Education: Culture Economy Society*, Oxford: Oxford University Press.

Hamilton, D. (1989) *Towards a Theory of Schooling*, London: Falmer Press.

Hammersley, M. and Atkinson, I. (1995) *Ethnography: Principles in Practice*, 2nd edn, London: Routledge.

Hammersley, M. and Woods, P. (1984) *Life in School: The Sociology of Pupil Culture*, Milton Keynes: Open University Press.

Hargreaves, D. (1967) *Social Relations in a Secondary School*, London: Routledge and Kegan Paul.

Hargreaves, D. (1972) *Interpersonal Relations and Education*, London: Routledge and Kegan Paul.

Hargreaves, D. (1996) 'Teaching as a research based profession: possibilities and prospects', Teacher Training Agency, Annual Lecture, Birmingham.

Hargreaves, D., Hestor, S. and Mellor, F. (1975) *Deviance in Classrooms*, London: Routledge and Kegan Paul.

Harlen, W., Gipps, C., Broadfoot, C. and Nuttall, D. (1994) 'Assessment and the improvement of education' in B. Moon and A.S. Mayes (eds), *Learning to Teach in the Secondary School*, London: Routledge.

Harris, D. and Bell, C. (1990) *Evaluating and Assessing for Learning*, London: Kogan Page.

Hart, S. (ed.) (1996) *Differentiation and the Secondary Curriculum: Debates and Dilemmas*, London: Routledge.

Harter, S. (1985) 'Competence as a dimension of self-evaluation: toward a comprehensive model of self-worth', in R.L. Leay (ed.), *The Development of the Self*, Orlando, FL: Academic Press.

Hartley, D. (1997) *Re-Schooling Society*, London: Falmer Press.

Harvey, D. (1991) *The Condition of Postmodernity*, Oxford: Blackwell.

Hayek, F. (1976) *Law, Legislation and Liberty*, London: Routledge.

Hayes, N. (1993) A First Course in Psychology. Third Edition. Walton on Thames: Nelson.

Hayes, N. and Orrell, S. (1987) *Psychology: An Introduction*, London: Longman.

Hebb, D.O. (1949) *The Organisation of Behaviour*, New York: Wiley.

Helsby, G. (1999) *Changing Teachers' Work: The 'Reform' of Secondary Schooling*, Buckingham: Open University Press.

Her Majesty's Inspectorate (HMI) (1977) *Curriculum 11–16: A Contribution to Current Debate*, London: HMSO.

Her Majesty's Inspectorate, (HMI) (1994) 'The entitlement curriculum', in B. Moon and S. Mayes, *Teaching and Learning in the Secondary School*, London: Routledge.

Herrnstein, R.J. and Murray, C. (1994) *The Bell Curve: Intelligence and Class Structure in American Life*, New York: Free Press.

Hess, R.D. and Azuma, M. (1991) 'Cultural support for schooling: contrasts between Japan and the United States', *Educational Researcher*, 20: 2–8.

Hillyard, S.A. (1993) 'Electrical and magnetic brain recordings: contributions to cognitive neuroscience', *Current Opinion in Neurobiology*, 3: 217–24.

Hines, B. (1974) *Kes: A Kestrel for a Knave*, London: Michael Joseph.

Hirst, P.H. (1975) *Knowledge and the Curriculum*, London: Routledge and Kegan Paul.

Hitchcock, G. and Hughes, D. (1993) *Research and the Teacher*, London: Routledge.

Hodkinson, P, Sparkes, A. and Hodkinson, H. (1996) *Triumphs and Tears: Young People, Markets and the Transition from School to Work*, London: Fulton.

Honey, P. and Mumford, A. (1986) *Using Your Learning Styles*, Maidenhead: Honey.

Horn, P. (1989) *The Victorian and Edwardian Schoolchild*, Gloucester: Sutton.

Hoyle, E. (1980) 'Professionalisation and deprofessionalisation in education', in E. Hoyle and J. Megarry (eds), *World Yearbook of Education 1980: Professional Development of Teachers*, London: Kogan Page.

Hughes, M. (1975) 'Egocentricity in children', unpublished PhD thesis, Edinburgh University.

Hunter, I. (1994) *Rethinking the School*, Sydney: Allen and Unwin.

Hurt, J.S. (1979) *Elementary Schooling and the Working Classes*, London: Routledge and Kegan Paul.

Illich, I. (1971) *Deschooling Society*, Harmondsworth: Penguin.

Jackson, B. (1964) *Streaming: An Education System in Miniature*, London: Routledge and Kegan Paul.

Jackson, B. and Marsden, D. (1962) *Education and the Working Class*, Harmondsworth: Penguin.

James, W. (1890) *The Principles of Psychology*, 2 vols, Dover reprint 1950, New York: Dover.

Jameson, G., Maines, B. and Robinson, G. (1995) *Invisible Support: Delivering the Differentiated Curriculum*, Bristol: Lame Duck.

Jenkins, D. and Shipman, M.D. (1976) *Curriculum: an Introduction*, London: Open Books.

Jensen, A.R. (1969) 'How Much Can we Boost IQ and Scholastic Achievement?', *Harvard Educational Review*, 33: 1–23.

Jensen, A.R. (1973) *Educational Differences*, London: Methuen.

Johnson, D. and Johnson, R. (1992) 'Encouraging thinking through constructivist controversy', in N. Davidson and T. Worsham (eds), *Enhancing Thinking through Co-operative Learning*, New York, Teachers' College.

Johnson, R. (1991) '*A new road to serfdom? A critical history of the 1988 Act'*, in Department of Cultural Studies, University of Birmingham *Education Limited: Schooling and Training and the New Right since 1979*, London: Unwin Hyman.

Jones, D. (1990*)* 'The genealogy of the urban schoolteacher', in S. Ball (ed.), *Foucault and Education: Disciplines and Knowledge*, London: Routledge.

Jones, D.K. (1977) *The Making of the Education System*, London: Routledge and Kegan Paul.

Jones, G. and Carter, G. (1994) 'Verbal and non-verbal behaviour of ability-grouped dyads', *Journal of Research in Science Teaching*, 31: 603–19.

Jones, K. (2000). 'Rhetorics of educational reform 1945–1947', unpublished conference paper, European Conference on Education Research, Edinburgh, 20–23. Also forthcoming in U. Mietzner, K. Myers and N. Peim (eds) (2002) *Visualizing Subject and Object in the History of Education*, London: Peter Lang.

Jones, S. (1991) 'We're all cousins under the skin', *The Independent*, 12 December.

Jones, T. (1993) *Britain's Ethnic Minorities: An Analysis of the Labour Force Survey*, London: Policy Studies Institute.

Karabel, J. and Halsey, A.H. (eds) (1977) *Power and Inequality in Education*, New York: Oxford University Press.

Keddie, N. (1971) 'Classroom knowledge', in M.F.D. Young (ed.), *Knowledge and Control*, London: Collier-Macmillan.

Keddie, N. (1973) 'Classroom knowledge', in J. Young (ed.), *Tinker, Tailor: The Myth of Cultural Deprivation*, Harmondsworth: Penguin.

Kelly, A.V. (1999) *The Curriculum: Theory and Practice*, 4th edn, London: Paul Chapman Publishing.

Kelly, G.A. (1955) *The Psychology of Personal Constructs*, New York: Norton.

Kember, D. and Gow, L. (1990) 'Cultural specificity of approaches to learning', *British Journal of Educational Psychology*, 60: 356–63.

Kemmis, S. and Wilkinson, M. (1998) 'Participatory action research and the study of practice', in B. Atweh, S. Kemmis and P. Weeks (eds), *Action Research in Practice*, London: Routledge.

Kerry, T. (1984) 'Analysing the cognitive demands made by classroom tasks in mixed ability classes', in E.C. Wragg (ed.), *Classroom Teaching Skills*, Beckenham: Croom Helm.

Klein, G. (1993) *Education Towards Race Equality*, London: Cassell.

Koffka, K. (1935) *Principles of Gestalt Psychology*, New York: Harcourt Brace.

Kohlberg, L. (1976) 'Moral stages and moralization: the cognitive-developmental approach', in T. Lickona (ed.), *Moral Development and Behaviour: Theory, Research, and Social Issues*, New York: Holt, Rinehart and Winston.

Kohler, W. (1940) *Dynamics in Psychology*, New York: Liveright.

Kolb, D.A. (1976) *The Learning Style Inventory: Technical Manual*, Boston, MA: McBer and Company.

Kolb, D.A. (1985) *The Learning Style Inventory: Technical Manual*, revd edn, Boston, MA: McBer and Company.

Kong, C.K. and Hau, K.T. (1996) 'Students' achievement goals and approaches to learning: the relationship between emphasis on self-improvement and thorough understanding', *Research in Education*, 55: 74–85.

Kozulin, A. (1998) *Psychological Tools. A Sociocultural Approach to Education*, Cambridge, MA: Harvard University Press.

Kumar, K. (1995) *Post-Industrial to Post-Modern Society: New Theories of the Contemporary World*, Oxford: Blackwell.

Labov, W. (1972a) 'Rules for ritual insults', in T. Kochman (ed.), *Rappin' and Stylin' Out: Communication in Urban Black America*, Urbana, IL: University of Illinois Press.

Labov, W. (1972b) 'The logic of nonstandard English', in V. Lee (ed.), *Language Development*, London: Croom Helm/Open University.

Labov, W. (1973) 'The logic of nonstandard English', in J. Young (ed.), *Tinker, Tailor: The Myth of Cultural Deprivation*, Harmondsworth: Penguin.

Labov, W. (1997a) 'How I got into linguistics and what I got out of it' (http://www.ling.upenn.edu/~labov/Papers.HowIgot.html: 1997: 4–5).

Labov, W. (1997b) Testimony submitted by William Labov, Professor of Linguistics at the University of Pennsylvania', January, 23 (http://www.ling.upenn.edu/~labov/L102?Ebonics_test.html; + Winterson).

Lacey, C. (1970) *Hightown Grammar: The School as a Social System*, Manchester: Manchester University Press.

Lave, J. (1988) *Cognition in Practice: Mind, Mathematics and Culture in Everyday Life*, Cambridge: Cambridge University Press.

Lave, J. and Wenger, E. (1991) *Situated Learning: Legitimate Peripheral Participation*, Cambridge: Cambridge University Press.

Lawrence, D. (1996) *Enhancing Self-Esteem in the Classroom*, London: Paul Chapman Publishing.

Lawton, D. (1975) *Class, Culture and the Curriculum*, London: Routledge and Kegan Paul.

Lawton, D. (1989) *Education, Culture and the National Curriculum*, London: Hodder and Stoughton.

Lawton, D. (1992) *Education and Politics in the 1990s: Conflict or Consensus?* London: Falmer Press.

Lawton, D. (1994) *The Tory Mind on Education 1979–1994*, London: Falmer Press.

Lawton, D. (1999) *Beyond the National Curriculum*, London: Hodder and Stoughton.

Lawton, D. and Chitty, C. (eds) (1988) *The National Curriculum*, Bedford Way Paper 33, London: Institute of Education, University of London.

Leo, E.L. and Galloway, D. (1996) 'Evaluating research on motivation: generating more heat than light?', *Evaluation and Research in Education*, 10: 35–47.

Lim, T.K. (1994) 'Relationships between learning styles and personality types', *Research in Education*, 52: 99–100.

Lowe, R. (1997) *Schooling and Social Change, 1964–1990*, London: Routledge.

Lowe R. and Seaborne, M. (1977) *The English School: Its Architecture and Organization*, vol. 2, London: Routledge and Kegan Paul.

Lundgren, U.P. (1983) *Between Hope and Happening: Text and Context in Curriculum*, Victoria: Deakin University Press.

Lyotard. J.-F. (1984) *The Postmodern Condition*, Manchester: Manchester University Press.

Lyotard, J.-F. (1986) *The Postmodern Condition*, 2nd edn, Manchester: Manchester University Press.

Mac an Ghaill, M. (1994) *The Making of Men: Masculinities, Sexuality and Schooling*, Buckingham: Open University Press.

Macdonald, B. and Walker, R. (1976) *Changing the Curriculum*, London: Open Books.

Macdonald, M. (1981) 'Schooling and the reproduction of class and gender relations', in R. Dale, G.F. Esland and M. Ross MacDonald (eds), *Politics, Patriarchy and Practice*, London: Falmer Press.

Mackinnon, D., Statham, J. and Hales, M. (1999) *Education in the UK: Facts and Figures*, London: Hodder and Stoughton.

Madeus, G.F. (1994) 'A technological and historical consideration of equity issues associated with proposals to change the nation's testing policy', *Harvard Educational Review*, 64: 76–95.

Maehr, M.L. and Midgley, C. (1991) 'Enhancing student motivation: a school-wide approach', *Educational Psychologist*, 26: 399–427.

Majors, R. (2000) *The Black Education Revolution: 'Race' and Culture in Britain and America*, London: Routledge.

Mann, J.F. (1979) *Education*, London: Pitman.

Maqsud, M. (1997) 'Effects of metacognitive skills and non-verbal ability on academic achievement of high school pupils', *Educational Psychology*, 17: 387–97.

Marples, R. (1999) *The Aims of Education*, London: Routledge.

Marsh, C.J. (1997) *Perspectives: Key Concepts for Understanding Curriculum 1*, London: Falmer Press.

Marton, F. and Saljo, R. (1976) 'On qualitative differences in learning, 1: Outcome and process', *British Journal of Educational Psychology*, 46: 4–11.

Maslow, A.H. (1954) *Motivation and Personality*, New York: Harper.

Maybin, J., Mercer, N., and Stierer, B. (1992) 'Scaffolding learning in the classroom', in K. Norman (ed.), *Thinking Voices: The Work of the National Oracy Project*, London: Hodder and Stoughton.

Mayes, A.S. and Moon, B. (eds) (1994) *Teaching amd Learning in the Secondary School*, London: Routledge.

Maykut, P. and Morehouse, R. (1994) *Beginning Qualitative Research*, London: Falmer Press.

Mboya, M.M. (1995) 'Perceived teachers' behaviours and dimensions of adolescent self concepts', *Educational Psychology*, 15: 491–9.

McCarthy, B. (1987) *The 4MAT System*, Barrington: Excel.

McClelland, D.C. (1955) *Studies in Motivation*, New York: Appleton-Century-Crofts.

McClelland, D.C. (1985) *Motives, Personality and Society*, New York: Praeger.

McGarrigle, J. and Donaldson, M. (1974) 'Conservation accidents', *Cognition*, 3: 341–50.

McGregor, D. (1960) *The Human Side of Enterprise*, New York: McGraw-Hill.

McNeil, C. (1990) 'The National Curriculum: a black perspective', in B. Moon (ed.), *New Curriculum – National Curriculum*, London: Hodder and Stoughton.

McNiff, J. (1988) *Action Research. Principles and Practice*, London: Macmillan.

McPherson, A.F. and Willms, J.D. (1987) 'Equalization and improvement: some effects of comprehensive reorganization in Scotland', *Sociology*, 21 (4) 509–539.

Mead, G.H. (1934) *Mind, Self and Society*, Chicago: University of Chicago Press.

Meighan, R. and Siraj-Blatchford, I. (1998) *A Sociology of Educating*, London: Cassell.

Middlewood, D. and Lumby, J. (1999) *Human Resource Management in Schools and Colleges*, London: Paul Chapman Publishing.

Miles, M. and Huberman, M. (1994) *Qualitative Data Analysis*, London: Sage.

Miller, G. (1956) 'The magical number seven plus or minus two: some limits on our capacity for processing information', *Psychological Review*, 63: 81–97.

Millet, K. (1971) *Sexual Politics*, London: Hart Davis.

Minsky, M. (1975) 'A framework for representing knowledge', in P.H. Winston (ed.), *The Psychology of Computer Vision*, New York: McGraw-Hill.

Mitchell, J. and Oakley, A. (eds) (1986) *What Is Feminism?* Oxford: Blackwell.

Mitchell, R. (1994) 'The communicative approach to language teaching: an introduction', in A. Swarbrick (ed.), *Teaching Modern Languages*, London: Routledge/Open University.

Montgomery, D. (1996) 'Differentiation of the curriculum in primary education', *Flying High*, 3: 14–28 (Worcester: The National Association for Able Children in Education).

Moon, B. (2000) *A Guide to the National Curriculum*, Oxford: Oxford University Press.

Moran, K. (2000) *Phenomenology*, London: Routledge.

Morrison, K. and Ridley, K. (1989) 'Ideological contexts for curriculum planning', in M. Preedy (ed.), *Approaches to Curriculum Management*, Milton Keynes: Open University Press.

Mortimore, P. (1997) 'Can Effective Schools Compensate for Society?', in A.H. Halsey, H. Lauder, P. Brown and A. Stuart Wells (eds), *Education. Culture Economy Society*, Oxford: Oxford University Press.

Mortimore, P. (2000) 'Does Educational Research Matter?', *British Educational Research Journal*, 26 (1): 5–24.

Mullard, C. (1981) *Racism in School and Society*, London: University of London, Institute of Education Centre for Multicultural Studies.

Mulryan, C. (1992) 'Student passivity during co-operative small groups in mathematics', *Journal of Educational Research*, 85: 261–73.

Munn, P. and Drever, E. (1991) *Using Questionnaires in Small-Scale Research*, Edinburgh: SCRE.

Murphy, P. and Gipps, C. (1996) *Equity in the Classroom: Towards Effective Pedagogy for Girls and Boys*, Lewes: Falmer Press and UNESCO Publishing.

National Advisory Committee on Creative and Cultural Education (NACCCE) (1998) *All our Futures: Creativity, Culture and Education*, London: DfEE.

National Curriculum Council (NCC) (1993) *Teaching Science at Key Stage 1&2*, York: NCC.

Naylor, S. and Keogh, B. (1999) 'Constructivism in the classroom: theory into practice', *Journal of Science Teacher Education*, 10 (2): 93–106.

Neisser, U. (1976) *Cognition and Reality*, San Francisco: Freeman.

Newbold, D. (1977) *Ability Grouping: The Banbury Enquiry*, Windsor: NFER/Nelson.

Newbolt Report (1921) Board of Education, *The Teaching of English in England*, London: HMSO.

Newsom Report (1963) Ministry of Education, *Half our Future*, London: HMSO.

Nicholls, J.G. (1989) *The Competitive Ethos and Democratic Education*, London: Harvard University Press.

Norman, K. (ed.) (1992) *Thinking Voices: The Work of the National Oracy Project*, London: Hodder and Stoughton.

Norwood Report (1943) Board of Education, *Curriculum and Examinations in Secondary Schools*, London: HMSO.

Oakley, A. (1975) *Sex, Gender and Society*, London: Temple Smith.
Office for Standards in Education (OFSTED) (2000) *The Annual Report of Her Majesty's Chief Inspector of Schools. Standards and Quality in Education 1998/99*, London: The Stationery Office.
Ogbu, J. (1994) 'Racial stratification and education in the United States: why inequality persists', *Teachers College Record*, 96: pp. 264–71.
Ogbu, J. (1997) 'Racial stratification and education in the United States: why inequality persists', in A.H. Halsey, H. Lauder, P. Brown, A. Stuart Wells (eds), *Education: Culture, Economy, Society*, Oxford: Oxford University Press.
Ozga, J. (1995) 'Deskilling a profession', in H. Busher, and R. Saran (eds), *Managing Teachers in Schools*, London: Kogan Page.
Ozga, J. and Lawn, M. (1988) 'Schoolwork: interpreting the labour process of teaching', *British Journal of Sociology of Education*, 9 (3): 323–36.
Paechter, C. (1998) *Educating the Other: Gender, Power and Schooling*, London: Routledge.
Parker, S. (1997) *Reflective Teaching in the Postmodern World*, Buckingham: Open University Press.
Parsons, T. (1937) *The Structure of Social Action*, New York: McGraw-Hill.
Parsons, T. (1951) *The Social System*, New York: Free Press.
Parsons, T. (1964) *Social Structure and Personality*, New York: Free Press.
Parsons, T. (1970) 'Hobbes and the problem of order', in P. Worsley (ed.), *Modern Sociology: Introductory Readings*, Harmondsworth: Penguin Education.
Pavlov, I.P. (1927) *Conditioned Reflexes: An Investigation of the Physiological Activity of the Cerebral Cortex*, New York: Dover.
Peters, R.S. (1966) *Ethics and Education*, London: Allen and Unwin.
Peters, R.S. (1967) 'What is an educational process?', in R.S. Peters (ed.), *The Concept of Education*, London: Routledge and Kegan Paul.
Piaget, J. (1932) *The Moral Judgment of the Child*, New York: Macmillan.
Piaget, J. (1952) *The Origins of Intelligence in Children*, New York: International University Press.
Piaget, J. (1954) *The Construction of Reality in the Child*, New York: Basic Books.
Piaget, J. (1959) *The Thought and Language of the Child*, London: Routledge and Kegan Paul.
Plato (1955) *The Republic*, Harmondsworth: Penguin.
Porter, J. (1999) *Reschooling and the Global Future: Politics, Economics and the English Experience*, Oxford: Symposium.
Postman, N. and Weingartner, C. (1969) *Teaching as a Subversive Activity*, Harmondsworth: Penguin.
Price, G.E., Dunn, R. and Dunn, K. (1991) *Productivity Environmental Preference Survey (PEPS Manual)*, Lawrence, KS: Price Systems.
Pring, R. (1989) *The New Curriculum*, London: Cassell.
Prosser, J. (ed.) (1999) *School Culture*, London: Paul Chapman Publishing.
Purdie, N. and Hattie, J. (1996) 'Cultural differences in the use of strategies for self-regulated learning', *American Educational Research Journal*, 33: 845–871.
Pyke, N. (1996) 'Schools focus on "D-graders" to boost ranking', *Times Educational Supplement*, 22 November: 4.
Quality Assurance Agency (QAA) (2000) *Benchmarking Academic Standards*: Education Studies. (www.qaa.ac.uk).
Ranson, S. (1994) *Towards the Learning Society*, London: Cassell.
Ranson, S. (2000) 'The pedagogy of voice and communicative action in a learning community', Centre for Policy Studies in Education lecture, University of Leeds, 15 June.
Ravenette, A.T. (1999) *Personal Construct Theory in Educational Psychology: A Practitioner's View*, London: Whurr.
Rayner, S. and Riding, R.J. (1997) 'Towards a categorisation of cognitive styles and learning styles', *Educational Psychology*, 17: 5–27.

Reid, D. (1999) 'Investigating teachers' perceptions of the role of theory in Initial Teacher Training through Q methodology', *Mentoring and Tutoring*, 7 (3): 241–55.

Reynolds, D. (1997) 'Now we must tackle social inequality not just assess it', *Times Educational Supplement*, 21 March: 23.

Reynolds, D., Creemers, B., Bird, J., Farrell, S. and Swint, F. (1994) 'School effectiveness: the need for an international perspective', in D. Reynolds, B. Creemers, P. Nesselrodt, E. Schaffer, S. Stringfield and C. Teddlie (eds), *Advances in School Effectiveness Research and Practice*, Oxford: Pergamon Press.

Riding, R.J. (1991) *Cognitive Styles Analysis*, Birmingham: Learning and Training Technology.

Riding, R.J. (1996) *Learning Styles and Technology-Based Training*, Sheffield: DfEE.

Riding, R.J. and Burton, D. (1998) 'Cognitive style, gender and behaviour in secondary school pupils', *Research in Education*, 59, May: 38–49.

Riding, R.J., and Cheema, I. (1991) 'Cognitive styles: an overview and integration', *Educational Psychology*, 11: 193–215.

Riding, R.J. and Rayner, S. (1998) *Cognitive Styles and Learning Strategies*, London: Fulton.

Rist, R. (1970) 'Student social class and teacher expectations; the self-fulfilling prophecy in ghetto education', *Harvard Educational Review*, 40: 441–451.

Robbins Report (1963) *Higher Education: A Report of the Committee Appointed by the Prime Minister Under the Chairmanship of Lord Robbins, 1961–63* (Cmnd 2154), London: HMSO.

Roberts, P. (1994) 'Business sponsorship in schools: a changing climate', in D. Bridges and T. McLaughlin (eds), *Education and the Market Place*, London: Falmer Press.

Rogers, C.R. (1983) *Freedom to Learn for the 80s*, New York: Macmillan.

Rogoff, B. (1990) *Apprenticeship in Thinking: Cognitive Development in Social Context*, Oxford: Oxford University Press.

Rosenthal, R. and Jacobson, L. (1968) *Pygmalion in the Classroom*, New York: Holt, Rinehart and Winston.

Ross, A. (2000) *Curriculum: Construction and Critique*, London: Falmer Press.

Rotter, J.B. (1966) 'Generalised expectancies for internal versus external control of reinforcement', *Psychological Monographs*, 80 (609).

Rowbotham, S. (1989) *The Past Is Before Us: Feminism in Action Since the 1960s*, London: Pandora.

Rumelhart, D.E. and McClelland, J.L. (1986) *Parallel Distributed Processing: Explorations in the Microstructure of Cognition*, Cambridge, MA: MIT Press.

Rutter, M., Maughan, B., Mortimore, P. and Oulston, J. (1979) *Fifteen Thousand Hours: Secondary Schools and their Effects on Children*, London: Open Books.

Sahin, A. (2000) 'Researching the construction of identity among British Muslim youth', unpublished paper presented to the ISREV conference, Jerusalem, August.

Said, E. (1978) *Orientalism*, Harmondsworth: Penguin.

Salovey, P., and Mayer, J.D. (1990) 'Emotional intelligence', *Imagination, Cognition, and Personality*, 9: 185–211.

Salthouse, T. (1999) 'Aging and cognition', in R.A. Wilson and F.C. Weil (eds), *The MIT Encyclopedia of the Cognitive Sciences*, Cambridge, MA: MIT Press.

Sampson, G. (1952) *English for the English*, Cambridge: Cambridge University Press.

Scholtes, P.R. (1998) *The Leaders Handbook: Making Things Happen, Getting Things Done*, New York: McGraw-Hill.

Schon, D (1983) *The Reflective Practitioner: How Professionals Think in Action*, New York: Basic Books.

Scott, D. (1996) 'Ethnography and education', in D. Scott and D. Usher (eds), *Understanding Educational Research*, London: Routledge.

Scott-Baumann, A. (1995) *Review of the Learning Process*, Cheltenham: Cheltenham and Gloucester College of Higher Education.

Scrimshaw, P. (1983) *Educational Ideologies. Unit 2 E204. Purpose and Planning in the Curriculum*, Milton Keynes: Open University Press.

Seifert, C. (1999) 'Situated cognition and learning', in R.P. Wilson and F.C. Keil (eds), *The MIT Encyclopedia of the Cognitive Sciences*. Cambridge, MA: MIT Press.

Selman, R.L. (1980) *The Growth of Interpersonal Understanding*, New York: Academic Press.

Sereny, G. (2000) *The German Trauma*, Harmondsworth: Penguin.

Shallcross, T. and Robinson, J. (1999) 'A model of participation in continuing professional development and evaluation through action research in educating for sustainability', *Journal of In-service Education*, 25 (3): 403–22.

Sharpe, S. (1976) *Just Like a Girl: How Girls Learn to be Women*, Harmondsworth: Penguin.

Sigston, A., Curran, P., Labram, A. and Wolfendale, S. (eds) (1996) *Psychology in Practice with Young People, Families and Schools*, London: David Fulton.

Silver, H. (1973) *Equal Opportunity in Education: A Reader in Social Class and Educational Opportunity*, London: Methuen.

Silver, H., Strong, R. and Perini, M. (1997) 'Integrating learning styles and multiple intelligences', *Educational Leadership*, September: 22–7.

Simon, B. and Taylor, W. (eds) (1981) *Education in The Eighties*, London: Batsford.

Skilbeck, M. (1984) *School-Based Curriculum Development*, London: Harper and Row.

Skilbeck, M. (1994) 'The core curriculum: an international perspective', in B. Moon and A. Shelton-Mayes (eds), *Teaching and Learning in the Secondary School*, London: Routledge/Open University.

Skinner, B. (1957) *Verbal Behavior*, New York: Appleton-Century-Crofts.

Slater, J. (2000) 'Great expectations', *Times Educational Supplement*, 23 June: 22.

Slavin, R.E. (1990) 'Achievement effects of ability grouping in secondary schools: a best evidence synthesis', *Review of Educational Research*, 60: 471–99.

Slavin, R.E. (1993) 'Students differ: so what?', *Educational Researcher*, 22: 13–14.

Smith, A. (1996) *Accelerated Learning in the Classroom*, London: Network Educational Press.

Smith, P.K. and Cowie, H. (1988) *Understanding Children's Development*, London: Blackwell.

Smitherman, G. (2000) *Talkin' That Talk: Language, Culture and Education in African America*, London: Routledge.

Sotto, E. (1994) *When Teaching Becomes Learning: A Theory and Practice of Teaching*, London: Cassell.

Spearman, C. (1927) *The Abilities of Man*. London: MacMillan.

Spender, D (1982) *Invisible Women: The Schooling Scandal*, London: Writers and Readers.

Spivak, G. (1990) *The Post-Colonial Critic*, London: Routledge.

Stenhouse L. (1975) *An Introduction to Curriculum Research and Development*, Oxford: Heinemann Educational.

Sternberg, R. (1985) *Beyond IQ: A Triarchic Theory of Human Intelligence*, New York: Cambridge University Press.

Sternberg, R.J. (1999) 'Intelligence', in R.A. Wilson and F.C. Keil (eds), *The MIT Encyclopedia of the Cognitive Sciences*, Cambridge, MA: MIT Press.

Sternberg, R.J. and O'Hara, L.A. (1999) 'Creativity and intelligence', in R.J. Sternberg (ed.), *Handbook of Creativity*, Cambridge: Cambridge University Press.

Stones, E. (1979) *Psychopedagogy: Pyschological Theory and the Practice of Teaching*, London: Methuen.

Stones, E. (1992) *Quality Teaching: A Sample of Cases*, London: Routledge.

Storey, J. (1993) *Cultural Theory and Popular Culture*, London: Harvester Wheatsheaf.

Stradling, R., Saunders, L. and Weston, P. (1991) *Differentiation in Action: A Whole School Approach for Raising Attainment*, London: NFER/HMSO.

Taylor, I. and Hayes, N. (1990) *Investigating Psychology*, Harlow: Longman.

Terman, L.M. (1924) 'The mental tests as a psychological method', *Psychological Review*, 31: 93–117.

Terwel, J. (1992) 'Co-operative learning and adaptive instruction in a mathematics curriculum', *Journal of Curriculum Studies*, 26: 143–62.

Thorndike, E.L. (1911) *Animal Intelligence: Experimental Studies*, New York: Macmillan.

Thurstone, L.L. (1938) *Primary Mental Abilities*. Chicago: University of Chicago Press.

Tight, M. (1999) 'Lifelong learning: opportunity or compulsion?', *British Journal of Educational Studies*, 46 (3): 251–63.

Toogood, P. (1984) *The Head's Tale*, Ironbridge: Dialogue Publications.

Tooley, J. (1993) *A Market-Led Alternative for the Curriculum: Breaking the Code*, London: Tufnell Press.

Tooley, J. and Darby, D. (1998) *Educational Research: A Critique*, London: OFSTED.

Townsend, M.A.R. and Hicks, L. (1997) 'Classroom goal structures, social satisfaction and the perceived value of academic tasks', *British Journal of Educational Psychology*, 67: 1–12.

Tropp, A. (1957) *The School Teachers: The Growth of the Teaching Profession in England and Wales*, London: Heinemann.

Troyna, B. and Carrington, B. (1990) *Education, Racism and Reform*, London: Routledge.

Tubbs, N. (1996) *The New Teacher: An Introduction to Teaching in Comprehensive Education*, London: Fulton.

Tuden, A. and Plotnikov, L. (eds) (1970) *Social Stratification in Africa*, New York: Free Press.

Tulving, E. (1972) 'Episodic and semantic memory', in E. Tulving and W. Donaldson (eds), *Organisation of Memory*, New York: Academic Press.

Tulving, E. and Craik, F. (eds) (2000) *The Oxford Handbook of Memory*, Oxford: Oxford University Press.

Tyler, R.W. (1949) *Basic Principles of Curriculum and Instruction*, Chicago: University of Chicago Press.

Verma, G. and Mallik, K. (1999) *Researching Education. Perspectives and Techniques*, London: Falmer Press.

Visser, J. (1993) *Differentiation: Making it Work; Ideas for Staff Development*, Stafford: NASEN.

Viswanathan, G. (1989) *Masks of Conquest: Literary Study and British Rule in India*, New York: Columbia University Press.

Vygotsky, L.S. (1978) *Mind in Society: The Development of Higher Psychological Processes*, London: Harvard University Press.

Walford, G. (1994) *Choice and Equity in Education*, London: Cassell.

Wardle, D. (1970) *English Popular Education, 1780–1970*, Cambridge: Cambridge University Press.

Watson, J. (1913a) 'Psychology as the behaviorist views it', *Psychological Review*, 20: 159–77.

Watts, J. (ed.) (1977) *The Countesthorpe Experience*, London: Allen and Unwin.

Weber, M. (1958) *The Protestant Ethic and the Spirit of Capitalism*, New York: Charles Scribner's Sons.

Weber, M. (1963) *The Sociology of Religion*, Boston, MA: Beacon Press.

Weedon, C. (1987) *Feminist Practice and Poststructuralist Theory*, Oxford: Blackwell.

Weinberg, R.A. (1989) 'Intelligence and IQ: landmark issues and great debates', *American Psychologist*, 44: 98–104.

Weiner, B.J. (1972) *Theories of Motivation*, Chicago: Markham.

Weiner, B.J. (1979) 'A theory of motivation for some classroom experiences', *Journal of Educational Psychology*, 71: 3–25.

Weiner, B.J. (1992) *Human Motivation: Metaphors, Theories and Research*, London: Sage.

Weinstock, A. (1976) 'I blame the teachers', *Times Educational Supplement*, 23 January: 2.

Wertheimer, M. (1923) 'Untersuchungen zur Lehre von der Gestalt', II. *Psychologische Forschung*, 4: 301–50.

Weston, P. (1996) 'Learning about differentiation in practice', *TOPIC*, 16 (4) (London: NFER).

Wheeler, D.K. (1967) *Curriculum Process*, London: University of London Press.

Wheldall, K. and Merrettt, F. (1985) *The Behavioural Approach to Teaching Package*, Birmingham: Positive Products.

Whitty (1990) 'The New Right and the National Curriculum: state control or market forces?', in B. Moon (ed.), *New Curriculum – National Curriculum*, Sevenoaks: Hodder and Stoughton.

Whyte, J. (1983) *Beyond the Wendy House: Sex-Role Stereotyping in Primary Schools*, York: Longman.

Williams, J. (1981) 'Race and schooling' *British Journal of Sociology*, 2 (2): 221.

Williams, R. (1983) *Keywords*, London: Fontana.

Willis, P. (1979) *Learning to Labour*, Aldershot: Gator.

Willmott, R. (1999) 'School effectiveness research: an ideological commitment?', *Journal of Philosophy of Education*, 33 (2): 253–67.

Wilson, R.A. (ed.) (1999) *Species: New Interdisciplinary Essays*, Cambridge, MA: MIT Press.

Wintour, P. (1994) 'Blair gives "modern voice to Labour views" ', *Guardian*, 24 June: 8.

Withers, R. and Eke, R. (1995) 'Reclaiming "Match" from the critics of primary education', *Educational Review*, 47: 59–73.

Wolcott, H. (1990) 'On seeking – and rejecting – validity in qualitative research', in E. Eisner and A. Peshkin (eds), *Qualitative Inquiry in Education: The Continuing Debate*, New York: Teachers College Press.

Wong, N.Y, Lin, W.Y. and Watkins, D. (1996) 'Cross-cultural validation of models of approaches to learning: an application of confirmatory factor analysis', *Educational Psychology*, 16 (3): 317–27.

Wood, D. (1988) *How Children Think and Learn*, Oxford: Blackwell.

Woodrow, D. (1997) 'Social construction of theoretical beliefs', in D. Woodrow, G.K. Verma, M.B. Rocha-Trinidada, G. Campani, and C. Bagley (eds), *Intercultural Education: Theories, Policies and Practices*, Aldershot: Ashgate.

Woods, P. (1999) *Successful Writing for Qualitative Researchers*, London: Routledge.

Wragg, E. (1997) 'Oh Boy!' TES/Greenwich Lecture, *Times Educational Supplement*, 16 May: 4–5.

Wright, C. (1992) 'Early education: multicultural primary school classrooms', in D. Gill, B. Mayor and M. Blair (eds), *Racism and Education: Structures and Strategies*, London: Sage.

Wright, C., Weekes, D. and McGlaughlin, A. (1999) *'Race', Class and Gender in Exclusion from School*, London: Routledge.

Wright Mills, C. (1959) *The Sociological Imagination*, Oxford: Oxford University Press.

Young, M.F.D. (1971) *Knowledge and Control*, London: Collier-Macmillan.

Young, M.F.D. (1998) *The Curriculum of the Future: From the 'New Sociology of Education' to a Critical Theory of Learning*, London: Falmer Press.

Zimmerman, B.J. and Martinez-Pons, M. (1986) 'Development of a structured interview for assessing student use of self-regulated learning strategies', *American Educational Research Journal*, 23: 614–28.

Zimmerman, B.J. and Martinez-Pons, M. (1988) 'Construct validation of a strategy model of student self-regulated learning', *Journal of Educational Psychology*, 80: 284–90.

Zimmerman, B.J. and Martinez-Pons, M. (1990) 'Student differences in self-regulated learning: relating grade, sex, and giftedness to self-efficacy and strategy uses', *Journal of Educational Psychology*, 82: 51–9.

Index